MATTHEW

Brazos Theological Commentary on the Bible

Series Editors

R. R. Reno, General Editor
Creighton University
Omaha, Nebraska

Robert W. Jenson
Center of Theological Inquiry
Princeton, New Jersey

Robert Louis Wilken
University of Virginia
Charlottesville, Virginia

Ephraim Radner
Ascension Episcopal Church
Pueblo, Colorado

Michael Root
Lutheran Theological Southern Seminary
Columbia, South Carolina

George Sumner
Wycliffe College
Toronto, Ontario

MATTHEW

STANLEY HAUERWAS

Brazos Press
Grand Rapids, Michigan

Published by Brazos Press
a division of Baker Publishing Group
P.O. Box 6287, Grand Rapids, MI 49516-6287
www.brazospress.com

Printed in the United States of America

Library of Congress Cataloging-in-Publication Data
Hauerwas, Stanley, 1940–
    Matthew / Stanley Hauerwas.
        p.   cm. — (Brazos theological commentary on the Bible)
    Includes bibliographical references and index.
    ISBN 10: 1-58743-095-9 (cloth)
    ISBN 978-1-58743-095-4 (cloth)
    1. Bible. N.T. Matthew—Commentaries. I. Title. II. Series.
    BS2575.53.H38 2006
    226.2′077—dc22   2006018210

Dedicated to
David Aers
Ellen Davis
Richard Hays

CONTENTS

Series Preface   9
Preface   15
Abbreviations   17
Introduction   18

Matthew 1: In the Beginning   *23*
Matthew 2: Terror and Escape   *37*
Matthew 3: The Baptist   *43*
Matthew 4: Ministry   *50*
Matthew 5: The Sermon   *58*
Matthew 6: Practicing Prayer   *74*
Matthew 7: The Way of the Church   *84*
Matthew 8–9: The Power of the Kingdom   *93*
Matthew 10: The Sending   *105*
Matthew 11–12: "Are You the One to Come?"   *113*
Matthew 13: The Parable of the Kingdom   *126*

Matthew 14–15: John's Death, Jesus's Miracles, and Controversies   *137*
Matthew 16: "You Are the Messiah"   *146*
Matthew 17: The Transfiguration   *154*
Matthew 18: The Church   *160*
Matthew 19–20: Marriage, Wealth, and Power   *168*
Matthew 21–22: Jerusalem and the Temple   *181*
Matthew 23: Jesus on the Attack   *195*
Matthew 24–25: Enduring   *201*
Matthew 26: Betrayal and Arrest   *213*
Matthew 27: Crucifixion   *229*
Matthew 28: Resurrection   *244*

Bibliography   251
Subject Index   255
Scripture Index   263

SERIES PREFACE

Near the beginning of his treatise against Gnostic interpretations of the Bible, *Against the Heresies*, Irenaeus observes that Scripture is like a great mosaic depicting a handsome king. It is as if we were owners of a villa in Gaul who had ordered a mosaic from Rome. It arrives, and the beautifully colored tiles need to be taken out of their packaging and put into proper order according to the plan of the artist. The difficulty, of course, is that Scripture provides us with the individual pieces, but the order and sequence of various elements are not obvious. The Bible does not come with instructions that would allow interpreters to simply place verses, episodes, images, and parables in order as a worker might follow a schematic drawing in assembling the pieces to depict the handsome king. The mosaic must be puzzled out. This is precisely the work of scriptural interpretation.

Origen has his own image to express the difficulty of working out the proper approach to reading the Bible. When preparing to offer a commentary on the Psalms he tells of a tradition handed down to him by his Hebrew teacher:

> The Hebrew said that the whole divinely inspired Scripture may be likened, because of its obscurity, to many locked rooms in our house. By each room is placed a key, but not the one that corresponds to it, so that the keys are scattered about beside the rooms, none of them matching the room by which it is placed. It is a difficult task to find the keys and match them to the rooms that they can open. We therefore know the Scriptures that are obscure only by taking the points of departure for understanding them from another place because they have their interpretive principle scattered among them.[1]

1. Fragment from the preface to *Commentary on Psalms 1–25*, preserved in the *Philokalia* (trans. Joseph W. Trigg; London: Routledge, 1998), 70–71.

As is the case for Irenaeus, scriptural interpretation is not purely local. The key in Genesis may best fit the door of Isaiah, which in turn opens up the meaning of Matthew. The mosaic must be put together with an eye toward the overall plan.

Irenaeus, Origen, and the great cloud of premodern biblical interpreters assumed that puzzling out the mosaic of Scripture must be a communal project. The Bible is vast, heterogeneous, full of confusing passages and obscure words, and difficult to understand. Only a fool would imagine that he or she could work out solutions alone. The way forward must rely upon a tradition of reading that Irenaeus reports has been passed on as the rule or canon of truth that functions as a confession of faith. "Anyone," he says, "who keeps unchangeable in himself the rule of truth received through baptism will recognize the names and sayings and parables of the scriptures."[2] Modern scholars debate the content of the rule on which Irenaeus relies and commends, not the least because the terms and formulations Irenaeus himself uses shift and slide. Nonetheless, Irenaeus assumes that there is a body of apostolic doctrine sustained by a tradition of teaching in the church. This doctrine provides the clarifying principles that guide exegetical judgment toward a coherent overall reading of Scripture as a unified witness. Doctrine, then, is the schematic drawing that will allow the reader to organize the vast heterogeneity of the words, images, and stories of the Bible into a readable, coherent whole. It is the rule that guides us toward the proper matching of keys to doors.

If self-consciousness about the role of history in shaping human consciousness makes modern historical-critical study critical, then what makes modern study of the Bible modern is the consensus that classical Christian doctrine distorts interpretive understanding. Benjamin Jowett, the influential nineteenth-century English classical scholar, is representative. In his programmatic essay "On the Interpretation of Scripture," he exhorts the biblical reader to disengage from doctrine and break its hold over the interpretive imagination. "The simple words of that book," writes Jowett of the modern reader, "he tries to preserve absolutely pure from the refinements or distinctions of later times." The modern interpreter wishes to "clear away the remains of dogmas, systems, controversies, which are encrusted upon" the words of Scripture. The disciplines of close philological analysis "would enable us to separate the elements of doctrine and tradition with which the meaning of Scripture is encumbered in our own day."[3] The lens of understanding must be wiped clear of the hazy and distorting film of doctrine.

Postmodernity, in turn, has encouraged us to criticize the critics. Jowett imagined that when he wiped away doctrine he would encounter the biblical text in its purity and uncover what he called "the original spirit and intention

---

2. *Against the Heretics* 9.4.
3. Benjamin Jowett, "On the Interpretation of Scripture," in *Essays and Reviews* (London: Parker, 1860), 338–39.

of the authors."[4] We are not now so sanguine, and the postmodern mind thinks interpretive frameworks inevitable. Nonetheless, we tend to remain modern in at least one sense. We read Athanasius and think him stage-managing the diversity of Scripture to support his positions against the Arians. We read Bernard of Clairvaux and assume that his monastic ideals structure his reading of the Song of Songs. In the wake of the Reformation, we can see how the doctrinal divisions of the time shaped biblical interpretation. Luther famously described the Epistle of James as a "strawy letter," for, as he said, "it has nothing of the nature of the Gospel about it."[5] In these and many other instances, often written in the heat of ecclesiastical controversy or out of the passion of ascetic commitment, we tend to think Jowett correct: doctrine is a distorting film on the lens of understanding.

However, is what we commonly think actually the case? Are readers naturally perceptive? Do we have an unblemished, reliable aptitude for the divine? Have we no need for disciplines of vision? Do our attention and judgment need to be trained, especially as we seek to read Scripture as the living word of God? According to Augustine, we all struggle to journey toward God, who is our rest and peace. Yet our vision is darkened and the fetters of worldly habit corrupt our judgment. We need training and instruction in order to cleanse our minds so that we might find our way toward God.[6] To this end, "the whole temporal dispensation was made by divine Providence for our salvation."[7] The covenant with Israel, the coming of Christ, the gathering of the nations into the church—all these things are gathered up into the rule of faith, and they guide the vision and form of the soul toward the end of fellowship with God. In Augustine's view, the reading of Scripture both contributes to and benefits from this divine pedagogy. With countless variations in both exegetical conclusions and theological frameworks, the same pedagogy of a doctrinally ruled reading of Scripture characterizes the broad sweep of the Christian tradition from Gregory the Great through Bernard and Bonaventure, continuing across Reformation differences in both John Calvin and Cornelius Lapide, Patrick Henry and Bishop Bossuet, and on to more recent figures such as Karl Barth and Hans Urs von Balthasar.

Is doctrine, then, not a moldering scrim of antique prejudice obscuring the Bible, but instead a clarifying agent, an enduring tradition of theological judgments that amplifies the living voice of Scripture? And what of the scholarly dispassion advocated by Jowett? Is a noncommitted reading, an interpretation unprejudiced, the way toward objectivity, or does it simply invite the languid intellectual apathy that stands aside to make room for the false truism and easy answers of the age?

4. Ibid., 340.
5. *Luther's Works*, vol. 35 (ed. E. Theodore Bachmann; Philadelphia: Fortress, 1959), 362.
6. *On Christian Doctrine* 1.10.
7. *On Christian Doctrine* 1.35.

This series of biblical commentaries was born out of the conviction that dogma clarifies rather than obscures. The Brazos Theological Commentary on the Bible advances upon the assumption that the Nicene tradition, in all its diversity and controversy, provides the proper basis for the interpretation of the Bible as Christian Scripture. God the Father Almighty, who sends his only begotten Son to die for us and for our salvation and who raises the crucified Son in the power of the Holy Spirit so that the baptized may be joined in one body—faith in *this* God with *this* vocation of love for the world is the lens through which to view the heterogeneity and particularity of the biblical texts. Doctrine, then, is not a moldering scrim of antique prejudice obscuring the meaning of the Bible. It is a crucial aspect of the divine pedagogy, a clarifying agent for our minds fogged by self-deceptions, a challenge to our languid intellectual apathy that will too often rest in false truisms and the easy spiritual nostrums of the present age rather than search more deeply and widely for the dispersed keys to the many doors of Scripture.

For this reason, the commentators in this series have not been chosen because of their historical or philological expertise. In the main, they are not biblical scholars in the conventional, modern sense of the term. Instead, the commentators were chosen because of their knowledge of and expertise in using the Christian doctrinal tradition. They are qualified by virtue of the doctrinal formation of their mental habits, for it is the conceit of this series of biblical commentaries that theological training in the Nicene tradition prepares one for biblical interpretation, and thus it is to theologians and not biblical scholars that we have turned. "War is too important," it has been said, "to leave to the generals."

We do hope, however, that readers do not draw the wrong impression. The Nicene tradition does not provide a set formula for the solution of exegetical problems. The great tradition of Christian doctrine was not transcribed, bound in folio, and issued in an official, critical edition. We have the Niceno-Constantinopolitan Creed, used for centuries in many traditions of Christian worship. We have ancient baptismal affirmations of faith. The Chalcedonian definition and the creeds and canons of other church councils have their places in official church documents. Yet the rule of faith cannot be limited to a specific set of words, sentences, and creeds. It is instead a pervasive habit of thought, the animating culture of the church in its intellectual aspect. As Augustine observed, commenting on Jeremiah 31:33, "The creed is learned by listening; it is written, not on stone tablets nor on any material, but on the heart."[8] This is why Irenaeus is able to appeal to the rule of faith more than a century before the first ecumenical council, and this is why we need not itemize the contents of the Nicene tradition in order to appeal to its potency and role in the work of interpretation.

8. 8. *Sermon* 212.2.

Because doctrine is intrinsically fluid on the margins and most powerful as a habit of mind rather than a list of propositions, this commentary series cannot settle difficult questions of method and content at the outset. The editors of the series impose no particular method of doctrinal interpretation. We cannot say in advance how doctrine helps the Christian reader assemble the mosaic of Scripture. We have no clear answer to the question of whether exegesis guided by doctrine is antithetical to or compatible with the now-old modern methods of historical-critical inquiry. Truth—historical, mathematical, or doctrinal—knows no contradiction. But method is a discipline of vision and judgment, and we cannot know in advance what aspects of historical-critical inquiry are functions of modernism that shape the soul to be at odds with Christian discipline. Still further, the editors do not hold the commentators to any particular hermeneutical theory that specifies how to define the plain sense of Scripture—or the role this plain sense should play in interpretation. Here the commentary series is tentative and exploratory.

Can we proceed in any other way? European and North American intellectual culture has been de-Christianized. The effect has not been a cessation of Christian activity. Theological work continues. Sermons are preached. Biblical scholars turn out monographs. Church leaders have meetings. But each dimension of a formerly unified Christian practice now tends to function independently. It is as if a weakened army had been fragmented, and various corps had retreated to isolated fortresses in order to survive. Theology has lost its competence in exegesis. Scripture scholars function with minimal theological training. Each decade finds new theories of preaching to cover the nakedness of seminary training that provides theology without exegesis and exegesis without theology.

Not the least of the causes of the fragmentation of Christian intellectual practice has been the divisions of the church. Since the Reformation, the role of the rule of faith in interpretation has been obscured by polemics and counterpolemics about *sola scriptura* and the necessity of a magisterial teaching authority. The Brazos Theological Commentary on the Bible series is deliberately ecumenical in scope, because the editors are convinced that early church fathers were correct: church doctrine does not compete with Scripture in a limited economy of epistemic authority. We wish to encourage unashamedly dogmatic interpretation of Scripture, confident that the concrete consequences of such a reading will cast far more light on the great divisive questions of the Reformation than either reengaging in old theological polemics or chasing the fantasy of a pure exegesis that will somehow adjudicate between competing theological positions. You shall know the truth of doctrine by its interpretive fruits, and therefore in hopes of contributing to the unity of the church, we have deliberately chosen a wide range of theologians whose commitment to doctrine will allow readers to see real interpretive consequences rather than the shadow boxing of theological concepts.

Brazos Theological Commentary on the Bible has no dog in the current translation fights, and we endorse a textual ecumenism that parallels our diversity of ecclesial backgrounds. We do not impose the thankfully modest inclusive-language agenda of the New Revised Standard Version, nor do we insist upon the glories of the Authorized Version, nor do we require our commentators to create a new translation. In our communal worship, in our private devotions, in our theological scholarship, we use a range of scriptural translations. Precisely as Scripture—a living, functioning text in the present life of faith—the Bible is not semantically fixed. Only a modernist, literalist hermeneutic could imagine that this modest fluidity is a liability. Philological precision and stability is a consequence of, not a basis for, exegesis. Judgments about the meaning of a text fix its literal sense, not the other way around. As a result, readers should expect an eclectic use of biblical translations, both across the different volumes of the series and within individual commentaries.

We cannot speak for contemporary biblical scholars, but as theologians we know that we have long been trained to defend our fortresses of theological concepts and formulations. And we have forgotten the skills of interpretation. Like stroke victims, we must rehabilitate our exegetical imaginations, and there are likely to be different strategies of recovery. Readers should expect this reconstructive—not reactionary—series to provide them with experiments in postcritical doctrinal interpretation, not commentaries written according to the settled principles of a well-functioning tradition. Some commentators will follow classical typological and allegorical readings from the premodern tradition; others will draw on contemporary historical study. Some will comment verse by verse; others will highlight passages, even single words that trigger theological analysis of Scripture. No reading strategies are proscribed, no interpretive methods foresworn. The central premise in this commentary series is that doctrine provides structure and cogency to scriptural interpretation. We trust in this premise with the hope that the Nicene tradition can guide us, however imperfectly, diversely, and haltingly, toward a reading of Scripture in which the right keys open the right doors.

R. R. Reno

PREFACE

It seemed like such a good idea. An idea whose time had come. Rusty Reno had the idea that theologians should write commentaries on books of the Bible. I suppose, given my past work, it seemed like a good idea to ask me to write on Matthew. So when Rusty called asking me to write on Matthew I thought, "What a good idea. I am honored to be asked." Now that I have finished trying to do what he asked, I am not at all sure I want to thank him for his "good idea." But thank God, Rusty got us into this. I must also thank Rusty and Ephraim Radner for their critical comments on the first draft of this commentary. They made this a much better book.

Thanks also needs to be given to Rodney Clapp and his fellow conspirators at Brazos Press for publishing this commentary series. God only knows if they know what they are doing, but we must all be glad that they are willing to do what they do even when they do not know what they are doing. They seem willing to live ready to be surprised, which, if I am right about Matthew, is at least one aspect of what it means to live apocalyptically.

Perhaps my deepest debt is to the students who took the two seminars I have taught on Matthew. I seldom say I learn more from my students than they learn from me, but in this case I certainly did learn much from those gracious enough to bear with me as we read Matthew together. I am particularly grateful to my colleague Douglas Campbell, who co-taught the second seminar on Matthew with me. Douglas is one of those rare people who know theology as well as he does the historical-critical literature represented by New Testament scholarship. He taught me more than he knows.

I am indebted to Sarah Musser, Jonathan Tran, and Sheila McCarthy not only for helping me get the manuscript in shape, but for their insightful criticism and suggestions about what I had written. I am particularly grateful to

Carole Baker for her ability to make many of my misshapen sentences capable of being read with understanding. She accomplished this amazing feat during the last months of her pregnancy, giving birth to Sophia about the same time this commentary was finished. I have no doubt about which birth gives God the greatest joy. The final preparation of the manuscript fell again to Sarah Freedman, who returned from retirement while Carole was on maternity leave. It means a great deal to me that Sarah had a hand in bringing this to light.

As always I have learned much from Paula Gilbert. She has now said Eucharist for the Wesley Fellowship at Duke every Thursday for seventeen years. I have heard her preach often on Matthew. I have no doubt that many of the themes developed in this commentary I learned from her homilies.

Finally it gives me great pleasure to dedicate this book to David Aers, Ellen Davis, and Richard Hays. They are remarkable close readers of texts who have taught me much by their example. I am sure many reading this commentary will think that I have not learned enough from them, but I try. As remarkable as their patience with my reading habits, they honor me by allowing me to count them as close friends. I hope at least here or there in this commentary they may see some indication that I have learned a little from their attempts to teach me to be a better reader. Even more, I hope they see how much their friendship has meant for making me a follower of Christ.

ABBREVIATIONS

Acts	Acts	Judg.	Judges
Amos	Amos	1 Kgs.	1 Kings
1 Chr.	1 Chronicles	2 Kgs.	2 Kings
2 Chr.	2 Chronicles	Lam.	Lamentations
Col.	Colossians	Lev.	Leviticus
1 Cor.	1 Corinthians	Luke	Luke
2 Cor.	2 Corinthians	Mal.	Malachi
Dan.	Daniel	Mark	Mark
Deut.	Deuteronomy	Matt.	Matthew
Eccl.	Ecclesiastes	Mic.	Micah
Eph.	Ephesians	Nah.	Nahum
Esth.	Esther	Neh.	Nehemiah
Exod.	Exodus	Num.	Numbers
Ezek.	Ezekiel	Obad.	Obadiah
Ezra	Ezra	1 Pet.	1 Peter
Gal.	Galatians	2 Pet.	2 Peter
Gen.	Genesis	Phil.	Philippians
Hab.	Habakkuk	Phlm.	Philemon
Hag.	Haggai	Prov.	Proverbs
Heb.	Hebrews	Ps.	Psalms
Hos.	Hosea	Rev.	Revelation
Isa.	Isaiah	Rom.	Romans
Jas.	James	Ruth	Ruth
Jer.	Jeremiah	1 Sam.	1 Samuel
Job	Job	2 Sam.	2 Samuel
Joel	Joel	Song	Song of Songs
John	John	1 Thess.	1 Thessalonians
1 John	1 John	2 Thess.	2 Thessalonians
2 John	2 John	1 Tim.	1 Timothy
3 John	3 John	2 Tim.	2 Timothy
Jonah	Jonah	Titus	Titus
Josh.	Joshua	Zech.	Zechariah
Jude	Jude	Zeph.	Zephaniah

INTRODUCTION

Writing a theological commentary on the gospel of Matthew is an honor, a burden, and a daunting task. I have few examples to draw on in our times to know how to write such a commentary. Moreover, most of the habits that come with being a theologian in modernity do not help us know how to write a theological commentary. Theologians are trained to write articles and books, not commentaries. We may use or comment on this verse or book of the Bible, but we do not write theology as an ongoing comment on scripture. So, few could be as ill prepared as I was for this task.

However, the only way I knew to do the task I had been given was to do it. I taught the gospel of Matthew twice. Each student read a commentary and reported on what the reading offered. I have learned much from my students and the commentaries I have read. I have learned much from the historical work done on the book of Matthew over the past two centuries. I have learned much from the commentaries written by the church fathers as well as Reformation figures. But finally I realized I simply had to write what I thought should be said in and for our time. Accordingly I have tried not to write about Matthew. I have tried to write with Matthew, assuming that the gospel was written for us.

By writing "with" Matthew I mean to indicate how I have tried to retell the story that Matthew tells as, Ephraim Radner suggests, a ruminative overlay. As a result I should like to think that the commentary imitates the form of commentaries common in the Middle Ages and Reformation that were moral allegories. Readers will discover that Herod becomes "Herods" who represent the politics of death, that scribes and Pharisees become "intellectuals for hire" to such a politics, and the journey of the wise men after their encounter with the Christ child is one we must take if we are to escape Herod's politics. Such a "method"—and I certainly have no stake in claiming to know what I am doing—risks being heavy-handed. I hope the readers will discover that by following along they may discover how we are read by the story Matthew tells.

Indeed I hope that those reading my commentary will discover that reading what I have written does no more than make them hungry to reread Matthew. I have not tried to be smarter than Matthew; but rather I have tried to submit to Matthew's discipline. Indeed, as the reader will discover, I believe Matthew wrote to make us disciples of Christ. I have tried to show the "how" of that project in how I have written, that is, by retelling the story Matthew tells.

Insofar as this commentary has an organization, I have simply written a commentary chapter that corresponds to a chapter in Matthew (sometimes grouping two chapters together in order to sustain continuity of the story). There are many intriguing suggestions about Matthew's mode of organization of his gospel, but I have not made much of those. Instead I simply thought it best to accept the chapter divisions as helpful devices for reading. Therefore I advise those kind enough to read this commentary to first read the respective chapter in Matthew and then read my commentary on that chapter. I hope the reader would then reread Matthew's chapter and that the second reading will be illumined by the commentary.

I have written with the strong conviction that it is not the task of the commentary to be a substitute for the gospel. I have, therefore, written in hope that I have done nothing more than highlight what Matthew says. I try to illumine the grammar of his text through the grammar of the text I have written. I take it that this is what commentaries are meant to do—that is, make us more competent readers of the text on which the commentary comments. Matthew's gospel is meant to train us to be disciples of Jesus. I should like to think that learning to read Matthew's gospel through the commentary I have written might be a small aid in helping Matthew's gospel do the work it was written to do.

I have also tried to write the commentary in the hope that those reading the commentary will want to read it as a book. In other words, I hope that the reader will read the commentary the way they read a novel. Matthew's gospel is a compelling story. We know how it will end, but that we know the ending does not make the story any less compelling. I have tried to write with the dramatic urgency characteristic of the story that Matthew tells. The reader may wish to read what I have to say about this or that passage, but the intelligibility of the commentary depends upon its being read in sequence.

I have tried to comment on every passage in Matthew, but I have not burdened the text by citing each verse. Indeed, readers may find at times that they are not sure where I am in the text, but I hope that will make their reading more interesting. Whatever it may mean for this commentary to be a theological commentary, I have tried to write in a manner that the reader is encouraged to discover and make connections. That such connections are made will often be signaled by the reaction, "Oh! Now I see." At least that is the reaction I often experienced, and I hope that some readers will share that reaction with me.

I hope I have written in a leisurely manner. The temptation is to say everything early. The first line of the gospel says everything, but it did not seem wise to try to say all that the gospel has to say in the first chapter of the commentary. So I hope the reader will be patient and wait to see if I develop a theme that they may well think should have been developed earlier. For example, I do not in the first chapter develop a full-blown Christology (I am not even sure what a "full-blown Christology" would look like). But I follow Matthew's lead in letting christological reflections be developed while following Jesus through his ministry.

I have also avoided making any big argument or concentration on one motif to organize the diverse material of the text. Matthew has some central concerns: the relation between church and Israel, the continuing status of the law, the significance of the temple, the political character of Jesus's challenge to the elites of Israel and the implications for Rome. I have, however, tried to avoid making every text in Matthew conform to a singular agenda. I do stress the politics of Matthew as well as the role of nonviolence in Jesus's ministry, but I hope I have avoided making the political character of Matthew "what Matthew is all about." Jesus the Son of God is what Matthew is all about. That means the subject of Matthew's gospel is inexhaustible and, therefore, defies any attempt to make the story that Matthew tells conform to an overarching theme.

I discovered that writing a commentary is an invitation to indulge in assertions. I have not tried to resist asserting what I know to be true. But assertions are not meant to end the conversation. Rather, assertions are intertwined in a manner that hopefully illumines why, faced with the reality of God, all we can do is proclaim what we have been given. Assertions are the grammar required by the story being told, but the story being told should illumine why the assertions are required if what we say is to be considered true. In short, assertions are reports on judgments that require further inquiry. The proof will always be in the pudding.

I have tried to respect what I regard as the reticence and austerity of Matthew's gospel. We often want Matthew to tell us more. Who were the disciples of John the Baptist and how were they positioned in relation to Jesus's disciples? What was Jesus like as a boy? Matthew has told us what we need to know to be transformed into a follower of Jesus. I have tried to respect Matthew's refusal to tell us more than we need to know. I have assumed that this is one of the aspects that make this commentary theological.

The reader will also discover that I have in general tried to avoid all consciousness words. I have tried to avoid, for example, locutions such as, "Matthew must have decided to tell the story this way" or "Jesus clearly must have thought such and such." What we know is what the text says. There is no "behind" behind the text in the form of what either Matthew or Jesus must have been thinking, nor is there any more determinative historical explanation for what must have "really been going on." What is really going on is that Jesus the Messiah has inaugurated the kingdom of God.

Therefore there is no recognition of the so-called Synoptic Problem in this commentary. Nor do I assume that the destruction of the temple in AD 70 is crucial for reading Matthew. Instead I assume that John's gospel, the Pauline epistles, and the letter to the Hebrews provide good commentaries on Matthew's gospel. I am not sure if this makes me an intertextual or extratextual interpreter, but I try to let some texts read other texts.

Throughout the commentary I try to read our lives into the story that Matthew tells. For example, I am not hesitant to suggest how the accommodation of the church to American presumptions cannot help but distort our reading of Matthew's gospel. Nor do I make any apology for assuming that the challenge of reading Matthew after the Shoah is not to be avoided. The continuing significance of Israel is one of Matthew's concerns, offering an opportunity to reflect on the relation between the church and the people of Israel.

Some may find disconcerting that some of the readings of Matthew that I offer confirm positions that I have taken in previous work. Though often accused of not taking scripture seriously enough, I have, however, always tried to be faithful to scripture. Those who criticize me for being insufficiently exegetical may find that what I have done in this commentary confirms their view that I pay insufficient attention to the text. I hope that this will not be the case, even though I cannot deny that my readings often confirm judgments made prior to my close engagement with Matthew. I have tried to avoid forcing the texts to say what I want them to say, but that does not mean I think it possible to come to the text innocent. I continue to think, as I argued in *Unleashing the Scripture* (1993), that a church committed to nonviolence is a more likely faithful reader of Matthew.

I have found writing this commentary hard. To be asked to comment on the word of God is a daunting task. It does not get any more serious than that. What I have written cannot be *my* theology. What I have written, I hope, will be read as the theology of the church. Indeed I hope I have never written *my* theology, but to write a commentary on scripture is certainly a different task than to write on this or that theological issue. This commentary has been hard work, but I hope that some will find in reading it the joy of the gospel.

MATTHEW 1

In the Beginning

"The book of the genesis of Jesus Christ" is not a modest beginning. Matthew starts by suggesting that the genealogy of this man Jesus requires our revisiting the very beginning of God's creative acts: "In the beginning when God created the heavens and the earth" (Gen. 1:1). That is, for Matthew, to rightly understand the story of this man Jesus, we must begin with God because this is God's Messiah. Therefore just as the book of Genesis provides us with the generation of the heavens and the earth (Gen. 2:4), so Matthew provides us with the genealogy of Jesus. And, for Matthew, the reverse is also true. Namely, it is necessary to understand the genesis of Jesus if we are to understand "in the beginning when God created the heavens and the earth." In Jesus we now rightly understand the beginning because we can now see the end.

For some time—that is, in the time often identified as modern—Christian and non-Christian alike have thought that belief in God primarily depends on whether you think the world had a beginning: "Something had to start it all." God, therefore, becomes an explanation for why there is something rather than nothing. However, the god that must exist in order to show that what exists has a beginning too often, due to our fantasies, is not a god who comes to us in Jesus Christ. It is the Christian conviction, a conviction shaped by the grammar of the first verse of the gospel of Matthew, that we can know there was a beginning, because we have seen the end in the life, death, and resurrection of Jesus Christ.

Eschatology is the word that Christians use to describe this understanding of the way things are. Eschatology indicates that the world, including ourselves, is storied. The gospels and especially Matthew assume there is no more determinative way to understand existence than through the story found in scripture. Creation is the first movement in the story that, as we shall see spelled out in Matthew, involves the election of Israel, kingship, sin, exile, and redemption. For Matthew, indeed for all the gospels, Jesus is the "summing up" of the history of Israel so that Jew and Gentile alike can now live as God's people.

This is also an apocalyptic story making apparent what had been hidden since the foundation of the world. Creations, after all, are not everyday affairs, and Matthew believes that the story of Jesus is the story of a new creation. Apocalyptic language suffuses the story that Matthew tells because such dramatic language signals the difficult task that Matthew undertakes to help us discover how we must learn to see and live in the world under the lordship of Christ.

Apocalyptic is the disruption of time by God's time so that time might be redeemed. Apocalyptic means that there is another world, another time, than the one in which we live; but it turns out to be the same world in which we live. As Rainer Maria Rilke puts it: "There is another world, the same as this one." We simply must learn to see the world in which we live as the world that the Father created and redeemed through the Son. That seeing, moreover, entails a politics that challenges our most fundamental assumptions about the way things are. Matthew's gospel is, therefore, an ongoing exercise to help us see the world through Christ.[1]

In *Believing Three Ways in One God*, Nicholas Lash notes that the spring festival, rather than midwinter, once marked New Year's Day. Lash calls attention to a fifth-century calendar known as the Martyrology of Jerome that designates March 25 as the day that

> "our Lord Jesus Christ was crucified, and conceived, and the world was made." On this day God brings all things alive, *ex nihilo*. Out of nothing, by his word, he makes a world, a home. Out of the virgin's womb, Christ is conceived. Out of the world-threatening death on Calvary, life is new-born from an empty tomb. Christ's terror is God's Word's human vulnerability. But, it is just this vulnerability, this surrender, absolute relationship, which draws out of darkness finished life, forgiveness of sin. (Lash 1993, 118)

The boldness of the claim made by the Martyrology of Jerome is matched by the prologue of the gospel of John. Indeed John's prologue provides a fitting

---

1. Hart 2005, 60–61 puts it this way: "To see the world as it should be seen, and to see the true glory of God reflected in it requires the cultivation of charity, of an eye rendered limpid by love . . . the Christian should see two realities at once, one world (as it were) within another: one the world as we know it, in all its beauty and terror, grandeur and dreariness, delight and anguish; and the other the world in its first and ultimate truth, not simply 'nature' but 'creation,' an endless sea of glory, radiant with the beauty of God in every part, innocent of all violence. To see in this way is to rejoice and mourn at once, to regard the world as a mirror of infinite beauty, but as glimpsed through the veil of death; it is to see creation in chains, but beautiful as in the beginning of days."

commentary on the first verse of the book of Matthew: "In the beginning was the Word, and the Word was with God, and the Word was God. He was in the beginning with God. All things came into being through him, and without him not one thing came into being. What has come into being in him was life, and the life was the light of all people. The light shines in the darkness, and the darkness did not overcome it." The word has a name, Jesus Christ, the second person of the Trinity, present with the Father and the Spirit in the creation of the world. These are grand claims that animate every word of Matthew's gospel, which makes us wonder who this Matthew could possibly be that would tell such a story.

Historians speculate that Matthew was a Greek-speaking Christian Jew living in Antioch toward the end of the first century. The historical project to determine who the author of Matthew's gospel may have been is useful and interesting. No doubt that scholarship will inform many of the judgments made in this commentary. But, given this commentary's objectives, references to the writer of Matthew are simply meant to indicate Matthew as the one to be known, in the words of Lewis Ayres, from "the way the words run" (2004, 32).[2] And this is consonant with Matthew's assumption that his task be nothing less than to witness to God's desire to save all creation through the life of Jesus Christ. Matthew writes to make us disciples of this man, Jesus, which means that we must be transformed if we are to live in obedience to the new reality of a redeemed world. After Jesus there is no "normal," or, put differently, after Jesus we are able to live "normally" only because of his extraordinary work.

For Matthew, Jesus has changed the world, requiring that our lives be changed if we are to live as people of the new creation. Accordingly, the gospel is not information that invites us to decide what we will take or leave. Our task is not to understand the story that Matthew tells in light of our understanding of the world. Rather, Matthew would have our understanding of the world fully transformed as the result of our reading of his gospel. Matthew writes so that we might become followers, be disciples, of Jesus. To be a Christian does not mean that we are to change the world, but rather that we must live as witnesses to the world that God has changed. We should not be surprised, therefore, if the way we live makes the change visible.

Paul Minear suggests that the gospel of Matthew is a training manual for disciples and prophets:

> The entire story of Jesus was intelligible and powerful only as it reflected the hidden purposes of God from the foundation of the world and only as it was

2. Ayres observes that "the way the words run" reflects the plain sense of the text, that is, the techniques that a community used for following the argument of the text. He notes that early Christian readers frequently equated the plain sense with the author's intention, but such a view was qualified by the claim that the ultimate author of the text was God. Accordingly, it was assumed that God may well intend that the words of a text carry multiple plain senses.

instrumental in initiating a mission that was to be continued through the school of prophets. To attempt to distill from this document data for an earthly biography of Jesus that is divorced from its heavenly roots and its later fruits is to destroy the possibility of conversation with Matthew. Unfortunately, such is the result of many current treatments of the Gospel. The same distortion occurs when we separate study of the later mission of Jesus' students from its grounding in the design of God mediated through the vocation of Jesus. (Minear 2000, 6)

This commentary on the gospel of Matthew is meant, therefore, to do no more than to call attention to what Matthew has done so well, that is, to position the reader to be a follower of Jesus. Matthew wrote knowing that many of his readers knew, as he knew, that Jesus would be killed and raised from the dead. The problem was that such knowledge did his readers no good unless they were trained in a manner that Jesus had trained his own disciples: to be a follower of Jesus through the reading of gospel. Matthew understands that most of us will be tempted to be a member of the ever-present crowd depicted in the gospel. The crowd was often impressed by Jesus's teachings and his miracles, but when push came to shove, the crowd called for his crucifixion. Jesus's disciples also abandoned him at the end, but Jesus had called them to follow him, making them the continuation of the story. Matthew rightly hopes that through the reading of the gospel we may be no less.

The story, of course, is a complex one with many characters, plots, defeats, and victories. In the first seventeen verses of his gospel, Matthew manages to tell us a great deal about the background story necessary to understand the story of Jesus. We need not worry, however, if we miss some aspect of the story early on; Matthew is not afraid of being repetitive. Indeed he seems to understand that, given the extraordinary story he is telling, we will need many repetitions. Yet with every repetition we learn different aspects of the story of Jesus. Every word of Matthew's gospel is precious.

Creation is the subject of the opening line of Matthew's gospel, suggesting that the very destiny of God's creation is at stake in the life of this Jesus the Messiah. But if this is about the renewal of God's creation by a new creation, it can well be asked, why is Jesus the Messiah identified as "the son of David, the son of Abraham"? It seems that Matthew would have been better advised, like Luke, to have traced Jesus's genealogy back to Adam. Yet by identifying Jesus as "the son of David, the son of Abraham," Matthew testifies to Israel's faith and emphasizes God's faithfulness to Abraham, through whom all people will be blessed. God's response to the history of human sinfulness, graphically depicted in the first eleven chapters of Genesis, is to call Abraham from his country to be the father of a new people.

In response to humanity's rebellious attempt to replace their dependence on God by creating their own heaven, in response to the attempt of people to overcome their contingency, God benevolently scattered the people of the world so that they might learn to respect the other and to learn humility. John Howard Yoder observes that the "confusion" of Babel is such only when measured against the simplicity of an imperially enforced uniformity: "Thus the 'confusion of tongues' is not a punishment or a tragedy but the gift of new beginnings, liberation from a blind alley" (1994a, 63). Yet the gift of difference was, like all gifts, capable of being perverted by us. The humility required to know others like us but different from us gave birth to unending fear and led to unending violence and war. Yet God had a response: he called Abraham to be the father of Israel, a people who would be given his law that they might learn to live among the nations, trusting only in God for their protection. Such a people were called to be holy, to be sanctified, so that their very existence would be unintelligible if the God who had called them to be a light to the nations did not exist.

Jesus is identified as "the son of David, the son of Abraham" because he is the one who recapitulates Israel's life. Matthew reminds us time and time again that "this happened to Jesus" or Jesus did or said this or that so that the scriptures could be fulfilled. Joseph, for example, is told by God to flee to Egypt and to return only after the death of Herod so that "what had been spoken by the Lord through the prophet, 'Out of Egypt I have called my son'" (Matt. 2:15, quoting Hos. 11:1) might be fulfilled. Richard Hays observes, "Matthew is not merely looking for random Old Testament prooftexts that Jesus might somehow fulfill; rather he is thinking about the *shape* of Israel's story and linking Jesus' life with key passages that promise God's unbreakable redemptive love for his people" (2005, 176).

The shape of that story is suggested by the genealogy that begins with the identification of Jesus as "the son of David, the son of Abraham." It is interesting to ask why Matthew names Jesus as the son of David prior to being the son of Abraham. The answer may be simply that Matthew thinks naming Abraham second provides a useful transition to the list of descendents beginning with Isaac. Yet no words or ordering of words in scripture is without significance. Matthew knows he is telling the story of one that was born a king, yet a king to be sacrificed. God had tested Abraham by commanding him to sacrifice Isaac. By beginning with "son of David," Matthew prepares us to recognize that this is a king who will end up on the cross.

So at the very beginning of his gospel Matthew introduces us to the central question that animates the story he will tell: How can it be that the one long expected, the Messiah, the one Israel believes will free it from political servitude, will not triumph as kings do with their armies? To be trained as a disciple is to learn why this Jesus, the son of David, the one true king, must suffer crucifixion. Matthew's gospel is meant to train us, his readers, just as Jesus had to train his disciples, to recognize that the salvation wrought in the cross is the Father's refusal to save us according to the world's understanding of salvation, which is that salvation depends on having more power than my enemies.

The crucial turning point in Matthew's gospel is Peter's confession at Caesarea Philippi. In response to Jesus's question regarding his identity, Peter rightly confesses he is "the Messiah, the Son of the living God." Yet Peter rebukes Jesus when he begins to "show" the disciples that he must go to Jerusalem to "be killed, and on the third day be raised" (Matt. 16:13–23). Peter cannot imagine that the one to save Israel, the successor to David, should undergo crucifixion. Jesus's prediction of his resurrection does not, however, prevent Peter from rebuking Jesus, for Peter is unable to hear anything other than what he takes to be a prediction of failure. Peter, as well as the other disciples, is not yet prepared to comprehend how God will save not only Israel but all of God's creation through a crucifixion.

The crucifixion of the Messiah, Jesus, also explains his identification as "the son of Abraham." Abraham was told by God to sacrifice Isaac, his only son, the very embodiment of God's promise to make Abraham the father of a nation. We must confess, Peter-like, that we find the story of the sacrifice of Isaac profoundly offensive. We do so because as modern people the language of sacrifice simply makes no sense to us. Israel may have continued to make animal sacrifices on the altar in the temple to expiate the sins of the people, but we side with the prophets (Hos. 6:6) and Jesus (Matt. 12:7), who suggest that what God requires is "steadfast love and not sacrifice, / the knowledge of God rather than burnt offerings."

Yet it seems that if we are to read Jesus's struggle in Gethsemane rightly (Matt. 26:36–46), as well as his trial and crucifixion, a sacrifice must be made so that we might be free from the sacrificial systems that dominate our lives, for whether we acknowledge it, our lives continue to be dominated by the language of sacrifice, particularly the sacrifice of war. Indeed, sacrifice is the preeminent human action that gestures our rightful desire to return to God, but we are subtle creatures capable of perverting any good gift. So we have tried, as Israel tried, to make our sacrifices a way to control God's good gift. We continue to do so even as we are told in the book of Hebrews that Jesus abolished forever burnt offerings and sin offerings because it was the Father's will that a people be "sanctified through the offering of the body of Jesus Christ once and for all" (Heb. 10:10).

God had given Israel the law to provide the means through which Israel might become a holy people capable of sacrifice. Israel, however, became the exemplification of our ability to make God's law serve the devices and desires of our own hearts. So the Father sent the Son, humbled in human form, obedient to the point of death, even death on a cross, to end forever any sacrifice not determined by his cross. Our Father restrained Abraham, providing a ram in place of Isaac; but the Father did not spare his only Son's becoming for us the sacrifice necessary to free us from our endless attempts to secure salvation for ourselves on our own terms.

We dare not miss, moreover, the political character of this king's sacrifice. This human being, Jesus, the Son of God (as Pilate insisted), is a king who puts an end to all the sacrifices that leaders of this world use to give their rule the appearance of sanctity. Christ's sacrifice is the one true sacrifice calling into question all sacrifices asked on behalf of lesser causes and lesser gods.[3] That is why the rulers of this world—who war against the cross or try to co-opt it—must finally tremble before the cross. The cross of Christ challenges their very right to ask that sacrifices be made on their behalf. Thus Augustine can say:

> It is we ourselves—we, his City—who are his best, his most glorious sacrifice. The mystic symbol of this sacrifice we celebrate in our oblations, familiar to the faithful. . . . It follows that justice is found where God, the one supreme God, rules an obedient City according to his grace, forbidding sacrifice to any being save himself alone; and where in consequence the soul rules the body in all men who belong to this City and obey God, and the reason faithfully rules the vices in a lawful system of subordination; so that just as the individual righteous man lives on the basis of faith, which is active in love, so the association, or people, of righteous men lives on the same basis of faith, active in love, the love in which a man loves God as God ought to be loved, and loves his neighbour as himself. But where this justice does not exist, there is certainly no "association of men united by a common sense of right and by a community of interest." Therefore there is no commonwealth; for where there is no "people," there is no "weal of the people." (Augustine 1977, 889–90)

Augustine quite rightly identifies politics with questions of sacrifice. But Augustine also knows well that power is constitutive of politics. Indeed we will soon see political power exposed in Herod's response to the news of the birth of one who is identified by the "wise men from the East" as the "king of the Jews." Herod does not hesitate to murder in order to secure his power. So Matthew's gospel is about "the politics of Jesus," which entails an alternative to the power politics of the world.[4] The politics of Jesus, moreover, entails not only the politics *in* the gospel but also the politics of reading the gospel. A right reading of the gospel requires a people who are shaped by the "oblation familiar to the faithful," that is, a community whose fundamental political act is the sacrifice of the altar—an alternative to Herodian power politics.

A theological reading of Matthew, therefore, reaffirms that the church be an alternative politics to the politics of the world. The reading I try to provide of

3. Hart 2005, 52–53 notes that, starkly put, nature itself is a cycle of sacrifice and that religion has often been an attempt to reconcile us to this reality through "sacrificial ceremonies and myths designed to soothe the anguish of that estrangement by seeming to unite us again to the perennial order of things." In contrast, the God we worship as Christians, the Father of the Son, is one who reveals all such sacrificial schemes idolatrous. Needless to say, the close association of politics with religion often involves such idolatry.

4. "The politics of Jesus" echoes the title of Yoder's book. Yoder observes that Jesus is often appealed to as a political figure, but such appeals have a sloganlike formal quality that fails to be linked to "a substantial concern for the *kind* of politics Jesus incarnated" (1994b, 3). I hope that my sympathies with Yoder's account of the politics of Jesus will be obvious.

Matthew's gospel is not for "anyone," though I hope many "anyones" will be attracted to Matthew through the reading offered. Rather, this commentary is guided by the presumption that the church is the politics that determines how Matthew is to be read. That politics, moreover, is one that presumes, as the gospel of Matthew presumes, that the whole life of Jesus is to be understood as determinative for the life of the church.

In more strictly theological terms, the political character of Jesus "the son of David, the son of Abraham" means that the person and work of Christ cannot be separated. That Jesus's teachings have been separated from what some understand to be salvation reflects the accommodation of Christians to the world. The doctrine of the incarnation has unfortunately been used by an accommodated church to give itself the illusion it is faithful because it believes the right doctrine. But incarnation properly understood means that Jesus's person and work cannot be separated because Jesus saves by making us participants in a new way of life. The name of that way of life is church.

Too often the emphasis on the incarnation leads some to focus on the birth or the crucifixion and resurrection as the defining events of Jesus's life. To emphasize the birth as the central event of Jesus's life is often associated with Eastern Christianity, whereas the West is thought to have focused on the death and resurrection.[5] Whatever the truth may be in these characterizations of Eastern and Western theology, what is clearly the case in the light of the gospel of Matthew is that either emphasis fails to do justice to the gospel. Both ways of locating the significance of Jesus fail to account for the significance of his calling the disciples, his teachings, his miracles, his controversies with the leaders of Israel, his call to obey the law and the prophets. Too narrow a focus on either his birth or death can become one of the ways that Jesus is depoliticized. Incarnation rightly reminds us that Jesus is very God and very man, but that formula does not mean we do not have to attend to Jesus's whole life.

Matthew's narration of the salvation wrought in Jesus requires a full disclosure of Jesus's life, including his birth, his relation to the disciples, his teaching and controversies, his miracles, his crucifixion and resurrection. The shape of the gospel, the narrative of this life, is an indication of the kind of politics required for the kingdom that Jesus proclaims. For example, too often those in the Christian tradition who represent quite orthodox theologies of the incarnation ignore or provide tendentious readings of the Sermon on the Mount in order to justify Christian participation in war. Yet the one who surely is very God and very man is also, as is clear from Matthew's gospel, the one who heals, teaches, calls disciples, and was crucified and raised. A high Christology is but a correlative of a community that has learned what it means to forgive enemies.

5. Ayres 2004 argues quite successfully that the alleged strong difference between Eastern and Western theology does not do justice to figures such as Augustine.

Moreover, attention to the whole life of Jesus makes it impossible to ignore Matthew's understanding of the politics that God has been enacting through his people Israel. Matthew believes that God, through Israel, has been about the redemption of all that is and that that redemption entails the creation of a people called to be holy. Accordingly, Matthew seeks to show how the story of this man Jesus requires that we see how the story of Israel is open to the inclusion of the Gentiles. This is why the first verse of Matthew's Gospel announces nothing less than his intention to tell the story of the genesis of a new age begun in this man Jesus, the Messiah long expected, "the son of David, the son of Abraham."

The genealogy that Matthew provides from Abraham to Jesus is but a commentary on the extraordinary claim that with Jesus we have a new beginning. The genealogy is divided into three series, the first two consisting of fourteen generations and the last of thirteen generations. The last group has only thirteen generations because the church that Jesus calls into existence constitutes the fourteenth generation. It is not clear why Matthew may have thought fourteen to be significant, but what is crucial is the story of Israel that Matthew tells through the genealogy.

The first generational history is meant to tell the story of Israel's triumph as a nation, for it ends with King David, who clearly represents for Matthew the climax of Israel's history. David, the mighty king, the lover of justice, ruled Israel in fulfillment of the law given to Moses (Ps. 99). However, the history that Matthew tells in the genealogy is also one of loss, because the next series climaxes with the Babylonian captivity, an exile that still haunts Israel's life even after the return to Palestine. Matthew, like the writers of the Old Testament, does not try to hide Israel's failure to trust God or God's judgment on Israel's unfaithfulness through exile. That Israel continues to tell the stories of her failure is a witness to the community's conviction—a conviction learned through the hard discipline of prophetic lives and one that affirms the story it has to tell—to the God who makes her very existence intelligible. Matthew becomes part of that witness, testifying to God's continued faithfulness to Israel through the coming of Jesus.

Accordingly the last genealogical series is about the restoration of Israel through the birth of Jesus. To be Israel's Messiah means that Jesus does not simply represent Israel, but that he is the renewing of the law, he is the promise of the land, and he is the temple. Jesus is the long-awaited king. He is the restoration of all that makes Israel the promised people. Through Joseph's adoption, Jesus stands in the line of David, becoming for Israel its king unlike the kings of this world. Jesus is the climax of Matthew's genealogical story of Israel's past, at once representing Israel's story while profoundly transforming the very categories of its existence.

Matthew's genealogy also includes the names of four women: Tamar (Gen. 38), Rahab (Josh. 2), Ruth, and Bathsheba wife of Uriah (2 Sam. 11–12; 1 Kgs.

1). That Matthew names these women is unusual because the genealogies of Israel (e.g., those in Gen. 5; 10; 11) are lists consisting of only males. That Matthew names these women, therefore, cannot be insignificant. Some suggest that they represent women who engaged in sexually doubtful activity, thus preparing the reader for the irregularity of Jesus's conception. Such a reading, however, does not seem to do justice to Ruth's relationship with Boaz.[6] It seems more likely, given the role that Gentiles will play throughout his gospel, that Matthew names these women, who are in different ways outsiders to Israel, to indicate how God has used them to sustain the promise people. These women are not clearly from the people of Israel, yet they serve God's providential care of Israel by quite literally making the Davidic line possible. Confronted with untenable situations that seem to preclude their full inclusion, these women use their wits to force the men of Israel to claim them as members of God's promise. They prefigure the Canaanite woman who calls to Jesus to cure her daughter tormented by a demon (Matt. 15:21–28). Jesus at first refuses to answer her, responding that he was sent only to "the lost sheep of the house of Israel." But she kneels before him, confessing, as we confess in the prayer of humble access, that she is ready like the dogs, an Israelite description of Gentiles, to eat the crumbs that fall from the master's table. Jesus commends her faith and heals her daughter.

These women (and it is not accidental that they are women) represent the undeniable reality that God's promise to Israel has spread to the Gentiles. Matthew's gospel is the ongoing commentary on this reality and the tension it represents for understanding Jesus's mission. Matthew does not try to resolve the tension created by the brute fact that Jesus is acknowledged by those who are not Israel. And we, from our position two thousand years later, cannot assume that we know how to resolve the tension created by the promise of Israel including the Gentiles. All we know, because Matthew makes it a point to show us, is that Gentiles recognize Jesus. Therefore, it is crucial that we not seek solutions that would make it impossible for us to read Matthew's gospel with a faith like that of the Canaanite woman. Like her, we must recognize that Jesus has the power to restore us to life even if it means we receive God's gifts as crumbs from the table.

In his wonderful sermon "The Genealogy of Christ," Herbert McCabe suggests that in his genealogy Matthew was reminding us that Jesus was tied to the squalid reality of human life often exemplified in our sexual behavior as well as our politics. McCabe runs through the list of characters that make up the genealogy, noting they are anything but an admirable group of folk. The unscrupulous but entertaining Jacob won his position in the line that leads to

6. See, for example, Davis's discussion of Ruth. Davis notes that the question of whether sexual intercourse is suggested in Ruth 3:9–10 is often debated, but since the text is silent there is no way to know. Accordingly, Davis suggests that "we must conclude from the perspective of the narrator, settling the matter beyond reasonable doubt is simply not the point" (2003, 79).

Christ by lying and cheating his blind father; David, the ruthless and highly successful bandit, unites the tribes of Israel through intrigue and murder; Rehoboam son of Solomon loses most of David's gains through arrogance and greed; Ahaziah son of Ahab continued his father's ways as a sadistic mass murderer. McCabe notes that things get only relatively better with the exile partly because the line of kings ends or at least we do not know their names.

Matthew's genealogy, therefore, is a stark indication that God's plan is not always accomplished through pious people, but through "passionate and thoroughly disreputable people." According to McCabe, the moral is almost too obvious to belabor: Jesus did not belong to the nice clean world of middle-class respectability, but rather he "belonged to a family of murders, cheats, cowards, adulterers and liars—he belonged to *us* and came to help *us*, no wonder he came to a bad end, and gave *us* some hope" (1987, 246–49, at 249).

Matthew's genealogy is thus made possible by the resurrected Jesus's charge to the disciples to "make disciples of all nations, baptizing them in the name of the Father and of the Son and of the Holy Spirit, and teaching them to obey everything that I have commanded you" (Matt. 28:19–20). The gospel has gone to the Gentiles, but this does not mean that the special character of the people of Israel is denied, for God's promise of salvation to Israel through the law—as the women named in the genealogy indicate—was never restricted to Israel.

The story of Jesus's birth makes clear the extraordinary story that Matthew has to tell of God's action on our behalf. Mary, engaged to Joseph, is pregnant with a child "from the Holy Spirit." This is no ordinary conception, but rather this is God acting on our behalf by becoming fully one of us. We stand, therefore, before what the church will learn to describe as the mystery of the incarnation. The timeless one is here conceived in time through the work of the Holy Spirit, that is, the third person of the Trinity. It is often said that the Holy Spirit is an afterthought in modern theology, but the Spirit is certainly present in Matthew's gospel from the beginning (Rogers 2005, 117). For Matthew, the work of the Spirit is to point to the humanity of Christ. Thus at the baptism of Jesus the heavens open, and "he saw the Spirit of God descending like a dove and alighting on him" (Matt. 3:16). It is the same work of the Spirit that we seek when we pray, "And we most humbly beseech thee, O merciful Father, to hear us, and with thy Word and Holy Spirit, to bless and sanctify these gifts of bread and wine, that they may be for us the Body and Blood of thy dearly beloved Son, Jesus Christ" (*Book of Common Prayer* 1979, 342).

That the Holy Spirit is necessary for our recognition of Jesus as the Son of God is not surprising, given our presumption that it is surely not possible for God to be one of us. Our temptation is to believe that if God is God then God must be the biggest thing around. Accordingly we describe God with an unending list of superlatives: omnipotent, omniscient, omnipresent. God is all powerful, all knowing, and everywhere present, but these descriptions make it difficult for some to understand how God can be conceived by the Spirit in

Mary. Yet that is to presume we know what it means for God to be omnipotent, omniscient, omnipresent prior to God being found in Mary's womb. Admittedly this challenges our presumption that we can assume we can know what God must be prior to knowing Jesus, but such presumption is just another word for sin. By Mary's conception through the Spirit, our prideful assumption that we are capable of knowing God on our own terms is challenged. As Jesus will later claim, a claim inherent in his conception: "All things have been handed over to me by my Father; and no one knows the Son except the Father, and no one knows the Father except the Son and anyone to whom the Son chooses to reveal him" (Matt. 11:27).

Too often those who worry about whether we are required to believe in the virgin birth do so assuming they are being asked to believe something for which there is no evidence. But Matthew is telling the story of the God who refuses to abandon us—and even becomes one of us that we might be redeemed. Virgin births are not surprising given that this is the God who has created us without us, but (as Augustine observes) who will not save us without us. What the Father does through the Spirit to conceive Mary's child is not something different than what God does through creation. God does not need to intervene in creation, because God has never been absent from creation.[7] Creation is not "back there," but is God's ongoing love of all he has willed and continues to will to exist.

What should startle us, what should stun us, is not that Mary is a virgin, but that God refuses to abandon us. Here, in the announcement of Mary's pregnancy is, in the words of Karl Barth, the humanity of God:

> God's high freedom in Jesus Christ is His freedom for *love*. The divine capacity which operates and exhibits itself in that superiority and subordination is manifestly also God's capacity to bend downwards, to attach Himself to another and this other to Himself, to be together with him. This takes place in that irreversible sequence, but in it is completely real. In that sequence there arises and continues in Jesus Christ the highest communion of God with man. God's deity is thus no prison in which He can exist only in and for Himself. It is rather His freedom to be in and for Himself but also with and for us, to assert but also to sacrifice Himself, to be wholly exalted but also completely humble, not only almighty but also almighty mercy, not only Lord but also servant, not only judge but also Himself the judged, not only man's eternal king but also his brother in time. And all that without in the slightest forfeiting His deity! All that, rather, in the highest proof and proclamation of His deity! He who *does* and manifestly *can*

---

7. Burrell 2000, 103 makes this point: "All divine action comes under the rubric of *creating*, as we have noted with God's conserving in being what God creates. Hence any talk of God's 'intervening' in creation will be at once misleading and inappropriate." Talk of intervention is misleading because it presupposes that God is part of the metaphysical furniture of the universe, thereby betraying that what it means for God to create involves a fundamental distinction between God and all that is.

do all that, He and no other is the living God. So constituted is His deity, the deity of the God of Abraham, Isaac, and Jacob. In Jesus Christ it is in this way operative and recognizable. If He is the Word of Truth, then the truth of *God* is exactly this and nothing else. (Barth 1960, 48–49 [emphasis original])

God's actuality means that any attempt to explain, to render the virgin birth explicable in naturalistic terms, is a mistake. Just as we cannot explain creation we cannot and should not try to explain how Jesus can at once be fully God and fully man. Nicea and Chalcedon do not explain the Trinity and incarnation, but rather they teach us how to speak of the mystery of God without explanation. Accordingly Nicea and Chalcedon reproduce the character of the gospels, that is, the only way to speak of what God has done for us in Jesus Christ is to tell the story, the story of Mary's being found with child though she and Joseph had not "known one another." That is why Matthew does not try to prepare us for the story of Mary by providing a transition from the genealogies to the story of Mary's pregnancy. Rather, he tells us in a straightforward, if not blunt, manner that "the birth of Jesus the Messiah took place in this way." Again we see that Matthew does not assume that it is his task to make God's work intelligible to us, but rather his task is to show us how we can live in light of Jesus's conception and birth.

"Christ has died, Christ has risen, Christ will come again," we rightly affirm at every Eucharist. But these affirmations should not tempt us to forget that "Christ was born." The second person of the Trinity was conceived and born needing the care of a mother.[8] To be human is to be vulnerable, but to be a baby is to be vulnerable in a manner we spend a lifetime denying. Indeed Jesus was a baby refusing to forego the vulnerability that would climax in his crucifixion. And as such, Jesus was entrusted to the care of Mary and Joseph. They could not save him from the crucifixion, but they were indispensable agents to making his life possible. We rightly celebrate, therefore, the Holy Family.

Matthew's story of Mary's pregnancy lacks the charm and detail of Luke's account, but that may well be its value. One of the great enemies of the gospel is sentimentality, and the stories surrounding Jesus's birth have proven to be ready material for maudlin sentiment. Matthew's account of Jesus's conception and birth is unapologetically realistic. Joseph, not Mary, is the main actor. John Chrysostom praises Joseph as a man of exceptional self-restraint since he must have been free of that most tyrannical passion, jealousy. Unwilling to cause Mary distress, to expose her to public disgrace, he planned to dismiss her discreetly. Joseph, therefore, refused to act according to the law, but rather chose to act in a manner that Jesus himself would later exemplify by his attitude toward known sinners (Matt. 9:10–13).

8. I am indebted to James Wetzel for the significant reminder that Jesus, like us, had to be born.

Yet Joseph still required a revelation so that he would know the character of Mary's pregnancy. He is also given the honor to name Jesus as the new Joshua capable of rescuing his people from their sins. The Joshua of old had been given the task of conquering the promised land, but this Joshua is sent to save his people from their sins, making it possible for them to live as the people of the promise. Joseph did as he was instructed, taking Mary for his wife and naming his son Jesus.

Moreover, Matthew tells us all this was done so that the prophecy of Isa. 7:14 would be fulfilled. This is the first time that Matthew uses the formula "all this took place to fulfill what had been spoken by the Lord," but he will use the formula often to show how Jesus fulfilled the prophecies of the Old Testament. It is tempting to suggest that Matthew is forcing his material to conform to a prior template, but that is to assume Mary was not in fact a virgin when in fact she must have been. We now rightly know how to read Isa. 7:14 because Mary is the young woman and she is a virgin.

Mary had to be a virgin, because Jesus is the Son of God. There is no way to prove Mary's virginity other than to observe that without Mary's virginity the story cannot be told. Mary's virginity is simply required by the way the story runs. The one to whom she gave birth is none other than Emmanuel, "God with us," and such a one can have no other father than the Father who is the first person of the Trinity. It is important that Isa. 7:14 be fulfilled, but that a virgin should give birth to the Son is crucial for our understanding of the character of the Father.

We do not have "here am I" in Matthew as we do with Luke's Mary, but that does not in any way lessen Mary's significance. Without Mary's obedience, without Mary's willingness to receive the Holy Spirit, our salvation would be in doubt. Raniero Cantalamessa, therefore, quite rightly entitles his 1992 book *Mary: Mirror of the Church*. With some justification Mary is often identified as the second Eve, but Mary is also our Abraham. Just as Abraham obeyed God's call for him to leave his familiar land to journey to a foreign destination, so Mary through her willingness to become the very Mother of God is the beginning of the church. She is the firstborn of the new creation faithfully responding to the Son who calls into being a new people. Just as Abraham is the father of Israel, so Mary is the mother of the church.

All of this means that when Christians lose the significance of Mary in the economy of salvation we also risk losing our relation with the people of Israel. Jesus is born of a Jewish mother. His flesh is Jewish flesh. To be sure Jewish flesh is human, but Christians dare not forget that the flesh that is "very man" is particularly the flesh of Mary. Matthew will not let us forget that the one born of Mary is he who has come to free Israel from its sins. Jesus is very God and very man, but that formula does not mean we can ever forget that the God he is, and the man he is, is the same God that has promised to always be faithful to the people of Israel.

MATTHEW 2

Terror and Escape

"In the time of King Herod" may seem like a return to reality. Apocalyptic time, creation time, the time of Jesus's conception—given the way we assume the world works—may seem unreal. But apocalyptic time intersects everyday time, the time of Herod, creating a political crisis. Jesus, the eternal Son of the Father, is born into Herod's time. The story of Jesus's conception and birth is not a mythical story, but rather a story that shapes the time in which we live. It is a time in which rulers rule, assuming that they determine the story that constitutes time—for those who rule assume that time is determined by power. For example, in recent time it is often said that we live in the American century. Like Herod, Americans believe we are in control of time because all people must tell their time, must tell their stories, in relation to the American story.

Herods, however, are seldom as powerful as they think. Herod is king only because it pleases the Romans to have him rule over this troublesome region peopled by the equally troubling Judeans. Herod is a pawn used by Rome to maintain order useful to Rome. Jesus is born in an occupied land, a small outpost, on the edge of a mighty empire. Jesus is eventually killed under Rome's authority, and at the time his death will mean nothing to Rome. How could Rome know that this man would be the most decisive political challenge it would face? Rome knew how to deal with enemies: you kill them or co-opt them. But how do you deal with a movement, a kingdom whose citizens refuse to believe that violence will determine the meaning of history? The movement that Jesus begins is constituted by people who believe that they have all the time in the world, made possible by God's patience, to challenge the world's impatient violence by cross and resurrection.

Too often the political significance of Jesus's birth, a significance that Herod understood all too well, is lost because the church, particularly the church in America, reads the birth as a confirmation of the assumed position that religion has within the larger framework of politics. That is, the birth of Jesus is not seen as a threat to thrones and empires because religion concerns the private. Such a view does not intentionally downplay the importance of the gospel, since it is assumed that the private deals with the most important aspect of our life, which is often labeled "morality." The gospel of Matthew, however, knows no distinction between the public (the political) and the private. Jesus is born into time, threatening the time of Herod and Rome. Jesus, as the genealogy makes clear, is king in the line of David, but he is a king who will redeem kingship from its former state of exile. Warren Carter is right, therefore, to claim that the

> divine presence is manifested in Jesus (Mt. 1:23; 28:20) and in the community committed to him (18:20). The revelation of God's presence in Jesus' conception and birth (Mt. 1:18–25) brings a violent response from one of the empire's vassal kings (Mt. 2). The scene's theme and vocabulary are reminiscent both of Pharaoh's opposition to Moses' freeing God's people from slavery in Egypt and of Jesus' crucifixion by the religious and political elite. . . . The gospel tells a story of a prophetic figure who suffers the worst that the empire can do to him, execution by crucifixion. But his resurrection and subsequent coming in power expose the limits of Roman power. The gospel constructs an alternative world. It resists imperial claims. It refuses to recognize that the world has been ordered on these lines. It offers an alternative understanding of the world and human existence centered on God manifested in Jesus. It creates an alternative community and shapes an anti-imperial praxis. (Carter 2003, 42–43)

"Repent, for the kingdom of heaven has come near" is John the Baptist's sermon (Matt. 3:2), which Jesus will also proclaim (4:17). The kingdom is not some inner sanctuary, but rather the kingdom is an alternative world, an alternative people, an alternative politics. That is what it means for Jesus to be an apocalyptic. He is, in his person and in his work, God's embodied kingdom. The temptation for Christians in modernity is to equate the kingdom with ideals that we assume represent the best of human endeavor: freedom, equality, justice, respect for the dignity of each person. These are all worthy goals that Christians have every reason to support, but goals that are not in themselves the kingdom. To equate these ideals with the kingdom is to separate the kingdom from the one who proclaims the kingdom. "Jesus is Himself the established Kingdom of God" (Barth 1936–77, 2.2.177). Or in Origen's classical phrase, Jesus is the *autobasileia*—the kingdom in person (1926, 498).

So Herod, upon hearing the news that "wise men from the East" have come to Jerusalem asking about a child who has been born "king of the Jews," was appropriately concerned. Herod's fear of this baby reveals the depth of his fragility. Herods know that their positions require constant vigilance, because any change may well make their insecure positions more insecure. Herods rule in fear by employing fear as a means to secure power: if you do not like my rule, if you do not obey me, you will like the direct rule of the Romans even less. So "all Jerusalem with him" is fearful, indicating that Herod's rule is possible because the fear of those he rules makes Herod's rule seem necessary. And like all who rule by fear, the last thing Herod, or those he rules, wants is to be surprised. It cannot, therefore, be good news that strangers appear believing a king has been born. Moreover, their reason for finding the new king is so they may worship him.

Herod has a reputation for being crafty. He is an experienced ruler. He could have told these strangers from the East that they were surely confused. Herod is the king of the Jews. But intrigue is a way of life for Herods. Although he is frightened by the new threat to his power, Herod knows what to do. He calls to him the chief priests and scribes (not always his natural allies) and inquires where the Messiah is to be born. They are the intellectuals of the day—educated, as intellectuals usually are, to serve those in power. They know their Bible and, like many who know the Bible in our day, know how to read the Bible in a manner most useful to suit their ruler's desire.

They direct Herod's attention to the prophecy in Mic. 5:2, which says that the ruler of Israel, the one who will be a shepherd for the people, will come not from Jerusalem but from Bethlehem. The difference between Herod's rule and the one to be born in Bethlehem could not be more stark. The one to come does not depend on the accouterments of power associated with past political regimes. He will enter Jerusalem when the time is right on a donkey (Matt. 21:1–2). He is to be born in Bethlehem, which has never been one of the power centers of Judah. Moreover, his rule is to be that of a shepherd. He will have no power but the power that comes from his love of the lost sheep of Israel.

The cosmic signs heralding this birth should not be surprising, given that the love born in this humble place is the love that moves the sun and the stars. It is the same love that Jesus will use later to calm the winds and the sea, amazing his frightened disciples (Matt. 8:21–27). And though the king comes to shepherd the lost sheep of Israel, this love is clearly not restricted to Israel. Wise men, non-Israelites, have observed a star signaling the king's birth.

The wise men confirm the church's conviction articulated at Vatican I that we should believe that God's existence is in principal open to rational demonstration. In 1 Cor. 14:22 Paul says that even those who speak in tongues may be a sign for unbelievers, that is, to those who do not know the prophecies made to Israel. That wise men from the East will find their way to Jesus by the sign of a star should, therefore, not be surprising. But it is also the case that this "natural knowledge" requires narration through the stories that have been given us in scripture. Guided by hope, the wise men follow the star, but it is not sufficient to lead them to the place of Jesus's birth. They assume that the king of the Jews will be born in Jerusalem, the capital city, but they need help;

and that help comes from the most unlikely of sources, Herod, who has been taught by his advisors who know the scriptures where to find the child.

Herod, informed by his wise men, in secret calls the wise men from the East to him, learns from them when the star appeared, and sends them to Bethlehem. He calls them in secret because he does not want to make credible the presumption that a king has been born. But he tells the wise men that he would also like to go and pay homage to the one who has been born a king. Herod's role in the narrative should not be overlooked, for without Herod the wise men might not have found the one they sought. The enemies of the kingdom often serve the movement begun in Jesus.

The wise men, heeding Herod's advice, continue to follow the star that goes before them. The star stops over the place where Jesus is born, paying homage to the child and eliciting from the wise men overwhelming joy. These wise men, men schooled to appreciate the complexity of the world, see the mother and child, and they worship him. If this is not the Messiah, if this is not the one born to be king, if this is not the Son of God, then what these wise men do is idolatry. That they are able to see the worthiness of this one who alone can be worshiped was surely a gift from the Father. The same gift gives hope to all Gentiles, for through this child we have been called to participate in the alternative world signaled by his birth. Moreover, like the wise men, it turns out that God has given us gifts of bread and wine to be offered so that the world may know that there is an alternative to Herod.

The wise men are warned in a dream not to return to Herod but to return to their own country by another road. It is quite significant that the wise men return to their own country. It seems that God did not mean for them to stay in Israel, which, given the joy they experienced, must have been a temptation. Rather, they are charged to return home, becoming an outpost, a witness, to the joy they have experienced. The journey they undertake becomes for us part of the story that brings us joy. That journey might well be called "another road" that we too must take. The kingdom is a journey, another road, whereby followers of Jesus may well find that they are strangers even when they are "at home."

Indeed Joseph soon discovers through another dream that he must take Mary and the child on a journey to Egypt to escape Herod's wrath. Joseph's namesake could interpret the dreams of the Egyptians, but Joseph is given the gift to trust his own dreams. So Jesus is taken to Egypt, fulfilling God's declaration in Hosea that he will call Israel, his son, out of Egypt. "The son of David, the son of Abraham" is also the new Moses called to lead his people to the land of faithfulness.

Jesus, the new Moses, will like Moses be burdened by his people's unfaithfulness. In Hos. 11:1–2 God says that the more he loved Israel, even calling them from Egypt, the more they sacrificed to Baal and idols. Jesus's disciples will be tempted to mimic Israel's unfaithfulness and idolatry. Like Moses, Jesus will give us the law to help us guard against the temptation to create our own gods, but even though the law is now embodied in Jesus's flesh, we still find ways to distort what we have been given.

The wise men do not return to Herod, but he is no fool. He trusts what he has been told. The threat to him is to be found in Bethlehem. We must remember that Herod is frightened by the news that a king of the Jews had been born. Realizing that power can never be secure, Herods know no limit when they sense that their tenuous holds on power are threatened. Such fear—fear born of power—recognizes no limit because it draws its strength from death. Accordingly Herod orders the killing of all children born in and around Bethlehem two years old and under, the time he estimates that it took the wise men to reach Israel.

Perhaps no event in the gospel more determinatively challenges the sentimental depiction of Christmas than the death of these children. Jesus is born into a world in which children are killed, and continue to be killed, to protect the power of tyrants. Christians are tempted to believe that the death of the children of Bethlehem "can be redeemed" by Jesus's birth, death, and resurrection. Donald MacKinnon, however, insists that such a reading of the gospels, in particular the destruction of the innocents of Bethlehem, is perverse. For MacKinnon, the victory of the resurrection does not mean that these children are any less dead or their parents any less bereaved, but rather resurrection makes it possible for followers of Jesus not to lie about the world that we believe has been redeemed (1979, 182–95).

Matthew's account of the death of the children of Bethlehem is stark. No attempt is made to explain or justify this horror. Rather, Matthew reminds us that Jeremiah prepared us for such a horror, warning of the loud lamentation that would come from Ramah. There Rachel would weep for her children, refusing to be consoled (Jer. 31:15). Rachel, moreover, rightly refuses to be consoled. The gospel—the crucifixion and resurrection of Jesus—is not a consolation for those whose children are murdered. Rather, those who would follow and worship Jesus are a challenge to those who would kill children. The Herods of this world begin by hating the child, Jesus, but, as Frederick Dale Bruner observes, end up hurting and murdering children (2004, 68). That is the politics, the politics of murder, to which the church is called to be the alternative.

Herods must be resisted, but we must also not forget that the fear that possessed Herod's life is not absent from our own lives. "All Jerusalem" was also frightened by the news of this child's birth. And the same fear continues to possess cultures—our culture—that believe they have no time or energy for children. Abortion is one of the names for the fear of time that children make real. Children rightly frighten us, pulling us as they do into the unknown future. But that pull is the lure of love that moves the sun and the stars, the same love that overwhelmed the wise men with joy. It is that love that makes the church an alternative to the world that fears *the* child.

The good news is that Herods die. Crafty as he was, his craftiness could not save Herod from death. Kings come and go, but God's people endure. They can endure, because God has made endurance possible through the kingdom begun in Jesus. So again, while in Egypt, an angel appears and tells Joseph of Herod's death, stating that he should return to Israel. Joseph never hesitates. With Mary and Jesus, Joseph returns, but the return is not without danger. Archelaus, Herod's son, now rules Judea. Again Joseph is warned in a dream to avoid Judea, and he instead goes to Galilee, to Nazareth, thereby, according to Matthew, fulfilling the prophecy that Jesus will be called a Nazarene (Matt. 2:23).

Even though no Old Testament text seems to say that Jesus will be called a Nazarene, we begin to sense the significance that geography has in Matthew's gospel. Galilee was a notorious area of Palestine peopled by Samaritans, Jews, and Gentiles. Throughout his ministry Jesus will move to and from Galilee, which means that he will inevitably encounter Gentiles who are as diverse as the people of Israel. Some of these Gentiles will recognize him as the Messiah. The one who has come to Israel to call Israel to repentance, to announce the advent of the kingdom, discovers that Gentiles will hear and respond. Matthew's gospel is the story of that great surprise.

MATTHEW 3

The Baptist

"In those days John the Baptist appeared in the wilderness of Judea." A vague beginning. What days? How long since Joseph had moved the family to Nazareth? What has it been like for Jesus to grow up? What is his relationship with his mother and father? What kind of education has he received? What brings him into Judea? Why might he consider undergoing the baptism of John? These are all good questions, but not interesting to Matthew, which is a reminder that none of the gospels—including Luke's, which tells us more about Jesus's early life—pretend to be biographies. This is the story of God with us. The abrupt transition from learning that Jesus will be called a Nazarene to the sudden appearance of John reminds us that "in those days" is God's time.

The reticence of the gospels frustrates us, but that frustration is necessary if we are to be trained to be good readers, disciples, of this man. In the gospel of John we are told that Jesus performed many signs that "are not written in this book," but the ones we have are shared so that "you may come to believe that Jesus is the Messiah, the Son of God, and that through believing you may have life in his name" (John 20:30–31). Matthew and John are not writing to provide information about which we can make up our mind, but rather they tell us what we need to know to be drawn into the kingdom of God. Yet our imaginations can go wild desiring to fill in what we can only regard as the gaps in the story. One of the forms that imagination takes in modernity is speculation about Jesus's "messianic consciousness." Did Jesus know he was the Messiah, and what kind of Messiah did he think he was? Attempts to answer these ill-formed questions often involve trying to show how Jesus reflected or was different from the developing Judaism that was beginning during his life.

It is important to remember that what we now call Judaism became a reality only after the destruction of the temple. The investigation of the relation of Jesus to Judaism has taught us much about how "Jewish" Jesus was, and that is to the good, but attempts to "get behind the gospels" betray a prideful attempt to get a handle on Jesus. Matthew shows no interest in Jesus's subjectivity, and neither should we.

Matthew provides no connecting story to prepare us for the appearance of John the Baptist. That Jesus comes from Nazareth, however, may help us understand John's significance. Nazarenes were those in Israel whose life was dedicated completely to God. Thus, Samson describes himself as a Nazirite from his mother's womb (Judg. 16:17), indicated by the sign that "a razor has never come upon my head." Nazarenes were called to live lives of holiness not unlike the role of monks in Christianity. John is not explicitly described as a Nazarene, but he seems to have shared much with those so designated in Israel's past.

We know, however, that John was conceived and born to be the one capable of first recognizing Jesus (Luke 1:5–25). Even while in Elizabeth's womb John "leaped for joy" in the presence of Mary's life-filled womb (1:44). And at his circumcision, John's father, Zechariah, is filled with the Holy Spirit and prophesies, proclaiming that God has raised up a mighty savior from the house of David (1:68–69). For a time, some may have thought that savior to be John, but God gifted John with the ability to recognize that the long-expected Messiah has come in Jesus.

What a strange figure John must have presented. He appeared in the wilderness of Judea. He was dressed in camel hair with a leather belt around his waist. He lived on locusts and wild honey. His dress reminds us of Elijah, who is described in 2 Kgs. l:8 as "a hairy man, with a leather belt around his waist." Elijah, the prophet who was taken to heaven in a chariot without dying, was long expected to be the one to return to pronounce judgment as well as to inaugurate the new age. The Old Testament ends with this admonition:

> Remember the teaching of my servant Moses, the statutes and ordinances that I commanded him at Horeb for all Israel.
> Lo, I will send you the prophet Elijah before the great and terrible day of the Lord comes. He will turn the hearts of parents to their children and the hearts of children to their parents, so that I will not come and strike the land with a curse. (Mal. 4:4–6)

John the Baptist is clearly this Elijah. Jesus explicitly identifies John with Elijah in Matt. 11:14. Moreover, in response to John's query if Jesus is the one to come, Jesus answers: "Go and tell John what you hear and see: the blind receive their sight, the lame walk, the lepers are cleansed, the deaf hear, the dead are raised, and the poor have good news brought to them. And blessed is anyone who takes no offense at me" (11:4–6). The jubilee year, the restoration of land and people outlined in Lev. 25 and interpreted by Isa. 61, the long-expected overturning of injustice that John said was coming—all these Jesus claims are accomplished in his ministry.[1]

John is found in the wilderness eating food that can only be gathered. John, as Elijah, recapitulates the wilderness wanderings that Israel experienced after its exodus from Egypt. Israel's experience in the wilderness was at once a punishment for its apostasy as well as the place of its formation. As is so often the case, God's punishment of Israel was also a gift through which it might learn how wonderful it is to be chosen by God. In the wilderness Israel learned to be dispossessed of possession so that it might learn to be led by God's fiery cloud as well as to live on food that came only as gift. Thus in Amos 2:10–11 God reminds his people:

> Also I brought you up out of the land of Egypt,
>   and led you forty years in the wilderness,
>   to possess the land of the Amorite.
> And I raised up some of your children to be prophets
>   and some to your youths to be nazirites.
>   Is it not indeed so, O people of Israel?

John's sermon, "repent, for the kingdom of heaven has come near," is, therefore, not as obscure as it may appear. John is the embodiment of what it means for Israel to repent. He is the fulfillment of Isa. 40:3, that is, that Israel can expect the voice of one crying out in the wilderness to prepare the way of the Lord. It is not surprising, therefore, that the people from Jerusalem and all Judea, as well as all the regions along the Jordan, went out to him. He was long expected. Moreover, they confessed their sins and were baptized in the river Jordan.

But what could it have meant for John to call for repentance? Our temptation is to think of repentance in individualistic terms, but John is a prophet of Israel. He represents God's decisive action on behalf of Israel to save Israel from its failure to live as God's people. That John baptizes in the Jordan is a reminder of Israel's baptism in Exodus by Moses's parting of the waters. Israel had to face death as it walked across the dry land between the walls of water. John's baptism calls Israel again to face death that it might live. Repentance is about the life and death of the people of Israel.

The repentance for which John calls, the same repentance that Jesus preaches in Matt. 4:17, is the call for Israel to again live as God's holy people, a holiness embodied in the law, requiring Israel to live by gift, making possible justice restored. To be called to such repentance is always a challenge. John Howard Yoder says:

1. I am drawing on Yoder's account of the jubilee year in 1994b, 21–60.

"The kingdom of God is at hand: repent and believe the good news!" To repent is not to feel bad but to think differently. Protestantism, and perhaps especially evangelical Protestantism, in its concern for helping every individual to make his own authentic choice in full awareness and sincerity, is in constant danger of confusing the kingdom itself with the benefits of the kingdom. If anyone repents, if anyone turns around to follow Jesus in his new way of life, this will do something for the aimlessness of his life. It will do something for his loneliness by giving him fellowship. It will do something for his anxiety and guilt by giving him a good conscience. So the Bultmanns and the Grahams whose "evangelism" is to proclaim the offer of restored selfhood, liberation from anxiety and guilt, are not wrong. If anyone repents, it will do something for his intellectual confusion, by giving him doctrinal meat to digest, a heritage to appreciate, and a conscience about telling it all as it is: So "evangelicalism" with its concern for hallowed truth and reasoned communication is not wrong; it is right. If a man repents it will do something for his moral weakness by giving him the focus for wholesome self-discipline, it will keep him from immorality and get him to work on time. So the Peales and the Robertses who promise that God cares about helping me squeeze through the tight spots of life are not wrong; they have their place. BUT ALL THIS IS NOT THE GOSPEL. This is just the bonus, the wrapping paper thrown in when you buy the meat, the "everything" which will be added, without taking thought for it, if we seek first the kingdom of God and His righteousness! (Yoder 1971, 31–32)

"But all this is not the gospel" jars us. We think we must know what repentance is. But Yoder reminds us, just as those who heard John the Baptist, that God gets to determine the character of repentance. John was not offering a better way to live, though a better way to live was entailed by the kingdom that he proclaimed was near. But it is the proclamation of the "the kingdom of heaven" that creates the urgency of John's ministry. Such a kingdom does not come through our trying to be better people. Rather, the kingdom comes, making imperative our repentance. John's call for Israel to repent is not a prophetic call for those who repent to change the world, but rather he calls for repentance because the world is being and will be changed by the one whom John knows is to come. To live differently, moreover, means that the status quo can be challenged because now a people are the difference.

That is why he refuses to baptize the Pharisees and Sadducees. John's condemnation of the Pharisees and Sadducees in some ways seems odd. The Pharisees and Sadducees represented alternative ways to negotiate the keeping of Israel's law under Roman occupation. John's refusal to baptize these leaders of the people anticipates Jesus's biting critique of how these so-called authorities fail to lead lives congruent with their advocacy of God's law. As we shall see, Jesus accuses them of attempting to make God's gifts to Israel a possession rather than a task. John says that they assume that being progeny of Abraham is sufficient to insure their status. As a result, they fail to bear fruit worthy of the repentance made possible by the coming kingdom. Jesus is the progeny of Abraham capable of raising children of promise from the stones themselves.

John's condemnation of the Pharisees and Sadducees will be extended by Jesus throughout his teaching and healing ministry. Matthew's gospel reports a string of controversies occasioned by Jesus's ministry that eventually results in the conspiracy to put him to death. Accordingly the leaders of Israel seldom appear in a favorable light in Matthew's gospel, inviting us to assume that the Jews rejected Jesus. Yet Jesus and his followers are Jews. Indeed Jesus's understanding of the righteousness required by the law may well have been quite similar to that of the Pharisees, who attempted to maintain the observance of the law in a very hostile context. It is not what the Pharisees and Sadducees say that John and Jesus condemn; but rather it is the inconsistency between their lives and what they commend.

Every tree must bear good fruit, according to John, or it will be thrown into the fire. Drawing on prophetic condemnation of Israel's refusal to trust in God, John says the ax now threatens the very root of the tree. Israel has often been pruned by God, and the pruning has even meant exile. Yet God had never abandoned his love for Israel, creating it anew through suffering. John's prophetic condemnation of Israel is but the form that God's care of Israel takes—from stones, indeed from hearts of stone (Ezek. 11:19), God will raise up his people again. Some of those stones, we will discover, are Gentiles who are grafted, according to Paul in Rom. 9–11, into the life of Israel.

Since the Protestant Reformation it has often been alleged that Paul's account of the relation of law and gospel, as well as his understanding of the continuing status of the people of Israel, is at odds with Matthew's gospel. Yet Paul maintains, as does Matthew, that Jesus is about Israel's redemption. Thus Paul in Rom. 9:30–33 elaborates John's appeal that God is able to raise up a people from the stones, because the stone turns out to be Jesus:

> What then are we to say? Gentiles, who did not strive for righteousness, have attained it, that is, righteousness through faith; but Israel, who did strive for the righteousness that is based on the law, did not succeed in fulfilling the law. Why not? Because they did not strive for it on the basis of faith, but as if it were based on works. They have stumbled over the stumbling stone, as it is written,
> > "See, I am laying in Zion a stone that will make people stumble, a rock that will make them fall,
> > and whoever believes in him will not be put to shame."

For Matthew and Paul it is not a question of law or gospel, but rather it is a question of Jesus; Jesus has come to draft us into the promise, into the story of Israel. When Christians presume that we are superior to the people of Israel, we ironically, like the Pharisees and Sadducees, claim a status rather than a calling. John refuses to baptize the Pharisees and Sadducees because they have not borne "fruit worthy of repentance." Surely it is the same presumption of status that led to the Christian persecution of Jews. No doubt, on this side of the Shoah, Christians rightly read and hear texts about "the ax . . . lying at the root of the trees" with apprehension and guilt. But guilt is seldom a useful position to assume for a faithful response to God's word. Far more important is that we respond, as John demands, to the one who has come to baptize with the Holy Spirit and fire.

John is the end of the prophets. He has come to prepare the way for the one who is God's refining fire. John's baptism is not the baptism that Jesus will charge his disciples to take to the nations. That baptism, the baptism into the life and death of Jesus, awaits Jesus's destiny, which is death by crucifixion. John knows that the one to come is "more powerful" because he will have, as we will learn, the authority to forgive sins. Only the Son of God can have that authority. John's humility is not feigned. He is the forerunner calling Israel to a repentance made possible and necessary by Jesus.

John's description of Jesus's task challenges all attempts to characterize his ministry in a manner that leaves the world as it is. John's sermon is the apocalyptic announcement anticipating Jesus's account of the destruction that accompanies God's judgment in Matt. 24. The new age begun in this man requires that the chaff of our lives be burned away. That fire, the fire of the Holy Spirit, is the fire of a love so intense that we fear its grasp. Yet it is the love unleashed in Jesus's life—the life into which we are baptized—that, as Paul tells us in Rom. 6, frees us from the sin revealed through the law but from which the law cannot in itself deliver us. A people freed by love, which is Jesus himself, can live with the joy that comes from no longer being subject to the fear of death.

Jesus comes from Galilee, from relative safety, to John at the Jordan to be baptized by him. The one who is free of sin, the one for whom it is John's whole mission to announce, comes to be baptized by John. We should not be surprised then that John recognizes it is he who should be baptized by Jesus. Yet Jesus, speaking for the first time in Matthew's gospel, tells John that he must undergo his baptism in order "to fulfill all righteousness." Jesus, who is the very embodiment of justice, of the law, submits to the law so that we might see justice done. This gives us a foretaste of Jesus, who is life itself, submitting to death so that death may be conquered once and for all.

John consents and baptizes Jesus. The heavens open, and Jesus, like Israel coming through the sea, sees the Spirit descending like a dove and hears a voice declaring: "This is my Son, the Beloved, with whom I am well pleased." This is Jesus's coronation. The Father anoints the Son to rule over the nations. Jesus is the son decreed in Ps. 2:7–9:

> He said to me, "You are my son;
>   today I have begotten you.
> Ask of me, and I will make the nations your heritage,
>   and the ends of the earth your possession.

> You shall break them with a rod of iron,
> and dash them in pieces like a potter's vessel."

Jesus is unleashed into the world. His mission will not be easy, for the kingdom inaugurated by his life and death is not one that can be recognized on the world's terms. He is the beloved Son who must undergo the terror produced by our presumption that we are our own creators. He submits to John's baptism just as he will submit to the crucifixion so that we might know how God would rule the world. His journey begins. Matthew would have us follow.

MATTHEW 4

Ministry

"Then Jesus was led by the Spirit into the wilderness to be tempted by the devil." We dare not miss the ominous resonance of this "then." With "then," Matthew gestures to the mystery of the incarnation. The Father willingly wills the Son to be subject to time, to be subject to our flesh, to be subject to the devil. Jesus, the Son of God, is led by the Spirit into the wilderness and abandoned to the "tempter." This "then," therefore, anticipates the agony of the cross and the cry, "My God, my God, why have you forsaken me?" (Matt. 27:46).

Jesus is to be subjected to Israel's testing in the wilderness, a testing in which Israel proved her inability to live faithfully despite God's good gifts. The Son, however, will be obedient, but we cannot overlook the cost of his obedience. His obedience depends on his trusting the Father's faithfulness to Israel through the scripture. Jesus is able to resist the devil, a devil able to quote scripture, by being a superior exegete to the one who would tempt him. Jesus, the faithful interpreter of Israel's scripture, teaches us how to read so that we might know how to resist the devil.

First, however, Jesus must fast for forty days and nights. He thus replicates the hunger that God gave Israel in the wilderness in the hope it might learn humility. Jesus, the very embodiment of humility, accepts our humiliation and undergoes a fast for our sake. His fast is not unlike that of Elijah in 1 Kgs. 19:4–9. Elijah has challenged Jezebel, and his life is in danger. He escapes to the wilderness, where he is ministered to by an angel, who gives him food to sustain him for a forty-day journey to Mount Horeb. Jesus has been fed by the Father's benediction, "This is my Son, the Beloved, with whom I am well pleased," but like Israel and Elijah he must now face the one who is always ready to threaten our ability to live by God's good gifts—the devil.

The devil, a fallen angel, is the embodiment of the mystery of disobedience. God would have us love him with the same love that gave birth to our existence. God's love risks our disobedience in the hope that we will freely return the love he has for us. God refuses to coerce us to participate in the love that is the interdependent life of the Trinity. Yet we mysteriously refuse God's peaceable love, preferring to secure our lives by our devices, which inexorably lead to violence against ourselves and one another. Our sin drives us mad because our very ability to revolt against our creator is dependent on the gifts we have been given by him.

That is why the devil is at once crafty but self-destructively mad, for the devil cannot help but be angry, recognizing as he must that he does not exist. Augustine gave classical theological expression to this understanding of sin and evil when he observed that there can be no evil where there is no good. This leads him to the surprising conclusion:

> If every being, insofar as it is a being, is good then when we assert that a defective thing is bad, it would seem we are saying that evil is in fact good, for any defect depends on the goodness that is always prior and therefore there is no evil apart from that which is good. In other words, nothing evil exists *in itself*, but only as an evil aspect of some actual entity because every actual entity is good [*omnia natura bonum est*]. Absurd as this sounds, the logical connections of the argument nevertheless compel us to its inevitability. (1955a, 344)[1]

It is significant, therefore, to recognize that the devil's only viable mode of operation is to "tempt." The devil can be only a parasite, which means that the devil is only as strong as the one he tempts. This is not to suggest, however, that the temptation of the devil is any less destructive for us. But it does mean that the temptation Jesus endures is unlike the temptation we endure, for the devil knows this is the very Son of God, who has come to reverse the history initiated by Adam and Eve's sin in the garden and continued in the history of revolt by the people whom God loves as his own, namely, Israel.

But this time the devil will lose. Hilary observes that it is fitting that the devil will be defeated by the same humanity whose death and misfortunes he effected: "It was the devil who envied God's gifts to humanity before the temptation of Adam, who was now unable to understand God's being present in a human being. The Lord was therefore tempted immediately after being baptized. His temptation indicates how sinister are the devil's attempts, especially against those who have been sanctified, for he eagerly desires victory over the saints" (quoted in Manlio 2001, 57).

1. For my extended reflections on Augustine's understanding of evil, see Hauerwas 2006.

The devil, therefore, thinking that Jesus's fast might have weakened him, approaches Jesus just as he had approached Eve. Eating may be the devil's first line of attack because eating gets to the heart of our dependency—a dependency we try to deny. He initiates a conversation with Jesus, as he had Eve, with what seems to be an innocent remark, but a remark designed to create doubt: "Did God say, 'You shall not eat from any tree in the garden?'" (Gen. 3:1). "If you are the Son of God, command these stones to become loaves of bread" (Matt. 4:3). The trick, of course, that Eve did not recognize is to try to answer the devil on the devil's own terms. Bonhoeffer observes that Eve's disobedience began as soon as she assumed that she could answer the serpent's question on God's behalf, for the question was designed to suggest that she and Adam could go behind the word of God and establish for themselves what the word entailed. In short, the devil's question invited them to assume that they were equal with God. Bonhoeffer notes, therefore, that the serpent is a representative of religion because his question is "religious," assuming that the questioner knows more about God than can be known by a creature (1962, 66–69).

The devil exists as rage, but his rage does not cloud his cleverness. He is crafty. He therefore suggests to Jesus that, if he is the savior of Israel, he should then do what God had done for Israel in the wilderness, that is, provide food. Jesus, who will feed thousands with a few loaves of bread and a small number of fish, could turn the stones into bread. But Jesus refuses, quoting Deut. 8:3, which tells the story of how God had humbled Israel by letting her go hungry before sending manna. God says, I fed "you with manna, with which neither you nor your ancestors were acquainted, in order to make you understand that one does not live by bread alone, but by the very word that comes from the mouth of the Lord." God is indeed in the business of providing food, but Jesus rejects Satan's proposal because Satan would have us believe that food and the word of God can be separated.

Christians believe that Jesus is the word that we now eat in his very body and blood in the Eucharist. But that gift, like the gift of manna to Israel, makes us vulnerable to the same temptations that the devil used to encourage Israel to abandon God's law, to tempt Jesus, and to make the church unfaithful. The very people whom God has gifted with his body to be his witness for all people are constantly tempted to betray that which has been given them. We become, like the Pharisees, scribes, and Sadducees, leaders who assume that our task is to protect "the people" from the demands of the gospel. We simply do not believe that God's word, God's love, can sustain us.

In "The Grand Inquisitor," Dostoevsky describes a confrontation between the Cardinal Grand Inquisitor and Jesus during the Inquisition. Jesus has appeared unmistakably present and recognized by the way love and power flow from him. Fearing the crowd, the cardinal orders him arrested. The cardinal comes to him in prison with the news that they, meaning the church, have finally finished the work done in Jesus's name. The church has managed to still the desire of freedom begun in Jesus by providing the earthly bread that people desire. The cardinal observes that the promise of freedom that Jesus proclaimed is too much for people. Humans are too simple and lawless to comprehend what it might mean to live free of the fear of death. "Nothing," observes the cardinal to the silent Jesus,

> has ever been more insufferable for man and for human society than freedom! But do you see these stones in this bare, scorching desert? Turn them into bread and mankind will run after you like sheep, grateful and obedient, though eternally trembling lest you withdraw your hand and our loaves cease for them. But you did not want to deprive man of freedom and rejected the offer, for what sort of freedom is it, you reasoned, if obedience is bought by loaves of bread? You objected that man does not live by bread alone, but do you not know that in the name of this very earthly bread, the spirit of the earth will rise against you and fight with you and defeat you, and everyone will follow him exclaiming: "Who can compare to this beast, for he has given us fire from heaven!" Do you know that centuries will pass and mankind will proclaim with the mouth of its wisdom and science that there is no crime, and therefore no sin, but only hungry men? "Feed them first, then ask virtue of them!"—that is what they will write on the banner they raise against you, and by which your temple will be destroyed. (Dostoevsky 2001, 44–45)

The cardinal has had Jesus arrested because of the cardinal's love for humankind. According to Dostoevsky the cardinal risks his own happiness in order that people may have the illusion of security as well as the happiness that is assumed to be the product of security. The cardinal, and the church he serves, knows that peace and even death are dearer to people than confronting the choice between good and evil. The cardinal, for example, accuses Jesus of failing to love us because he refused, as he was asked to do, to come down from the cross so that we might see his power and believe. Jesus refuses to enslave us by a miracle, which means that he wants us to love him for the love he is. But that, the cardinal maintains, is to ask too much of us, so the church has given those they serve bread: "And everyone will be happy, all the millions of creatures, except for the hundred thousand of those who govern them. For only we, we who keep the mystery, only we shall be unhappy" (2001, 51).

The devil, as Dostoevsky well knew, is not without resources. Failing to tempt Jesus to turn stones into bread, he tempts Jesus again. He, rather than the Spirit, leads Jesus to the holy city, to the pinnacle of the temple, tempting him to test the Father by throwing himself down. Moreover the devil quotes scripture: "for it is written" in Ps. 91:11–12 that God "will command his angels concerning you, / . . . so that you will not dash your foot against a stone." Jesus counters by quoting Deut. 6:16, stating that the Lord is not to be tested as Israel tested the Lord at Massah. Again, Jesus teaches us how to read scripture by refusing to "go behind the text" to discover what God must have "really meant." When you are in a struggle with the devil, it is unwise to look for "the meaning" of the text.

With this second temptation the devil tries to force God's hand, to make God rule as we desire to be ruled. Jesus will come to Jerusalem, he will cleanse the temple, but he will do so as the humble one riding on a donkey (Matt. 21:4–5). But the devil wants Jesus to seize the temple by force. The devil takes Jesus to the pinnacle of the temple to tempt Jesus to act as the priest of priests. Jesus is offered a heroic role, to take his life in his own hands, to be in control of his destiny, to force God's kingdom into reality by making a sacrifice that God cannot refuse. But such a role contrasts starkly with the man who will die on a cross subject to the will of others. In Jesus's refusal to act on his own we see that it is not his will but the Father's that is accomplished through Jesus's life and death. The resurrection is not, therefore, an event that renders Jesus's faithfulness unnecessary; rather it is a confirmation of his obedience to the Father's love manifest in his refusal to accept the devil's offer of power.

Jesus's response to the devil, his use of scripture, makes clear that Jesus is at once prophet, priest, and king. To be king of Israel, to be the true judge of Israel, requires the knowledge of the law acquired by having the law read every day of the king's life (Deut. 17:19). In contrast to Herod, Jesus rules through justice and thus becomes the king for whom Israel has longed.

It is not surprising, therefore, that the devil's third temptation makes explicit what has been at stake in the first two temptations, namely, the connection between worship and politics. The devil takes Jesus to a high mountain, offering him all the kingdoms of the world if Jesus will but worship him. At stake is the first and second commandments: "You shall have no other gods before me. You shall not make for yourself an idol, whether in the form of anything that is in heaven above, or that is on the earth beneath, or that is in the water under the earth. You shall not bow down to them or worship them" (Exod. 20:3–5). Give the devil his due. He understands, as is seldom acknowledged particularly in our day, that politics is about worship and sacrifice.

Jesus refuses to worship the devil and thus becomes the alternative to the world's politics based on sacrifices to false gods. Again he resists the devil by quoting Deuteronomy: "Worship the Lord your God, / and serve only him" (Matt. 4:10, quoting Deut. 6:13). The politics that Jesus represents has always been present in the first and second commandments. Jesus is the faithful incarnation of the right worship of the Father. By rejecting the devil Jesus calls into the world a people who, as Augustine suggests, can never obey the justice the world offers as an alternative to the justice found in the sacrifice of the Son. Yet too often the very people called into existence by Jesus, that is, the church, have betrayed Jesus's sacrifice by trying to rule using the means of power that the devil offered to Jesus.

Thus the Cardinal Grand Inquisitor tells Jesus that for a long time—eight centuries—"the church has not been with you but with him," that is, with the devil. It has been eight centuries since the church accepted what Jesus rejected, namely, "We took Rome and the sword of Caesar from him [the devil], and proclaimed ourselves sole rulers of the earth, the only rulers, though we have not yet succeeded in bringing our cause to its full conclusion" (Dostoevsky 2001, 49). But that is Jesus's fault for rejecting the last gift. Had Jesus accepted the third counsel of that mighty spirit, he could have furnished what all people seek on earth, that is:

> Someone to bow down to, someone to take over his conscience, and a means for uniting everyone at last into a common, concordant, and incontestable ant-hill—for the need for universal union is the third and last torment of men. . . . Great conquerors, Tamerlanes and Genghis Khans, swept over the earth like a whirlwind, yearning to conquer the cosmos, but they, too, expressed, albeit unconsciously, the same great need of mankind for universal and general union. Had you accepted the world and Caesar's purple, you would have founded a universal kingdom and granted universal peace. For who shall possess mankind if not those who possess their conscience and give them their bread? And so we took Caesar's sword, and in taking it, of course, we rejected you and followed *him*. (Dostoevsky 2001, 49)

The cardinal finally falls silent. His captive has said nothing in his defense. He has listened intently and calmly, offering no counterarguments. The cardinal wished him to say something but he remained silent. But suddenly the captive silently approaches the aged cardinal and gently kisses him on "his bloodless, ninety-year-old lips." That is Jesus's only response to the old cardinal, but the cardinal is shaken. The cardinal walks to the door, opens it, and says, "'Go and do not come again . . . do not come at all . . . never, never!' And he lets him out into the dark squares of the city. The prisoner goes away" (2001, 54).

The devil is but another name for our impatience. We want bread, we want to force God's hand to rescue us, we want peace—and we want all this now. But Jesus is our bread, he is our salvation, and he is our peace. That he is so requires that we learn to wait with him in a world of hunger, idolatry, and war to witness to the kingdom that is God's patience. The Father will have the kingdom present one small act at a time. That is what it means for us to be an apocalyptic people, that is, a people who believe that Jesus's refusal to accept the devil's terms for the world's salvation has made it possible for a people to exist that offers an alternative time to a world that believes we have no time to be just.

The devil's temptations are meant to force Jesus to acknowledge that our world is determined by death. Death creates a world of scarcity—a world without enough food, power, or life itself. But Jesus resists the devil because he is God's abundance. Jesus brings a kingdom that is not a zero-sum game. There is enough food, power, and life because the kingdom has come, making possible a people who have the time to feed their neighbors. Fear creates scarcity, but

Jesus has made it possible for us to live in trust. "Do not be afraid," the angel tells Mary Magdalene and Mary at the tomb (Matt. 28:4). By resisting the devil's temptations Jesus has made it possible for us to live without fear.

"Then the devil left him." "Then" remains ominous, but at least we have now seen what the struggle will entail. The devil leaves him, and Jesus is ministered to by angels—but the devil is certainly not gone. John the Baptist is arrested. The struggle has only begun. Some may find Jesus's reaction to John's arrest strange—he withdraws to Galilee. He escapes from Judea and the power of Archelaus. Jesus does not seek a direct confrontation with the powers, rather he begins to preach, declaring as John had, "Repent, for the kingdom of heaven has come near." Yet unlike John, Jesus proclaims the nearness of the kingdom in "Galilee of the Gentiles." Jesus goes to Galilee to fulfill Isaiah's prophecy that a light will dawn in the lands of Zebulun and Naphtali (Isa. 9:1). Isaiah identifies that light with the child on whose shoulders will rest all authority. He will be named

> Wonderful Counselor, Mighty God,
>   Everlasting Father, Prince of Peace.
> His authority shall grow continually,
>   and there shall be endless peace
> for the throne of David and his kingdom.
>   He will establish and uphold it
> with justice and with righteousness
>   from this time onward and forevermore.
> The zeal of the LORD of hosts will do this. (Isa. 9:6–7)

David's kingdom is now present in Jesus. Jesus now proclaims the advent of the kingdom in Galilee to the Gentiles—a remarkable development, but one that Israel itself anticipated, as we see from the prophet Isaiah. It is a kingdom that requires repentance. Repentance, moreover, requires a training called discipleship. So we should not be surprised that Jesus now calls his first disciples. He does not call his disciples from the powerful or the elites, but rather he calls fishermen, promising to make them fish for people.

When Jesus calls Simon and Andrew, James and John, they are working. Yet in both instances they immediately leave their nets and follow him. We are even told that James and John leave their father—a leaving signaling the sacrifices that the disciples will have to undergo in order to recognize who it is they follow, for the kingdom born in this man, the kingdom of David, requires a transformation that all his disciples must undergo. The new David is not one whose purple is immediately evident, but rather his power can be found only in his crucifixion. It will take new eyes and ears to see and hear the truth proclaimed through the cross.

Throughout the gospel Matthew is unsparing in his description of the incomprehension of the disciples, but they do follow Jesus. In that respect Matthew contrasts the disciples with the crowds that are attracted to Jesus. Jesus goes throughout Galilee teaching in the synagogues, proclaiming the good news, and curing those afflicted with diseases, demons, epileptics, and paralytics. We are told that great crowds follow him as he draws people to him from the Decapolis, Jerusalem, Judea, and even from beyond the Jordan. Those in the crowds will often be in awe of Jesus, they will express amazement at his teaching, but at the end of the day they will shout, "Let him be crucified!" (Matt. 27:22–23).

We are still in the early stages of Matthew's story, but we are already beginning to see what is required if we are to be followers rather than admirers of Jesus. A story that James McClendon tells about Clarence Jordan, the founder of the Koinonia Community, an interracial farm in Georgia, wonderfully illumines the difference between being a disciple and those who simply admire Jesus. In the early 1950s it is said that Clarence asked his brother, Robert Jordan, who would later be a state senator and a justice on the Georgia Supreme Court, to represent Koinonia Farm legally. His brother replied:

> "Clarence, I can't do that. You know my political aspirations. Why, if I represented you, I might lose my job, my house, everything I've got."
>
> "*We* might lose everything too, Bob."
>
> "It's different for you."
>
> "Why is it different? I remember, it seems to me, that you and I joined the church the same Sunday, as boys. I expect when we came forward the preacher asked me about the same question he did you. He asked me, 'Do you accept Jesus as your Lord and Savior?' And I said, 'Yes.' What did you say?"
>
> "I follow Jesus, Clarence, up to a point."
>
> "Could that point by any chance be—the cross?"
>
> "That's right. I follow him to the cross, but not *on* the cross. I'm not getting myself crucified."
>
> "Then I don't believe you're a disciple. You're an admirer of Jesus, but not a disciple of his. I think you ought to go back to the church you belong to, and tell them you're an admirer not a disciple."
>
> "Well now, if everyone who felt like I do did that, we wouldn't *have* a church, would we?"
>
> "The question," Clarence said, "is, 'Do you have a church?'" (McClendon 1990, 103 [emphasis original])

MATTHEW 5

The Sermon

The difference between those who admire Jesus and those who would be his disciples is indicated by his disciples' willingness to "come to him" on the mountain. Jesus has seen the crowds. Matthew will tell us often that Jesus had compassion for the crowds or that he felt sorrow for them, but before he delivers the sermon we are told that he simply "saw the crowds." He goes up the mountain, and the disciples follow him. That the disciples do so puts them at risk, because they cannot avoid being directly addressed by Jesus.

In Exodus, God calls Moses to ascend Mount Sinai to receive the law. Mount Sinai was wrapped in smoke, and the whole mountain trembled with the presence of God and the thunder of his voice. The Lord summoned Moses to join him on the mountain, warning that no others, except Aaron, were permitted to accompany Moses up the mountain (Exod. 19:16–25). It is, therefore, remarkable that the disciples had the courage to join Jesus on the mountain in order to receive his teaching. Jesus, the new Moses, is surrounded by his disciples so that they may be taught, as Israel was taught by Moses, to be holy.

Matthew does not suggest that Jesus addresses only the disciples from the mountain. We are told that he "taught them," which may indicate that he taught those in the crowd as well as the disciples. Yet Bonhoeffer suggests that with the disciples' movement to join Jesus on the mountain we begin to catch a glimpse of the tension that will develop throughout Matthew's gospel between the disciples and the crowd. Jesus has called the disciples from the people. The disciples will be sent to preach repentance to the people. "But," Bonhoeffer asks, "how will it end?"

Jesus sees: his disciples are over there. They have visibly left the people to join him. He has called each individual one. They have given up everything in response to his call. Now they are living in renunciation and want; they are the poorest of the poor, the most tempted of the tempted, the hungriest of the hungry. They have only him. Yes, and with him they have nothing in the world, nothing at all, but everything, everything with God. So far, he has found only a small community, but it is a great community he is looking for, when he looks at the people. Disciples and the people belong together. The disciples will be his messengers; they will find listeners and believers here and there. Nevertheless, there will be enmity between the disciples and the people until the end. Everyone's rage at God and God's word will fall on the disciples, and they will be rejected with him. The cross comes into view. Christ, the disciples, the people—one can already see the whole history of the suffering of Jesus and his community. (Bonhoeffer 2001, 101)

The Sermon on the Mount in Matt. 5–7 is unintelligible if it is isolated from its context within Matthew's gospel. The Sermon on the Mount cannot help but become a law, an ethic, if what is taught is abstracted from the teacher. When the sermon is isolated from the one alone who is the exemplification of righteousness, it seems natural to ask if all Jesus's teachings must be followed literally. Does Jesus really think it possible for us to live without lust? How would we be able to run the world if we do not resist evildoers?

Once such questions are allowed to determine how the sermon is read, strategies are developed to help us avoid thinking that it applies to our lives. For example, some suggest that the sermon is meant to govern our personal lives, but that it should not be thought relevant for public affairs. The problem with such a strategy is that nowhere in Matthew's gospel does such a distinction appear. Perhaps a more honest alternative reading acknowledges that the sermon is meant to apply to our lives, but such an application is useful only to make us "feel guilty."

Reformation polemics often shapes this strategy by suggesting that the sermon is law meant to drive us to recognize our need for forgiveness. So a strong distinction, allegedly derived from Paul, is drawn between law and gospel.[1]

1. Davies 1969, 97–99 challenges all attempts to drive a wedge between the Jesus of the gospels (in particular Matthew) and Paul. For example, he calls attention to the echoes of Jesus's teaching in Paul: "Bless those who persecute you; bless and do not curse them" (Rom. 12:14) seems quite similar to Jesus's command: "But I say to you, Love your enemies and pray for those who persecute you" (Matt. 5:44). Moreover, Jesus in Matt. 5:39 commands us not to resist one who is evil, which seems to be the source of Paul's admonition that Christians should "repay [no one] evil for evil, but take thought for what is noble in the sight of all" (Rom. 12:17). Davies also calls attention to the prohibition against judging in Rom. 14:10 and Matt. 7:1. Davies concludes "that Paul was steeped in the tradition of what Jesus had said and that the words of Jesus had become bone of his bone. It is erroneous to think that Paul was not interested in the details of Jesus's teaching. Paul's moral awareness, at least, was rooted in the teaching of Jesus about the good life."

From such a perspective, the sermon's hard sayings are at best considered "ideals" that Christians might try to achieve, but with the knowledge that whether we live or do not live the way the sermon seems to suggest we should live does not determine the character of our faith in God.

This way of reading the Sermon on the Mount often tries to distinguish Christianity from Judaism by suggesting that Christianity is a religion of forgiveness whereas Judaism is a religion of law. Protestants are fond of this reading, often casting Catholicism as the Christian form of Judaism, that is, as a legalism that denies Paul's understanding of justification by faith. These readings of the sermon, which presume the contrast between Protestants and Catholic readings, at least have the virtue of locating the question of how the sermon is to be read and followed in an ecclesial context.

But the ecclesial practices that have legitimated questions about whether Jesus's teachings in the sermon are meant to be followed are but reflections of Christologies that separate the person and work of Christ. When the church assumes it is at home in the world, that is, when the church loses the eschatological character of Jesus's proclamation of the kingdom, too often the salvation wrought in Christ is construed in individualistic and pietistic terms. Satisfaction theories of the atonement dominate accounts of Christ's work, making it possible for the "saved" to avoid the radical character of the discipleship depicted in Jesus's sermon. What is important, it seems, is that Jesus be accepted as one's "personal savior," which is then thought to make possible the attempt to follow the teachings of the Sermon on the Mount. The problem with this way of construing salvation is that the sermon becomes an ethic that is no longer constitutive of salvation.

Bonhoeffer called salvation so understood "cheap grace." By "cheap grace" he meant an understanding of grace "as doctrine, as principle, as system. It means forgiveness of sins as a general truth; it means God's love as merely a Christian idea of God. Those who affirm it have already had their sins forgiven" (2001, 43). Such an affirmation, according to Bonhoeffer, invites the assumption that since the whole world is justified by grace Christians should live like the rest of the world. This view of grace is often shared by conservative and liberal Christians who otherwise think they are in deep disagreement. But conservatives and liberals differ only in how they think Christians should conform to the world.

What cannot be forgotten is that the one who preaches the sermon is the Son of God, that is, he is the Messiah, making all things new. The sermon is the reality of the new age made possible in time. And so we must be careful not to distinguish the sermon from the one who delivers it:

> The Sermon on the Mount is the word of the one who did not relate to reality as a foreigner, a reformer, a fanatic, the founder of a religion, but as the one who bore and experienced the nature of reality in his own body, who spoke out of the depth of reality as no other human being on earth ever before. The Sermon

on the Mount is the word of the very one who is the lord and law of reality. The Sermon on the Mount is to be understood and interpreted as the word of God who became human. That is the issue at stake when the question of historical action is raised, and here it must prove true that action in accord with Christ is action in accord with reality.

Action in accord with Christ does not originate in some ethical principle, but in the very person of Jesus Christ. (Bonhoeffer 2005, 231)

The demands of the sermon are but ideals if this is not the Son of God. Indeed one could argue that the demands of the sermon are profoundly immoral, demanding as they seem to do that we do not resist one who is evil. Yet if these radical demands are abandoned, we abandon Jesus. As W. D. Davies observes, Jesus's very words "point beyond themselves to himself, as their source: they too become witnesses to the King-Messiah," expressions of the Lord's very being (1969, 148, 131). The sayings of the Sermon on the Mount are the interpretation of Jesus's life, and that same life is the necessary condition for the interpretation of the sermon.

Accordingly the sermon is not addressed to individuals but to the community that Jesus begins and portends through the calling of the disciples. The sermon is not a heroic ethic. It is the constitution of a people. You cannot live by the demands of the sermon on your own, but that is the point. The demands of the sermon are designed to make us depend on God and one another (Hauerwas 1993, 63–72). As Richard Lischer puts it:

> Our only hope of living as the community of the Sermon is to acknowledge that we do not retaliate, hate, curse, lust, divorce, swear, brag, preen, worry, or backbite because it is not in the nature of our God or our destination that we should be such a people. When we as individuals fail in these instances, we do not snatch up cheap forgiveness, but we do remember that the ecclesial is larger than the sum of our individual failures and that it is pointed in a direction that will carry us away from them. (Lischer 1987, 161–62)

The sermon, therefore, is not a list of requirements, but rather a description of the life of a people gathered by and around Jesus. To be saved is to be so gathered. That is why the Beatitudes are the interpretive key to the whole sermon—precisely because they are not recommendations. No one is asked to go out and try to be poor in spirit or to mourn or to be meek. Rather, Jesus is indicating that given the reality of the kingdom we should not be surprised to find among those who follow him those who are poor in spirit, those who mourn, those who are meek. Moreover, Jesus does not suggest that everyone who follows him will possess all the Beatitudes, but we can be sure that some will be poor, some will mourn, and some will be meek.

For the church to be so constituted, according to Bonhoeffer, requires the visibility of the church. To be salt, to be made light for the world, is a call for the church to be visible. For the followers of Jesus, "to flee into invisibility is to deny the call. Any community of Jesus which wants to be invisible is no longer a community that follows him" (2001, 113). Christians, however, are tempted to become invisible, justifying their identification with the surrounding culture in the name of serving the neighbor. One of the names given such invisibility is Constantinianism, a term that describes the strategy of Christians when they become an ally of Caesar.

John Howard Yoder makes the striking observation that after the Constantinian shift the meaning of the word "Christian" changes (1984, 135–49). Prior to Constantine it took exceptional conviction to be a Christian. After Constantine it takes exceptional courage not to be counted as a Christian. The establishment of Christianity had the ironic result of making paganism morally compelling. This change in status of what it meant to be Christian, according to Yoder, called forth a new theological development, "namely the doctrine of the invisibility of the church." Before Constantine, Christians assumed as a matter of faith that God was governing history even in the person of the emperor, but they knew that God was present in the church. After the Constantinian establishment, Christians knew that God was governing the world in Constantine, but they had to take it on faith that within the nominally Christian mass there was a community of true believers. No longer could being a Christian be identified with church membership, since many "Christians" in the church had not chosen to follow Christ. Now to be a Christian is transmuted to "inwardness" (1984, 136–37).[2]

But, according to Bonhoeffer, in the Sermon on the Mount and especially in the sayings of Jesus, Matthew challenges all attempts to make invisible what it means to follow Jesus: "You are the light of the world. A city built on a hill

2. The description "Constantinianism" is fraught with ambiguity and complexity. For example, Yoder certainly does not think the problem with the disappearance of the church began only with the legalization of Christianity. He is, moreover, quite well aware that Constantinianism has been more than able to mutate into various forms all the more pernicious by their subtlety. Yoder's extremely sophisticated analysis (1971, 148–82) of these developments provides a useful characterization of different neo-neo-neo-neo-Constantinianisms that help us see how Constantinian assumptions can be transmuted even into secular forms. According to Yoder the crucial axiom that determines Constantinianism is that "the true meaning of history, the true locus of salvation, is in the cosmos and not in the church. Then what God is really doing He is doing through the framework of society as a whole and not in the Christian community" (1971, 154). Of course, the belief that the true locus of salvation is the church does not mean that Christians do not believe that what Christ has done is not cosmic, which means it is extremely important to understand that many developments identified as Constantinianism may from Yoder's perspective be faithful forms of Christian witness. Indeed, Yoder argues that it is a mistake to try to establish speculatively or from historical examples a consistent anti-Constantinian model, because the "affirmative alternative underlying the critique of paganization is the concreteness of the visible community created by the renewed message. The alternative to hierarchical definition is local definition" (1994a, 253). In fact, it is Yoder's view that the drift toward Constantinianism began when Christians began to think they could make sense of what it means to be Christian without the Jews (see Yoder 2003).

cannot be hid" (Matt. 5:14). Bonhoeffer observes that any Israelite could not help but be reminded of Jerusalem by an appeal to such a city, only now that city is constituted by a community of disciples. Accordingly,

> the followers of Jesus are no longer faced with a decision. The only decision possible for them has already been made. Now they have to be what they are, or they are not following Jesus. The followers are the visible community of faith; their discipleship is a visible act which separates them from the world—or it is not discipleship. And discipleship is as visible as light in the night, as a mountain in the flatland.
>
> To flee into invisibility is to deny the call. Any community of Jesus which wants to be invisible is no longer a community that follows him. (Bonhoeffer 2001, 113)[3]

This does not mean that those who would follow Jesus do so that they may be seen. Nor are disciples called to be different in order to be different. Jesus clearly thinks that disciples will be different, but that difference is because of what he is—the Son of God. Bonhoeffer observes that Jesus's teachings in Matt. 6 help us to see that the righteousness of the disciple is hidden even from the disciple. Visibility and difference is the result of being pulled into the way of life made possible by Jesus. So the Sermon on the Mount is a description of a way of life of a people, a people of a new age that results from following this man.

That is what it means to be blessed. Given our everyday assumptions, we normally do not think that the poor in spirit, those who mourn, the meek, those who hunger and thirst for righteousness, the merciful, the pure in heart, peacemakers, those persecuted for righteousness sake, are "blessed." Yet that Jesus declares such people "blessed" indicates that the transformed world has begun with the proclamation that "the kingdom of heaven has come near." Each of the Beatitudes names a gift, but it is not presumed that everyone who is a follower of Jesus will possess each beatitude. Rather, the gifts named in the Beatitudes suggest that the diversity of these gifts will be present in the community of those who have heard Jesus's call to discipleship. Indeed, to learn to be a disciple is to learn why we are dependent on those who mourn or who are meek, though we may not possess that gift ourselves.

It is tempting to speculate what kind of person is the exemplification of each of the Beatitudes. For example, it is often suggested that the "poor in spirit" exemplify the virtue of humility; or that "those who mourn" repent of their sins; or that "the meek" imitate the gentleness of the Lord and endure offense rather than retaliate; or that "those who hunger and thirst for righteousness" desire nothing but God's justice; or that "the merciful" exemplify compassion for the poor; or that "the pure in heart" have been cleansed of fleshly desires;

---

3. For my more extended discussion of Bonhoeffer's understanding of the importance of the visibility of the church as well as a comparison to Yoder, see Hauerwas 2004b, 33–74.

or that "the peacemakers" preserve the unity of the church as well as seek the peace of the city; or that "those who are persecuted" endure hardship for the sake of the gospel. Each of these characterizations have merit and are useful for our edification.

But the source for any understanding of the Beatitudes must be Jesus.[4] It is from Jesus that we learn what it means to be "poor in the spirit." Thus Paul can commend the Philippians to have "the same mind . . . that was in Christ Jesus":

> Who, though he was in the form of God,
>   did not regard equality with God
>   as something to be exploited,
> but emptied himself,
>   taking the form of a slave,
>   being born in human likeness.
> And being found in human form,
>   he humbled himself
>   and became obedient to the point of death—
>   even death on a cross. (Phil. 2:5–8)

Paul does not assume that our poverty of spirit is the same as Jesus's self-emptying, but rather that Jesus's poverty has made it possible for a people to exist who can live dispossessed of possessions. To be poor does not in itself make one a follower of Jesus, but it can put you in the vicinity of what it might mean to discover the kind of poverty that frees those who follow Jesus from enslavement to the world. Not to be missed, moreover, is the political significance of such poverty. Too often we fail to recognize our accommodation to worldly powers because we fear losing our wealth—wealth that can take quite diverse forms.

Perhaps no beatitude is more christocentric than Jesus's commendation of those who mourn, for they are, like him, prepared to live in the world renouncing what the world calls happiness and even peace (Bonhoeffer 2001, 103). Like Jesus, moreover, the disciples endure injustice with the hard meekness that still hungers and thirsts for righteousness. Yet the righteousness of this new people is blessed by the mercy seen in the forgiveness that Christ showed even to those who would kill him. Such a people are capable of peacemaking because they

4. Origen observes: "Jesus confirms all of the beatitudes he speaks in the Gospel, and he justifies his teaching through his own example. 'Blessed are the meek' is what he says of himself. 'Learn of me, for I am meek.' 'Blessed are the peacemakers.' Who is a peacemaker like my Lord Jesus, who is our peace, who made enmity to cease and destroyed it in his flesh? 'Blessed are they who suffer persecution for righteousness' sake.' No one more than the Lord Jesus, who was crucified for our sins, endured persecution for righteousness' sake. The Lord, then, displays all the beatitudes as being realized in himself. Conforming to that which he said, 'Blessed are those who weep,' he himself wept over Jerusalem, to lay the foundation of this beatitude also" (quoted in Allison 2005, 150).

are sustained by the purity derived from having no other *telos* but to enact the kingdom embodied in Jesus. Yet such a people may well be persecuted, as Jesus was persecuted, because they are an alternative to the violence of the world that is too often called "peace."

That each of the Beatitudes is accompanied by a "reward" does not mean that a disciple might, for example, try to be poor in spirit in order to inherit the kingdom of heaven. As I suggested above, such an understanding of the Beatitudes would betray that they are gifts. That those who are merciful receive mercy is but an indication of the kind of life made possible for those called to live in Jesus's kingdom. Virtue may be its own reward, but for Christians the virtues, the kind of virtues suggested by the Beatitudes, are names for the shared life made possible through Christ.

Therefore, those who live in a manner described by the Beatitudes should rejoice and be glad when they are falsely accused and even persecuted "on my account." Such persecution marks these as standing in the tradition of the prophets. The office of the prophet has now fallen on this new community, who has become salt and light for the world. Just as the person of the prophets became God's presence to and in Israel, now those who follow Jesus become God's sign for the world. Accordingly, disciples cannot afford games of false humility. Too much is at stake. The cross is the light that illumines the works of the disciples, which makes possible, even for the Gentiles (Matt. 5:16), the ability to see the good works that give glory to the Father in heaven.

Jesus claims that he is the fulfillment of the law and the prophets. Therefore he calls his followers to keep the law, suggesting that the righteousness of those who would follow him should exceed that of the scribes and Pharisees. What could this possibly mean? Does it mean that Christians should keep, like the Jews, the law concerning what can and cannot be eaten or the law concerning sacrifice? Christians have rightly struggled to answer these challenges. For example, Thomas Aquinas suggests that we must distinguish between moral, juridical, and ceremonial law in the Old Testament. He does so in order to argue that only the moral law—that is, the law incumbent on all human beings by our participation in divine law—is to be observed by Christians (1981, part I-II QQ. 90–108).[5] According to Thomas, Christ has fulfilled through his life

---

5. Thomas calls our participation in the divine law the "natural law" (1981, part I-II Q. 94). This account of the natural law is dependent on his theological presuppositions, which means that he did not try to isolate the principles of natural law in an effort to establish a minimal set of obligations incumbent on all people, whether they were Christian or not. Those developments came later. According to Thomas, only the new law can justify. He quotes Augustine, who says in *The Spirit and the Letter* that in the Old Testament "*the Law was set forth in an outward fashion, that the ungodly might be afraid; here,* i.e. in the New Testament, *it is given in an inward manner, that they may be justified.*—The other element of the Evangelical Law is secondary: namely, the teachings of faith, and those commandments which direct human affections and human actions. And as to this, the New Law does not justify. Hence the Apostle says (2 Cor. iii.6): *The letter killeth, but the spirit quickeneth:* and Augustine explains this . . . by saying that the letter denotes

and death the juridical and ceremonial law, making it no longer necessary for Christians to observe that part of the law. Indeed from Thomas's perspective, for Christians to observe the ceremonial law would be idolatry.[6]

Thomas's account of the status of the law for Christians has shaped later discussion. The problem with Thomas's solution is that Jesus does not distinguish between the moral, juridical, and ceremonial law when he says that not one letter of the law will pass away "until all is accomplished." Moreover Jesus plainly says that his followers are to keep the law and that their righteousness should exceed that of the scribes and Pharisees. Everything, it seems, hangs on what it means for "all" to be "accomplished." Christians believe that all was accomplished in Jesus's death, resurrection, and ascension, but does that mean that every letter of the law in the Old Testament is no longer incumbent on Christians?

Jews rightly ask Christians to reconsider our assumption that the Jewish understanding of what it means to observe the law should not be incumbent on Christians. Of course it is important to remember that Jews do not agree among themselves about what it means to observe the law, but their very disagreements are also important for Christian obedience. Crucial for any Christian reflection on the status of the law in the Old Testament is what it means for Christian righteousness to exceed that of the Pharisees and scribes, for that "excess" should help us understand the appropriate context for assessing how Christian understanding of our discipleship to Jesus entails our fulfillment of the law. Accordingly, Christians must welcome the ongoing challenge concerning what it may mean for us to observe the law.

Jesus will criticize the Pharisees and scribes for hypocrisy (Matt. 15:1–9), for neglecting the weightier matters of the law while emphasizing minutiae (23:23), for greed and self-indulgence (23:25–26)—all criticisms made from within Israel's understanding of the purpose of the law. The prophets, for example, made similar criticisms of Israel's failure to observe the law. Yet it

---

any writing that is external to man, even that of the moral precepts such as are contained in the Gospel. Wherefore the letter, even of the Gospel would kill, unless there were the inward presence of the healing grace of faith" (1981, part I-II Q. 106 art. 2 [emphasis original]).

6. Thomas pays close exegetical attention to the ceremonial and juridical law, noting how the new law, which is nothing other than the law of the Holy Spirit, fulfills the old: "Some of the sacraments of the New Law had corresponding figurative sacraments in the Old Law. For Baptism, which is the sacrament of Faith, corresponds to circumcision. Hence it is written (Col. ii.11, 12): *You are circumcised . . . in the circumcision of* Our Lord Jesus *Christ; buried with Him in Baptism.* In the New Law the sacrament of the Eucharist corresponds to the banquet of the pascal lamb. The sacrament of Penance in the New Law corresponds to all the purifications of the Old Law. The sacrament of Orders corresponds to the consecration of the pontiff and of the priests. To the sacrament of Confirmation, which is the sacrament of the fulness of grace, there would be no corresponding sacrament of the Old Law, because the time of fulness had not yet come, since *the Law brought no man . . . to perfection* (Heb. vii.19)" (1981, part I-II Q. 102 art. 5 reply 3 [emphasis original]). Levering 2002 provides the best account of Thomas's analysis of the law.

is crucial that Jesus's criticisms of the Pharisees and scribes not overlook the challenge of the politics of the observance of the law. The righteousness of the scribes and Pharisees, their rightful desire to remain holy, was their attempt to be God's faithful people even when they were in exile or occupied by a foreign power. Yet too often Israel sought to be faithful in a manner that would not challenge the powers, and in particular the power of Rome. The Pharisees quite understandably tried to observe the law without that observance being recognized as subversive to those who ruled them.

Yet that is exactly what Jesus will not let those who would be faithful to God's calling of Israel, those who would be his disciples, do or be. Jesus does not seek to violently overthrow Rome, because his kingdom is an alternative to the violence of Rome as well as to those who would overthrow Rome with violence. His kingdom, however, cannot avoid being subversive. That subversion is the righteousness that exceeds that of the scribes and Pharisees and as such is a subversion that will result in his crucifixion, for rather than violently overthrowing the old order Jesus creates a people capable of living in accordance with the new order in the old. The antithesis that follows his admonition that his followers are to be salt and light for the world is but Jesus's description of the order of this new community. Yoder observes (1971, 28–29) that Jesus does what God had done in calling Abraham, Moses, Gideon, or Samuel. That is, he gathers people around his word so that a society comes into being like no other society the world has ever seen:

1. This was a voluntary society: you could not be born into it. You could come into it only by repenting and freely pledging allegiance to its king. It was a society with no second-generation members.
2. It was a society that, counter to all precedent, was mixed in its composition. It was mixed racially, with both Jews and Gentiles; mixed religiously, with fanatical keepers of the law and advocates of liberty from all forms; with both radical monotheists and others just in the process of disentangling their minds from idolatry; mixed economically with members both rich and poor.
3. When he called his society together Jesus gave its members a new way of life to live. He gave them a new way to deal with offenders—by forgiving them. He gave them a new way to deal with violence—by suffering. He gave them a new way to deal with money—by sharing it. He gave them a new way to deal with problems of leadership—by drawing upon the gift of every member, even the most humble. He gave them a new way to deal with a corrupt society—by building a new order, not smashing the old. He gave them a new pattern of relationship between man and woman, between parent and child, between master and slave, in which was made concrete a radical new vision of what it means to be a human

person. He gave them a new attitude toward the state and toward the "enemy nation."

That is the visibility that is at the heart of Jesus's calling of the disciples as well as the Sermon on the Mount. The details of that visibility follow in a series of contrasts: "You have heard that it was said, but I say to you." These antitheses serve, just as the Beatitudes, to spell out, to describe, the kind of community that the law requires.[7] Jesus has just told us that the law is to be observed, so murder, adultery, divorce, oaths, retaliation, and hatred of enemy are forbidden. Yet the community that Jesus calls into existence cannot be determined by what it avoids, but rather what is avoided is so because of the character of the community that is to exemplify Christ's life.

His life, moreover, makes possible our reconciliation with the Father and with one another. That reconciliation creates a community of reconciliation, a community of peace. So we should not be surprised that Jesus admonishes us not to harbor our anger at our brothers and sisters, but rather we are to seek reconciliation with them. He does not say that we are not to be angry, but rather that we are not to come to the altar of sacrifice unreconciled to the one with whom we are angry. Anger and sacrifice were cojoined by Cain's murder of Abel. Angered that God looked with favor on Abel's offering, Cain killed Abel (Gen. 4:1–16). Jesus now proclaims that the kingdom of repentance has drawn near, breaking the cycle of murder as sacrifice by commanding those who would follow him to be reconciled before offering their gifts at the altar. He not only commands that we be reconciled, but he tells us how we are to practice reconciliation (Matt. 18:15–20).[8]

Jesus charges members of the church to confront those whom we think have sinned against us. He does not say that if we think we have been wronged we might consider confronting the one we believe has done us wrong. Jesus tells us that we must do so because the wrong is not against us, but rather against the body, that is, the very holiness of the church is at stake. Moreover, to be required to confront those whom we believe have wronged us is risky business because we may find out that we are mistaken.

In 1 Cor. 6:1–8 Paul admonishes the Corinthians for taking one another to courts of law presided over by unbelievers. Paul reminds the Corinthians, a

---

7. Davenport suggests that the antitheses are not rules or regulations for mechanical or self-assertive righteousness, but rather Jesus's "descriptions" for the way of life that the new age makes possible. They are therefore not set over against Torah, but rather the fulfillment of Torah. Jesus is saying that one can now live this way. Moreover "since there can be no contradiction between the character of the Reign of God and the character of God himself, the Torah Jesus speaks is rooted in God's own character. Disciples, then, are free to abide by that Torah that others, seeing the manifestation of Torah in the disciples' lives, might be led to glorify God" (1988, 139).

8. Allison 2005, 65–72 provides a compelling argument for the Cain and Abel story as the background of this antithesis.

reminder that surely draws on Jesus's admonition not to remain angry with one another, that we should be ready to suffer a wrong rather than act against the body of Christ, for nothing less is at stake than the church offering the world an alternative to the world's justice. If such a community does not exist, then unbelievers will have no way to know God's peace.

The church, therefore, has rightly thought confession of sin, penance, and reconciliation necessary for the reception of the Eucharist. How could we dare come to the feast of reconciliation not in unity with our brothers and sisters? The name given that unity is love. The gifts of bread and wine must be brought by those at peace with God and with one another. If we are unreconciled, we best not receive; we dare not dishonor the holiness of the gifts from God.

Anger and lust are bodily passions. We simply are not capable of willing ourselves free of anger or lust. Jesus does not imply that we are to be free of either anger or lust; that is, he assumes that we are bodily beings. Rather, he offers us membership in a community in which our bodies are formed in service to God and for one another so that our anger and our lust are transformed. Too often technologies of the self, used to free ourselves of anger or lust, make those passions posses an even greater hold over our lives. Jesus, however, is not recommending that we will our way free of lust or anger, but rather he is offering us membership in a people that is so compelling we are not invited to dwell on ourselves or our sinfulness.

Alone we cannot conceive of an alternative to lust, but Jesus offers us participation in a kingdom that is so demanding we discover we have better things to do than to concentrate on our lust. If we are a people committed to peace in a world of war, if we are a people committed to faithfulness in a world of distrust, then we will be consumed by a way to live that offers freedom from being dominated by anger or lust.

Perhaps nothing is more indicative of the unexpected world that Jesus has brought into existence than his suggestion that some of his followers will not marry. For most of those who counted themselves members of the people of Israel, the idea that they could refrain from marriage and the having of children could be understood only as a challenge to the very character of what it means to be God's people, for to be a Jew means first and foremost to have a child, a child whose very existence is a sign of God's care of God's people. But the community called into existence by Jesus does not grow by biological reproduction, but by witness and conversion. Singleness and celibacy are practices constitutive of the mission to the Gentiles.

Jesus's teaching on adultery and divorce, the latter directed against male privilege, must be understood as expressions of the new body made ours through his crucified body. Bonhoeffer is, therefore, surely right to observe:

> Jesus does not make either marriage or celibacy into a required program. Instead, he frees his disciples from πορνεία, infidelity within and outside marriage,

which is a sin not only against one's own body, but a sin against the very body of Christ (1 Cor. 6:13–15). Even the body of the disciple belongs to Christ and discipleship; our bodies are members of his body. Because Jesus, the Son of God, assumed a human body, and because we are in communion with his body, that is why infidelity is a sin against Jesus' own body.

Jesus' body was crucified. The apostle says of those who belong to Christ that they have crucified the flesh with its passions and desires (Gal. 5:24). Thus, the fulfillment of even this Old Testament commandment becomes true only in the crucified, martyred body of Jesus Christ. The sight of that body, which was given for us, and our communion with it provide the disciples with the strength for the chastity Jesus commands. (Bonhoeffer 2001, 127)[9]

Those who use Matt. 5:32, in particular those trying to determine the meaning of "except on grounds of *porneias*" in order to decide if and when divorce may be justified, unfortunately transform the text from one of permission to a legalistic exchange. What is crucial is not the question of when a marriage may be dissolved, but given the new dispensation the question should be how Christians should understand marriage. In similar fashion the question is not whether a divorced woman should be allowed to marry, but what kind of community must a church be that does not make it a matter of necessity for such a woman to remarry. If Christians do not have to marry, if women who have been abandoned do not have to remarry, then surely the church must be a community of friendship that is an alternative to the loneliness of our world.

At the very least, any community capable of sustaining singleness as a way of life must be a community based on trust made possible by speaking the truth to one another. Bonhoeffer observes that oaths are a sign that we live in a world of lies. If we could trust ourselves to tell the truth not only to others but especially to ourselves, oaths would not be needed. Oaths hope to safeguard us from lying, but they also can encourage lying just to the extent that the very existence of the oath grants a certain right to the lie. Therefore to "let your word be 'Yes, Yes' or 'No, No'" is Jesus's way of saying that for disciples our speech always takes place in the presence of God: "Thus disciples of Jesus should not swear, because there is no such thing as speech not spoken before God. All of their words should be nothing but truth, so that nothing requires verification by oath. An oath consigns all other statements to the darkness of doubt. That is why it is 'from the evil one'" (Bonhoeffer 2001, 129–30).[10]

9. Jesus's use of bodily analogies to describe what must be done for those overwhelmed by lust suggests how our bodies have been transformed by the baptism into his body. Paul's understanding of baptism in Rom. 6 is a commentary on Jesus's admonition that if our right hand causes us to sin it is best "thrown away."

10. Griffiths observes that Augustine maintained that we should never tell a lie because to do so betrayed the very character of speech as a gift from God. According to Griffiths 2004, 89, Augustine maintained that only "God is the radiant truth-teller: we are liars shrouded in shadow. Approaching God makes truth-telling possible for us by shedding light on our darkness: moving

Christians are, thereby, committed to plain speech. We seek to say no more or no less than what needs to be said. Speech so disciplined is not easily attained. Too often we want to use the gift of speech as a weapon, often a very subtle weapon, to establish our superiority. To learn to speak truthfully to one another requires that we learn to speak truthfully to God, that is, we must learn to pray. That is why the Psalms are the great prayer book of the church because they teach us to pray without pretension. The Psalms allow us to rage against God and in our rage discover God's refusal to abandon us.

The Psalms, moreover, train us to speak truthfully because they force us to acknowledge our sins or at least to have our sins revealed. Jesus is God's psalm, for as we shall see, Matthew can tell the story of Jesus only through the Psalms. That is why Bonhoeffer is surely right that the truthfulness of the disciples has its basis in following Jesus, through whom their sins are revealed. Just as Israel refuses to hide its sins in the Old Testament, so Matthew refuses to be anything but honest about the sins of those who would follow Jesus.

> Only the cross as God's truth about us makes us truthful. Those who know the cross no longer shy away from any truth. Those who lie under the cross can do without the oath as a commandment establishing truthfulness, for they exist in the perfect truth of God. There is no truth toward Jesus without truth toward other people. Lying destroys community. But truth rends false community and founds genuine fellowship.
>
> There is no following Jesus without living in the truth unveiled before God and other people. (Bonhoeffer 2001, 131)

Such a community of truthfulness cannot be afraid of conflict. That Jesus requires us to confront one another if we believe we have been sinned against is not a recommendation for "just getting along." Moreover the truth that constitutes the church means that the lies of the world cannot help but be exposed by the way Christians are required to live. Such a people, as we are told in the Beatitudes, can expect to be persecuted. But it is surely the case that a people who have learned to "rejoice in the truth" find that they would desire no other life.

A people of truth is sure to have enemies. This makes Jesus's command against retaliation—as well as his call for those who would follow him to love

---

away from God guarantees that we lie by leaving us in the shadows. The liar speaks always and only *de suo*. . . . To speak by expropriation is the same as to speak *de suo*. It is also the same as to speak *secundum se* (according to oneself) or *secundum hominem* (according to humanity, humanly). All this is contrasted with using speech as gift, being filled up (*impletus*) from outside oneself—from God—and as a result becoming a participant (*particeps*) in God, who is, once again, the radiant and only source of truth. Abandoning the lie, then, requires acknowledgment of the fact that speech is a gift, something with which we are filled and by means of which we participate in the truth that is not ours. We cannot, when acting expropriatively (by theft, in an attempt to own), do anything but lie."

their enemies—all the more extraordinary. He does not promise that if we turn the other cheek we will avoid being hit again. Nonretaliation is not a strategy to get what we want by other means. Rather, Jesus calls us to the practice of nonretaliation because that is the form that God's care of us took in his cross. In like manner Christians are to give more than we are asked to give, we are to give to those who beg, because that is the character of God. Indeed, as we learn in Jesus's parable in Matt. 25, just to the extent we have not responded "to the least of these" we have failed to respond to him.

Jesus's charge that we are not to retaliate against those who would seek to do us harm—as well as his demand that we are to love our enemies—makes clear the apocalyptic character of the entire Sermon on the Mount. To so live requires the patience that has been made possible by God refusing to let our sin prevent him from becoming one of us, from joining our time, through the coming of Jesus. It is the same patience that animates those blessed in the Beatitudes, for they are examples of the kind of people who have the time in an unmerciful world to be merciful. To be a disciple of Jesus, to be ready to be reconciled with those with whom we are angry, to be faithful in marriage, to take the time required to tell the truth—all are habits that create the time and space to be capable of loving our enemies.

The patience required by the Beatitudes and the antitheses makes no sense if, as we are told in the Revelation of John, "the lamb that was slain is worthy to receive power!" The heart of the Sermon on the Mount is the conviction

> that the cross and not the sword, suffering and not brute power determines the meaning of history. The key to the obedience of God's people is not their effectiveness but their patience. The triumph of the right is assured not by the might that comes to the aid of the right, which is of course the justification of the use of violence and other kinds of power in every human conflict. The triumph of the right, although it is assured, is sure because of the power of the resurrection and not because of any calculation of causes and effects, nor because of the inherently greater strength of the good guys. The relationship between the obedience of God's people and the triumph of God's cause is not a relationship between cause and effect but one of cross and resurrection. (Yoder 1994b, 232)

We are called, therefore, to be perfect, but perfection names our participation in Christ's love of his enemies. Perfection does not mean that we are sinless or that we are free of anger or lust. Rather, to be perfect is to learn to be part of a people who take the time to live without resorting to violence to sustain their existence. To so live requires habits like learning to tell one another the truth, to be faithful in our promises to one another, to seek reconciliation. To so live can be called pacifism and/or nonviolence, but such descriptions do not do justice to the form of life described in the Beatitudes and antitheses, for that form of life can be lived truthfully only if Christ is who Matthew says he is, that is, the Son of God.

This ethic has often challenged Christians who have sought to be responsible for the social order. For example, Frederick Dale Bruner, commenting on the command not to take oaths, observes that obedience "to this Command will eventually raise serious questions about how far disciples can participate in government service where oaths are frequently required and administered. What of military service and its oaths?" (2004, 235). That question has often been answered by drawing a distinction between how I should respond to injury done to me personally and harm done that effects me as bearer of an office. I am in the former case to act as Jesus would have me act, but to the extent I occupy responsibility for maintaining order I am obligated to use violence in the name of that order. Indeed the latter obligation is understood to be an expression of the love demanded by Christ.[11]

Yet Bonhoeffer rightly observes that this distinction between the private person and the bearer of an office is unknown to Jesus. Jesus nowhere suggests that the disciples who have left all behind to follow him should not also leave behind their public responsibilities. Jesus has even asked them to leave behind their responsibilities as sons. Bonhoeffer notes that no one is ever a private person, but rather we always exist constituted by responsibilities. So if we are attacked we are so as parent to children, as pastor of a congregation, or as diplomat. Exactly because we are so situated is why Jesus commands us not to resist evil by using means that are evil. Jesus calls us to resist evil, but he does so by empowering us with the weapons of the Spirit. Those weapons must be shaped by the suffering of his cross:

> Only those who there, in the cross of Jesus, find faith in the victory over evil can obey his command, and that is the only kind of obedience which has the promise. Which promise? The promise of community with the cross of Jesus and of community with his victory. . . .
>
>   In the cross alone is it true and real that suffering love is the retribution for and the overcoming of evil. Participation in the cross is given to the disciples by the call into discipleship. They are blessed in this visible community. (Bonhoeffer 2001, 136–37)

---

11. Bruner tries to resolve what he regards as the tension between these two positions by suggesting that we need both: "Today we need both *pacifist* Christians who will work *outside* government in countercultural respect but distance under Jesus' Peacemaking commands as the Reformation Peace Churches did, *and* we need *pragmatic* Christians who will work *within* government pragmatically to seek peace and justice as the magisterial Reformation, under Jesus' Love command, decided to do" (2004, 246). Bruner's position on these matters is much different from the first edition of his book, which took a fairly straight Reformation line. So it is much to his credit that he has revised his position under the influence of John Howard Yoder, but his appeal to the love command abstracted from the one who commands us to love is unconvincing.

MATTHEW 6

Practicing Prayer

The visibility that Jesus calls for in the first part of the Sermon on the Mount seems qualified by his condemnation of those who practice righteousness in order to be seen. How are we to understand Jesus telling us that our light should shine before others (Matt. 5:16) and yet it seems that we are to give alms in secret (6:1)? Bonhoeffer argues that this is not a contradiction if we attend to the question from whom the visibility of discipleship is to be kept hidden. According to Bonhoeffer, the hiddenness that should characterize the disciples' action applies to the disciple. Disciples should "keep on following Jesus, and should keep looking forward to him who is going before them, but not at themselves and what they are doing. The righteousness of the disciples is hidden from themselves" (2001, 149).

Bonhoeffer suggests, therefore, that those who would follow Jesus can be characterized by a kind of "forgetfulness." Following Jesus requires that we lose our overpowering sense of self. Such a loss often accompanies participation in any grand movement, but the kind of forgetfulness required to follow Jesus is different from those moments that are briefly exhilarating but soon lost. The forgetfulness that Jesus offers is made possible by the compelling reality and beauty of participation in his time, a time that cannot be lost, because it is God's time.

Jesus's admonition that we guard against calling attention to ourselves through the practice of piety suggests that it matters not only that we follow Jesus but that how we do so is crucial for what it means to be his visible people. One of the languages the church has found helpful to explore this "how" has been the language of the virtues. That language, just as the language of the law, is not peculiar to the gospel but was first developed by Greek and Roman philosophers. Aristotle, for example, was aware that a person could not become good by simply copying the actions of a good or just person. For Aristotle, the just person is not one who does this or that action, but does what he or she does in the way in which a just person does them—which means that they must know what they are doing, that they must do what they do for no other reason than what they do is what a person of justice does, and that they must do what they do from a firm and unchanging character (1999, §1105a30–b10).

Aristotle has little use for those who think one can be made just or good through argument. Such people are like the sick who listen to the doctor but fail to act on the instructions the doctor gives. Rather, what is needed is training in the habits necessary for the acquisition of the virtues.[1] Such training requires apprenticeship to a master who has gained the wisdom necessary to gage our failures and our successes and also requires membership in a community that can direct us to the goods correlative to the virtues. There is a kind of forgetfulness to being so formed, because virtuous persons are virtuous for no other reason than that they would not desire to be other than they are.

There seem, therefore, to be some similarities between Jesus's admonition that we are not to act righteously in order to call attention to ourselves and what some understand to be the meaning of virtuous. Yet Christians are not called to be virtuous. We are called to be disciples. Such a calling may be analogous to the need for a master to acquire the virtues, but the kind of master that Jesus is makes all the difference. Those who are called to follow Jesus are able to do so because Jesus has no master to imitate. We are able to follow him only because he was able to do what we cannot do, that is, he alone was capable of freeing us from the grip of sin through his cross. That is why Christians believe, in contrast to Aristotle, that we are capable of becoming his disciples even if we acquired destructive habits early or late in our lives.

Augustine, therefore, insists that the virtues of the pagans are sinful unless they are transformed by the love of God. Only such a transformation can save us from the pride that cannot help but accompany the virtues that have not had God as their source and object (1955b, 115–17). Thomas Aquinas, who is often thought to have had a more positive view of the pagan virtues than did Augustine, insists that the "natural virtues" must be formed by charity if they are to make us follow the one alone from who we should learn humility (1981, part I-II Q. 62).

Bonhoeffer is surely right, therefore, to insist that "the genuine deed of love is always a deed hidden to myself" (2001, 151),[2] for Jesus is calling us not to

---

1. For a good account of the importance of habituation, see Wells 2004, 73–86.

2. Bonhoeffer makes the further claim, a claim that seems to be overstated, that this hidden love cannot be a visible virtue or a human habit. That the virtues are gifts makes them no less bodily. Milbank makes Bonhoeffer's point in a manner that does not entail the denial of the body: "Suppose it is the case that to be ethical is not to posses something, not even to possess

attend to our own goodness or our loves, but rather to follow him. Not to let our left hand know what our right hand does when giving alms is possible only by the overwhelming self-forgetfulness that comes from Jesus's call to discipleship. We are called to righteousness as well as called to give alms; these are possible because of what we have received.[3] That is why, for Christians, acquiring the virtues is not to be understood as what we do, but rather as what has been made possible by the gifts we have received. We can do only what we have been given.

Jesus, therefore, directs our attention to prayer. Prayer is perfect activity because it is done for no other purpose than itself. Jesus tells us to pray to our Father "in secret" and the Father will reward us "in secret." To so pray requires that we pray to the one whom Jesus has made known. So we learn to pray by following Jesus, who is the Father's prayer for us. That prayer, Jesus's prayer, is secret because it is directed to the Father. Prayer, like Jesus, makes the Father's will known, and the Father wills that we learn to pray.

It seems that if we are to know how to pray we must be taught to pray. Jesus says, however, that even the Gentiles pray, but they do not know how to pray, for the Gentiles think they need to impress whatever god or gods to whom they pray by the quality of their rhetoric. That the Gentiles pray is not surprising, because we believe that God created us to be animals who desire to pray, but that desire must be rightly formed. At the very least, we must know that we are to pray to our Father, but that is learned from the one alone who knows the Father. Jesus will tell us that "all things have been handed over" to him by his Father; "and no one knows the Father except the Son and anyone to whom the Son chooses to reveal him" (Matt. 11:27).

So our first lesson in prayer is to learn to discipline all our descriptions of God by the appellation to the Father. Whatever it may mean for God to be omnipotent, omnipresent, all knowing, eternal, infinite—none of these descriptions are more important or significant than Jesus teaching us to address the Father. What it means, for example, for God to be all powerful is that he does not disdain the sacrifice of his Son on the cross, a reminder that all theology must begin in prayer.

Some may worry that addressing God as Father depends on analogies derived from our experiences of our biological fathers. Yet Jesus's teaching us to call God Father challenges the presumption that we know who God is from our familial experiences. We do not call God Father because we have had or have not had a positive experience of being a father's child. Rather, all human fathers

---

one's own deed. Suppose it is, from the outset, to receive the gift of the other as something that diverts one's life, and to offer one's life in such a way that you do not know in advance what it is that you will give, but must reclaim it retrospectively" (2003, 147). Milbank is right that we know only retrospectively what we have done, even if we must live prospectively.

3. Alms can take many different forms. Giving money may be one of the lesser forms of alms. The virtues themselves are alms if we rightly understand that we are to give ourselves.

are measured and judged by the Father's love of the Son. To pray to God as the Father challenges the status quo of human fatherhood, just as calling the church our family challenges the limitations and sins of our human families. Jesus not only tells us that we must be taught to pray, he teaches us the prayer we must learn to pray. His prayer begins with "Our Father."

Though we may pray in secret, we always pray with others. We begin to learn to pray by praying to "our" Father. We are never alone when we pray because we pray as children who have been taught by the Spirit of the Son to cry "Abba! Father!" (Gal. 4:6). Through the Spirit our prayer is joined to Jesus's prayer so that when we pray we pray with the whole communion of saints who surround the Father in heaven.

We are able to pray to the Father in heaven because "we have a great high priest who has passed through the heavens, Jesus, the Son of God, [and] let us hold fast to our confession. For we do not have a high priest who is unable to sympathize with our weaknesses, but we have one who in every respect has been tested as we are, yet without sin. Let us therefore approach the throne of grace with boldness, so that we may receive mercy and find grace to help in time of need" (Heb. 4:14–16).

To pray to the Father in heaven means that our voice is joined with the "angels surrounding the throne and the living creatures and the elders; they numbered myriads of myriads and thousands of thousands, singing with full voice,"

> Worthy is the Lamb that was slaughtered
> to receive power and wealth and wisdom and might
> and honor and glory and blessing! (Rev. 5:11–12)

"Hallowed be your name," the name we have learned from Jesus, is at the heart of what it means to be called to holiness.[4] To hallow God's name is to live lives of prayer. It is to pray that we lead lives that glorify God. When we pray this prayer we do so as those commandeered by God, sanctified, set apart, ordained, made holy. We are commissioned to live lives that make visible to the world that the holy God, the same God before whom Moses hid his face when

---

4. In Exod. 3:13–15 we learn what a precious gift we have been given by the bestowal of God's name. "I AM WHO I AM" is, of course, an indication that we can never pretend to possess God's name. God's name is to be hallowed because it is unlike any other name. Rosenzweig puts it this way: "To utter God's name is entirely different from uttering the name of a man or a thing. True, they have something in common; the name of God, his proper name, and a term of designation are not identical with the bearers of these names. But except for this they differ widely. Man has a name so that he may be called by it. To be called by his name is for him an ultimate domestication. God does not have a name so that he may be called by it. To him it is irrelevant whether his name is called or not; he holds him who calls him by his name as well as those who call him by other names or those who speak to him in name-less silence. He bears a name for our sake, so that we may call him. It is for our sake he permits himself to be named and called by that name, since it is only by jointly calling upon him that we become a 'me'" (1999, 91).

he was told God's name (Exod. 3:6), reigns. God the Father has redeemed his creation through his Son. God has regained his territory from the enemy. God's newly won territory is those who pray, "Hallowed be thy name."

The same people pray that the disruption begun in Jesus, a disruption called the kingdom of God, continue. They pray that the kingdom come because they have become part of that coming. The devil left Jesus after failing to defeat him in the desert, but the struggle continues. So Jesus teaches us to pray for an end to the kingdoms of this world dominated by sin and the power of death. We are able to pray that the kingdom come because we now know we live between the times of Jesus's initial victory and the consummation. The prayer that Jesus teaches us, this prayer most appropriately prayed during our eucharistic celebration in which we affirm that "Christ has died, Christ is risen, Christ will come again," is the prayer required for the battle he has initiated.

The blessed, moreover, have seen in Jesus what the Father would will. And the Father wills that Jesus and his followers would pray that his will be done. They do so as those who know that the Father's will is not complete among them as they too must learn to pray for forgiveness. But they also pray that what the Father has willed in his Son will be done over the whole earth. To pray that God's will be done is to pray that our wills be schooled to desire that God's will be done. Our wills, the will of the world, will nail Jesus to the cross. But God defeated our willfulness, making it possible for us to pray that God's will be done on earth.

That is why we should not ask for more than our daily bread. Only on the basis of the work of Christ is it possible for us to ask for no more than our daily bread. Just as God supplied Israel daily with bread in the wilderness, so followers of Jesus have been given all they need in order to learn to depend on one another on a daily basis. Without the community that Jesus has called into existence, we are tempted to hoard, to store up resources, in a vain effort to insure safety and security. Of course our effort to live without risk not only results in injustice, but it also makes our own lives anxious, fearing that we never have enough (Matt. 6:19–21). In truth, we can never have enough if what we want is the bread that the devil offered Jesus. But Jesus is good news to the poor (11:4), for he has brought into existence a people who ask for no more than their daily bread.

A community of people capable of living daily is also a community that can forgive as well as be forgiven our debts. Jesus's proclamation of the jubilee year is unmistakably present in the prayer he is teaching us to pray. To be taught to pray is to be taught to beg. To be taught to beg requires that we recognize our status as debtors. The debts we have incurred as well as are owed us come in many shapes and sizes. In our day we are tempted to think of debts in terms of psychological exchanges, but the debts we owe and are owed us, at least if we remember Lev. 25, are as real as the next meal we eat. So we should not be surprised that debts owed us, debts as real as money and property, are to be forgiven.

This makes us wonder if we really do want to pray that our debts be forgiven as we have forgiven our debtors. In truth we find it easier to forgive than to be forgiven. We do so because so much of life is spent trying to avoid acknowledging we owe anyone anything. Yet to be a follower of Jesus, to learn to pray this prayer, means that we must first learn that we are the forgiven. To learn to be forgiven is no easy lesson, desiring as we do to be our own master—if not creator. But to be a disciple of Jesus demands that we recognize that our life is a gift that requires, if we are to live in a manner appropriate to our being a creature, our willingness to accept forgiveness with joy.

The forgiveness of debts signals that nothing is quite so political as the prayer that Jesus teaches us. To have debts forgiven certainly challenges our normal economic and political assumption. But the forgiveness of debts is also at the heart of truthful memory. No people are free from a past or present that is not constituted by injustices so horrific nothing can be done to make them right. There is, for example, nothing that can be done to "redeem" the slavery that defined early America. Faced with the tragedy of slavery, the temptation is simply to forget that America is a country of slavery or to assume that the wound of slavery has been healed by African Americans being given the opportunity to become as well-off as white Americans. But the forgetfulness that money names cannot forever suppress the wound of slavery.

The willingness to be forgiven, which may require that I have my "enemy" tell me who I am, is the only way that reconciliation can begin.[5] To pray "in this way," therefore, is to become a citizen of God's kingdom of forgiveness. There is no more fundamental political act than to learn to pray this prayer. To learn to have our sins forgiven, indeed to learn that we are sinners needing forgiveness, is to become part of the kingdom of God. If we do not learn to forgive then we will not be forgiven, we will not be part of the new reality, the new people, brought into existence by Jesus. To forgive and to be forgiven is not some crude exchange bargain to "get on with life," but rather to participate in a political alternative that ends our attempts to secure our existence through violence.

Learning to pray with Jesus, therefore, is to become part of his struggle with the powers of this world. In the last petition of the prayer, however, Jesus asks that we not be brought to the time of trial and that we be rescued from the evil one. As we have already seen in his struggle with the devil in the desert, and as we will see in the cross, Jesus alone is capable of that trial. He has told us that

5. Jones 1995, 213 suggests that the focus of forgiveness on isolated situations of wrongdoing and guilt fails to see that "our own moral histories *are* precisely what are at issue, because forgiveness is focused on the reconciliation and healing of our broken pasts, not simply the absolution of guilt." Jones quite rightly describes such forgiveness as a "craft" involving skillful use of language.

his followers may well be persecuted, but we can survive whatever trials we may face because he has already faced the trial. Those who follow Jesus, those who have been taught to pray this prayer, will be persecuted because they must be, as Jesus is. But his disciples will know how to persist in the face of persecution because they have been taught how to pray.

We should not, therefore, be surprised that after Jesus has given us instructions on how to pray he also tells us how we should fast. Prayer and fasting are closely related because they are disciplines necessary for learning to beg. Begging, moreover, is a determinatively bodily action. We beg to live because our body requires that if we are to live we must beg. The vulnerability of our bodies tempts us to deny that our bodies are the real "us." The real us, we think, must be the inward us. I may have, for example, many possessions, but they are not the real me. The real me is the "me" constituted by my "inner being."

Jesus will not let us engage in fantasy: "Where your treasure is, there your heart will be also." So the desire to be recognized for our piety, for our fasting, is not unrelated to our wealth. We think we can be something other than what we do and own, but Jesus challenges that assumption. We learn to see with our bodies because seeing is a bodily act. We are "thinking animals" but thinking itself is bodily. If our bodies are to learn to be free of the habits that tempt us to believe that we can secure our survival through possessions, then we must learn to fast. Fasting, however, is not a discipline only for Lent, though Lenten disciplines can be useful, but fasting is constitutive of the life of a disciple.

For those called to be disciples of Jesus, fasting is not dismal, though it may be hard, but rather fasting becomes a way of life that can be called joy. To fast is to discover the gifts that make our lives livable. To fast is to learn not to despise our bodies destined even to death. So to be drawn into a life of fasting is to learn to live without what I assumed I could not live without. True ascetics often deny that they are ascetics because they do not think their suffering to be that significant. Rather, they discover that their suffering is the source of freedom. Nothing enslaves more than that which we think we cannot live without. To be so enslaved, moreover, is to be captured by the powers of this world.

Fasting involves the discovery of who we serve. We cannot serve God and wealth, but we will also be told that we cannot serve God and the emperor (Matt. 22:15–22). There is, moreover, a close connection between wealth and the emperor because we believe that our wealth depends on the security offered by the emperor. After all, emperors always claim to be our benefactors. We may regret what emperors do in the name of our security, but we dare not oppose them because we fear losing what we have.

To be rich and a disciple of Jesus is to have a problem. Christians have often tried to deal with this problem by suggesting that it is not what we possess that is the problem but our attitude toward what we possess that is the problem. Some recommend, for example, that we learn to possess what we possess as if it is not really ours. This means we must always be ready to give out of our abundance or even be ready to lose all that we have. Christians, particularly in capitalist social orders, are told that it is not wealth or power that is the problem but rather we must be good stewards of our wealth and power.

However, Jesus is very clear. Wealth is a problem. That capitalism is an economic system justified by the production of wealth is therefore not necessarily good news for Christians. Alasdair MacIntyre observes that Christians have rightly directed criticisms toward capitalist systems for wrongs done to the poor and exploited in the name of producing wealth, but

> Christianity has to view any social and economic order that treats being or becoming rich as highly desirable as doing wrong to those who must not only accept its goals, but succeed in achieving them. Riches are, from a biblical point of view, an affliction, an almost insuperable obstacle to entering the kingdom of heaven. Capitalism is bad for those who succeed by its standards as well as for those who fail by them, something that many preachers and theologians have failed to recognize. And those Christians who have recognized it have often enough been at odds with ecclesiastical as well as political and economic authorities. (MacIntyre 1995, xiv)

MacIntyre's observations about capitalism are obviously contentious and controversial, but they have the virtue of making clear the radical character of Jesus's teaching on fasting, treasures, the body, and our inability to serve two masters. Moreover these teachings are but commentaries on the prayer we have just been taught. To so live is what it means to ask for no more than our daily bread. That does not mean we are encouraged to idleness (2 Thess. 3), but it means that we must learn what it means to live in a community of trust. Such a community offers the hope that habits can be developed that draw us from the forms of greed given legitimacy by capitalist practices and ideologies. Although almsgiving should be invisible for the disciples of Jesus, it will not be so for those who think our social order is sustained by each person pursuing their self-interest. To be formed in the habits, the virtues, of the prayer we are taught to pray means that Christians cannot help but appear as a threat to the legitimating ideologies of those who rule. Christians do not seek to be subversives; it just turns out that living according to the Sermon on the Mount cannot help but challenge the way things are.

The beautiful simplicity of the life to which Jesus calls his disciples is evocatively elicited by Jesus directing our attention to the birds of the air and the lilies of the field. Possessed by possessions, we discover that we cannot will our way free of our possessions. But if we can be freed our attention may be grasped by that which is so true, so beautiful, we discover we have been dispossessed. To seek first the righteousness of the kingdom of God is to discover that that for which we seek is given, not achieved.

It is not accidental that Jesus uses wisdom gained from human experience to argue for the radical demands of discipleship. Can we add a single hour to our span of life by worrying? Clearly not. The temptation, however, is to assume that Jesus's admonition not to worry is some general human truth that is true whether Jesus says it or not. But as we have seen, the content of the sermon cannot be abstracted from the one who delivers the sermon. That we are now able to live freed of possession is because the one has come who alone has the power to dispossess us. Jesus's recommendation, that we not worry about tomorrow because the trouble of today is enough, is not just good advice, but rather wisdom that reflects the character of God's new creation manifest in Christ's life and ministry.

Jesus's use of wisdom to help us understand the character of the kingdom made present in his ministry is sometimes mistakenly used as a general policy recommendation. Jesus is not suggesting that we should not plant crops or weave cloth, but rather if we plant crops or weave cloth to "store up treasures on earth" we can be sure that our lives will be insecure. We can perhaps know that the desire to be secure is a self-defeating project without being a disciple of Jesus. But that wisdom is transformed through the recognition of him who has come to call a people into existence capable of praying for their daily bread. They are able to do so because their lives have been transformed through the call to be a disciple, making it possible for them to live in recognition that God has given them all they need.

Abundance, not scarcity, is the mark of God's care for creation. But our desire to live without fear cannot help but create a world of fear constituted by the assumption that there is never enough. Such a world cannot help but be a world of injustice and violence because it is assumed that under conditions of scarcity our only chance for survival is to have more. Sam Wells suggests that God has given his people not just enough, but too much. The problem is that there is too much of God that we fearfully refuse to accept. Our refusal to imagine a world of abundance is sin and, in particular, the sin of sloth:

> The problem is that the human imagination is simply not large enough to take in all that God is and has to give. We are overwhelmed. God's inexhaustible creation, limitless grace, relentless mercy, enduring purpose, fathomless love: it is just too much to contemplate, assimilate, understand. This is the language of abundance. And if humans turn away it is sometimes out of a misguided but understandable sense of self-protection, a preservation of identity in the face of a tidal wave of glory. (Wells 2006, 7)

Yet those who would follow Jesus are taught that we have time to care for one another through small acts of mercy because God's mercy is without limit. Abundance, not scarcity, is the mark of God's kingdom. But that abundance must be made manifest through the lives of a people who have discovered that they can trust God and one another. Such trust is not an irrational gesture against the chaos of life, but rather a witness to the very character of God's care of creation. So it is no wonder that Jesus directs our attention to birds and lilies to help us see how it is possible to live in joyful recognition that God has given us more than we need.

MATTHEW 7

The Way of the Church

Those formed to live trusting in God's abundance will not find it odd that Jesus tells us not to judge. Yet no teaching of Jesus seems more paradoxical than his prohibition against judging. Any attempt to avoid judging is defeated by the judgment against those who judge. Moreover, Jesus obviously is in the business of judgment, particularly judgments against the scribes and the Pharisees who "sit on Moses' seat" (Matt. 23:2). Any attempt to avoid judging seems self-defeating. Yet the paradoxical character of Jesus's admonition against judging is the result of our attempt to separate Jesus's teaching from the teacher and the community he has come to establish.

To become a disciple of Jesus is to learn to see and accept the world as God's world. We are not called to be God, but rather we are called to learn to be a creature of God. Should we criticize birds, for example, for not sowing or reaping? Should we think lilies are any less than what God created them to be because "they neither toil nor spin"? Rather than remake God's good creation, our task is to learn why we persist in ways of life that deny, as the birds and the lilies do not, that we are God's good creation.

Bonhoeffer observes that there is an essential connection between the first two chapters of the Sermon on the Mount and the climatic admonitions that conclude the sermon in Matt. 7. According to Bonhoeffer, Matt. 5 describes the extraordinary character of being a disciple of Jesus. To be a follower of Jesus entails nothing less than becoming a visible alternative to the world. Matthew 6 displays the simple and hidden character of the life to which the disciples are called. Both chapters were designed to help us see that to be a disciple of Jesus requires separation from the community to which we had belonged, for we now belong to Jesus. Accordingly, the boundary between those who would follow Jesus and the world is unmistakably apparent, but nonetheless permeable. Matthew 7 consists of Jesus's instructions for how to negotiate that permeability.

The disciples have been called from the crowd, but does their being set apart mean they have special rights? Does it mean that the disciples have special powers, standards, or talents that give them authority over those who have not received these gifts? All this might have been the case, according to Bonhoeffer, if Jesus's disciples had assumed that they were to separate themselves from the world by sharp and divisive judgments. If they had done so, Bonhoeffer notes,

> people could have come to think that it was Jesus' will that such divisive and condemnatory judgments were to be made in the disciples' daily dealings with others. Thus Jesus must make clear that such misunderstandings seriously endanger discipleship. Disciples are not to judge. If they do judge, then they themselves fall under God's judgment. They themselves will perish by the sword with which they judge others. The gap which divides them from others, as the just from the unjust, even divides them from Jesus.
>
> Why is this so? Disciples live completely out of the bond connecting them with Jesus Christ. Their righteousness depends only on that bond and never apart from it. Therefore, it can never become a standard which the disciples would own and might use in any way they please. What makes them disciples is not a new standard for their lives, but Jesus Christ alone, the mediator and Son of God himself. (Bonhoeffer 2001, 169–70)

The disciples are not to judge because any judgment that needs to be made has been made. For those who follow Jesus to act as if they can, on their own, determine what is good and what is evil is to betray the work of Christ. Therefore, the appropriate stance for the acknowledgement of evil is the confession of sin. We quite literally cannot see clearly unless we have been trained to see "the log that is in [our] eye." But it is not possible for us to see what is in our eye because the eye cannot see itself. That is why we are able to see ourselves only through the vision made possible by Jesus—a vision made possible by our participation in a community of forgiveness that allows us to name our sins.

In his *Confessions*, Augustine describes his struggle with the problem of evil. Augustine finally came to understand, paradoxical though it may sound, that evil does not exist because "existence" names all that is created and everything created is good. He observes that there are separate parts of God's creation, which we think of as evil because they are at variance with other things. But there are other things with which they are in accord and so they are good. For example, the sky, which can be cloudy or windy, suits the earth for which it exists. Augustine observes, therefore, that it would be wrong for me to wish that these earthly things did not exist, for even if I saw nothing but them, I might wish for something better, but still I ought to praise you for them alone. . . . And since this is so, I no longer wished for a better world, because I was thinking of the whole of creation and in the light of this clearer discernment I had come to see that though the higher things are better than the lower, the sum of all creation is better than the higher things alone. (Augustine 1961, 7, 12)

Augustine had learned not to judge the birds of the air or the lilies of the field. But he tells us that this was but the beginning of his lesson in not judging. He had yet to come to terms with his pride. To find that "log" required that he encounter the stories of Victorinus and Anthony. It was their stories that led him to face the humiliation of the cross of Christ. Only then was Augustine able to confess that evil was "not out there," but rather resided in his will. Augustine confesses:

I began to search for a means of gaining the strength I need to enjoy you, but I could not find this means until I embraced the mediator between God and men, Jesus Christ, who is man, like them (I Timothy 2:5), and also rules as God over all things, blessed for ever (Romans 9:15). He it was who united with our flesh that which I was too weak to take. For I was not humble enough to conceive of the humble Jesus Christ as my God, nor had I learnt what lesson his human weakness was meant to teach. (Augustine 1961, 7, 18)

Augustine learned that judging makes us blind because, as Bonhoeffer puts it, "when I judge, I am blind to my own evil and to the grace granted the other person. But in the love of Christ, disciples know about every imaginable kind of guilt and sin, because they know of the suffering of Jesus Christ" (2001, 172). Following Christ requires our recognizing that the one I am tempted to judge is like me—a person who has received the forgiveness manifest in the cross. The recognition that the other person is like me—in need of forgiveness—prevents those who would follow Jesus from trying to force others to follow Jesus. We must, like Jesus, have the patience necessary to let those called deny that call. It means that the disciples are not called to make the world conform to the gospel, but rather the disciples are schooled to be patient, to be nonviolent—which means that the gospel is not a "conquering idea" that neither knows nor respects resistance. Rather, "the Word of God is so weak that it suffers to be despised and rejected by people. For the Word, there are such things as hardened hearts and locked doors. The Word accepts the resistance it encounters and bears it" (Bonhoeffer 2001, 173).

Therefore not to judge is to be schooled by the humility of the Son. That schooling begins through learning to confess our unwillingness to live as creatures that have been given all we need to be at peace with ourselves and one another. It does no good, therefore, to try to force on others what we have been given.

Jesus tells us we are not to give what is holy to those who have no capacity to receive what they are being given. Jesus does not deny that there will be those who are too afraid to receive the life he has come to offer. This fear is precisely why he has come into the world—that the world may know it is the world.

John Howard Yoder observes that the central affirmation of the New Testament is that Jesus Christ was sent to exercise dominion over the world. Before Jesus's ministry, our existence was dominated by powers and principalities that had revolted against their creator, but through Jesus's ministry the powers and principalities have been again restored to service in God's kingdom (1 Cor. 15). That Jesus has been victorious means that the time of the church, the time constituted by those called by Jesus into his kingdom of forgiveness, is characterized by the coexistence of two ages or what the New Testament calls eons (1964, 9).

According to Yoder, the two ages coexist but represent different directions: "The present aeon is characterized by sin and centered on man; the coming aeon is the redemptive reality which entered history in an ultimate way in Christ. The present age, by rejecting obedience, has rejected the only possible ground for man's own well being; the coming age is characterized by God's will being done" (1964, 9). The new age has yet to reach consummation, but it has clearly already begun to supersede the old. Jesus's admonition to his disciples not to judge, his charge to not give what is holy to those who will not receive what they are given, presupposes that the kingdom has come.

That Jesus expects and requires some to respond to his call to follow him creates a division between church and world. Crucial, though, is that this division not be understood as an ontological given, a dualism that frustrates the witness of the church. The difference between church and world is not a given, but rather a difference between agents. The difference between church and world is not that of realms or levels, but of response (Yoder 1964, 31–32). Therefore, Christians believe that all people can live the way Jesus would have us live. The world is merely the name for those who have chosen to use this time of God's patience to not live the way that Jesus has given us in the Sermon on the Mount. The only advantage the disciples have is that they are able to acknowledge their sinfulness, and in that acknowledgment they are able to embody, through community, the life of forgiveness.

We should not, therefore, be surprised that Jesus tells his disciples not to give what is holy, what is of great value, to those who will only profane what they have been given. Again Jesus recognizes that the kingdom he has begun can be rejected. Instead, those capable of receiving the kingdom are those able to ask and receive. Just as Jesus needed to teach us to pray, so he must teach us to ask that the door be opened. We can do so with the full confidence that the door will be opened. Even those who are evil know how to give appropriate gifts to their children. Therefore it is surely the case that those who follow Jesus can ask the Father to give the good things that only he can give. The trick, of course, is to learn how to live on the basis of gift. We fear receiving, requiring as it does the acknowledgment of our dependence and our need for forgiveness.

To be forgiven, to ask for forgiveness, forges a space, making possible a community that has learned to live by receiving. John Milbank observes that before a gift can be given it must have already started to be received (2003, 156).[1] The life to which Jesus calls us through the Sermon on the Mount is a life of renewed communion with God. The Father has refused to let our refusal determine our relationship with him. We are, therefore, being trained to ask through the sermon that Jesus delivers, and the asking is part of the way of life that makes it possible for us to be befriended by God and one another. Sacrifice may well be part of what such a life entails, but sacrifice is in service of the gift of mutuality otherwise unattainable.[2]

The so-called Golden Rule is an expression of the mutuality discovered through forgiveness. Oddly enough, however, when the rule is isolated from the eschatological context of the sermon, indeed when the rule is abstracted from Jesus's ministry in order to ground ethics, it is made to serve a completely different narrative than the one called the kingdom of God. For example, Jesus's admonition that everything we do to others should be done as we would have them do to us is often thought to have been given more exact formulation in Kant's famous statement of the categorical imperative: "Act only according to that maxim by which you can at the same time will that it should become a universal law" (1959, 39).

Yet Kant's statement of the categorical imperative is an attempt to free us of the need to rely on forgiveness and, more critically, a savior. Kant's hope was to make us what our pride desires, that is, that we be autonomous.[3] To be free in

1. Milbank puts this understanding of gift in a more theoretical mode. He argues that "to offer charity, whether as original gift or restorative forgiveness, is only possible if one is *already* receiving the infinite divine charity, since charity is not an empty disposition (as it later became), but the ontological bond between God and creatures, whereby creatures only are as the receiving of the divine gift and the unqualified return of this gift in the very act of receiving. . . . Hence giving, since it is not enacted in order to achieve purity of motive but to establish reciprocity, is already a receiving according to a reception transcendentally prior to any purely possessive calculation of what one might, perhaps, receive by giving. And, likewise, to forgive is to re-establish reciprocity only possible as the attainment of a mysterious harmony through its participation in the divine infinite harmony. As the human forgiver is himself a sinner, he must re-receive this harmony in order to be able to forgive. His forgiving of the other, therefore, shows that he is divinely forgiven, or rather his forgiving of the other is the very instance of himself being divinely forgiven" (2003, 57).

2. Milbank 2003, 159–60 observes that "parents who entirely sacrifice themselves for their children thereby betray them, since they fail to present them with any *telos* and example of a lived, enjoyed (and sexual) adult life."

3. Thus Kant says in the first paragraph of his essay "What Is Enlightenment?": "Enlightenment is man's release from his self-incurred tutelage. Tutelage is man's inability to make use of his understanding without direction from another. Self-incurred is this tutelage when its cause lies not in lack of reason but in lack of resolution and courage to use it without direction

Kant's sense requires that we rely on reason qua reason. To rely on any resource other than reason is to abandon ourselves to irrational authorities. According to Kant, no reasonable person should believe that his or her sins can be forgiven without that person doing the work necessary to transform his or her life. To be forgiven by another would force us to acknowledge that our lives depend on being capable of receiving a gift without regret. But from Kant's perspective such a capacity for reception makes the moral life impossible.[4]

Jesus knows nothing of a realm that Kant called "ethics." That we are to do to others as we would have others do to us is not ethics. According to Jesus it is the summation of the law and the prophets. Kant sought to free ethics from historical particularity. Jesus calls us to live faithful to the particularity of Israel's law and prophets. Jesus does not say that now that we know the Golden Rule—and the rule was known prior to Jesus—we no longer need to know the law and the prophets. On the contrary, we *must* know the law and the prophets if we are to know how to act toward others. Let us not forget that this is the same Jesus who told us earlier in the Sermon on the Mount that he has not come to abolish the law and the prophets, but to fulfill them.

Love is the fulfillment of the law. But this is not a sentimental love, rather this love is a radical politics that challenges the world's misappropriation of God's good gift. Christ's being the embodiment of God's love means that disciples cannot know love apart from loving one's enemies, for that is precisely what God has done regarding us: we are God's enemies yet God would still love us—even coming to die for us. We are, therefore, not surprised when, tested by the lawyer concerning which is the greatest commandment, Jesus's answer is twofold:

> "You shall love the Lord your God with all your heart, and with all your soul, and with all your mind." This is the greatest and first commandment. And a second is like it: "You shall love your neighbor as yourself." On these two commandments hang all the law and the prophets. (Matt. 22:37–40)

Jesus makes explicit what is implicit in the statement of the Golden Rule in the sermon, namely, that love of neighbor and love of God are interdependent. If we are to know how to love our neighbor we must love God as God has loved us. This is the presumption that animates the law and the prophets. The law and the prophets are now to be seen in the ministry of Jesus, where God's love for us is most intensely present. And yet we fear such intensity. We fear the intimacy of God's love, desiring instead to believe that we are separated from God by vast space. But in Christ, God has drawn near to us and to our neighbor. As a result we discover that we do not have a long journey to undertake

---

from another. *Sapere aude!* 'Have courage to use our own reason!'—that is the motto of the enlightenment" (1959, 85).

4. For Kant's reflections on the atonement, see 1960, 106–7.

to get to God; rather the long journey is the rigorous path necessary to accept our own, and our neighbor's, reality (Williams 2002, 35).

That journey takes place on the road called discipleship. Jesus does not try to entice us to undertake that journey by telling us that it will be easy or that many will join us along the way. The gate is narrow and the road is hard. Moreover, the journey is made even more difficult by false prophets who are quite good at disguising themselves as fellow travelers. Bonhoeffer bluntly tells us:

> To give witness to and to confess the truth of Jesus, but to love the enemy of this truth, who is his enemy and our enemy, with the unconditional love of Jesus Christ—that is the narrow road. To believe in Jesus' promise that those who follow shall possess the earth, but to encounter the enemy unarmed, to prefer suffering injustice to doing ill—that is the narrow road. To perceive other people as being weak and wrong, but to never judge them; to proclaim the good news to them, but never to throw pearls before swine—that is a narrow road. It is an unbearable road. (Bonhoeffer 2001, 176)

We are only able to walk such a road, Bonhoeffer suggests, because we can see Jesus walking ahead of us and with us. If, however, we begin to consider the threats along the road, if we fear losing our way and keep our eyes to the ground rather than on Jesus, we can be sure we will lose our way. We must keep our eyes on him because he is the gate and the way. How could we expect anything different, given that Jesus calls for us to abandon the world for the kingdom of God? Surely, Bonhoeffer rhetorically asks, we could not have expected a wide road to run between the kingdom of heaven and the world.

Jesus clearly does not expect that many will follow him on the road he must walk. Moreover he has already suggested that some who will follow him will do so falsely and, even more troubling, they will not be easily identified. Indeed, they may even, for a time, fool themselves. Jesus, however, suggests to his disciples that the only way to discover those who are false is to judge them by their fruit. Of course if we know ourselves and others by our fruits, we must have learned what constitutes good fruit. Jesus's sermon provides the outline for the discernment of those who are true.

Jesus's recommendation for discernment has important implications for what it means to believe that what we believe as Christians is true. In recent times, Christians have found themselves unable to explain to themselves or their neighbors why they believe what they believe to be true. Too often these attempts to establish the truth of what we believe try to separate the truth of our beliefs from how we live. But if we are to follow Jesus that is exactly what we cannot do.

The temptation to separate the truth of what we believe from our lives is the result of our fear of being held accountable. Moreover the idea that we can separate what we believe from how we live is a habit deeply rooted in culturally established Christianity. "True" is what everyone believes, which means it is assumed that the coercive character of Constantinian Christianity is assumed to be justified because what Christians believe is what anyone believes on reflection. But Jesus claims that by our fruits we will be known, making impossible any attempt to separate the content of the Christian belief from how we must live. To believe that this man Jesus is the Christ requires that we become his disciples. Christology and discipleship are mutually implicated, which entails that no account of the truthfulness of Christian belief can be abstracted from how lives are lived.

Therefore it is not enough to call him Lord, it is not enough to prophecy in his name, it is not enough to do deeds of power in his name, but rather only those who do the will of the Father will enter the kingdom of the Son. This means that during this time between the times we will need to be patient, often unable to identify the false prophets from the true. But Jesus has not left us without resources. We know that the poor, those who mourn, the meek, those who hunger and thirst for righteousness, the merciful, the pure in heart, the peacemakers, those persecuted for righteousness sake—all are signs of what it means to live truthfully.

Moreover, a community constituted by such people has no reason to fear the truth, nor would such a community need constant reassurance that what they believe is true. If they live confidently and joyfully, the truth will be seen for what it is—a witness to the one alone who is the truth—for the truth of the gospel cannot be known without witnesses because it is not a truth separable from lives lived according to Jesus's life. Jesus alone is the one who can be the truth because he shares his life with the Father.

There is no other way to the truth than the call to follow Jesus. Those who hear his words and act on them have lives founded on the only foundation capable of weathering the world. Jesus does not promise that those who follow him, those who become his people, will not experience difficulty. The exact opposite is the case. He tells us that we will be persecuted for his sake. Indeed, those who follow him will necessarily be exposed to dangers that those who are not his disciples can avoid, for his disciples offer the world an alternative to the violence of the world based on the lies thought necessary for people to survive in a world governed by mistrust. In such a world, a people of truth cannot help but be in danger because the world does not want its lies exposed.

Yet those who hear Jesus's call to follow him can do nothing else even if their response exposes them to danger. But they may take comfort in knowing that they are not alone, because Jesus calls them to be part of a people who have learned to need one another. Jesus does not call them to be heroes. He calls them to be disciples who have learned by living lives described in the Sermon on the Mount that to so live makes them dependent on God and one another. It should not be surprising, therefore, that such a people have lives capable of surviving good and bad fortune.

Matthew reminds us at the end of the sermon that the crowds have also been listening to Jesus's sermon. They are, moreover, astonished because he has taught, unlike the scribes, as one having authority. Scribes, it seems, exercise authority by citing another authority. In contrast, Jesus teaches as one who has the authority to determine what is authoritative. What he says cannot, therefore, be separated from who he is and how he says what he says. As we shall see, his life is but a commentary on the sermon, and the sermon is the exemplification of his life. What he teaches is not different from what he is.[5] Is it any wonder that the crowds are astonished at his teachings?

And yet astonishment is not the response that Jesus would have from those who hear him. He does not want our admiration. What he has taught, what he is, requires nothing else than our lives. We cannot serve two masters. Like those Athenians who heard Paul preach, we would like to respond to Jesus by saying, "We will hear you again about this" (Acts 17:32). But Jesus refuses to let us determine our relation to him. He teaches as one having authority. That authority, moreover, extends to asking us to be willing to lose our lives for his sake (Matt. 16:25). Only the Son of God has the authority to ask for our lives, and that is the authority behind every word of the Sermon on the Mount.

---

5. Bonhoeffer puts it this way: "The sayings of Jesus, . . . in the Sermon on the Mount, are the interpretation of his existence" (2005, 235).

MATTHEW 8–9

The Power of the Kingdom

Matthew indicates the peculiar character of Jesus's authority by telling us that Jesus "came down from the mountain." It seems insignificant to note Jesus's descent—of course he would have to come down from the mountain. But by pointing to Jesus's descent Matthew draws the subtle, yet significant, connection between Jesus and Moses. In Exod. 34:29 we are told that "Moses came down from Mount Sinai . . . with the two tablets of the covenant." This is the second time that Moses comes down Sinai with the tablets. The first time, confronted by the golden calf made by the people in his absence, Moses breaks the tablets by dashing them against the ground (32:19). The second time he returns with the tablets, and the skin of his face shines so brightly the people are afraid.

Jesus also descends from the mountain, but Jesus carries no tablets. He carries no tablets because he *is* the law. Like with Moses's descent, a crowd awaits Jesus's return. But the crowd in Matthew is unable to see that on this man rests the glory of the Lord. The crowd follows Jesus but they do not grasp who he is. He is the fleshly embodiment of the law, and he will, like the first tablets of the law, be broken by the disobedience of those he has come to save. Moses broke the tablets of the law at the foot of the mountain of the Lord. Jesus will be broken by being raised on a cross. That he will be broken on the cross remains for many the reason they cannot see how Jesus can be the Son of God.

In the midst of the crowd a leper approaches Jesus, kneels before him and, for the first time in Matthew, designates him "Lord." Lepers were subjected to a detailed regulation by the law. They were examined by priests to determine if they had leprosy; if they did they were forced to dwell "outside the camp" (Lev. 13:46). Matthew does not tell us anything about this leper other than that he recognizes Jesus as Lord. That a leper, one regarded as unclean, could recognize that Jesus has the power to make him clean is not accidental, for as Matthew leads us through the story of Jesus's ministry it will become increasingly clear that outsiders, those without status or power in Israel, are more likely to recognize Jesus as Lord.

It is not clear from this encounter what it might mean for the leper to identify Jesus as Lord. That is to say, it is not clear that the leper's recognition of Jesus's lordship includes the recognition of Jesus as the Messiah of Israel. Still, the leper kneels before Jesus, suggesting that he regards Jesus as one worthy to be worshiped because he knows that if Jesus chooses he can make him clean. Jesus not only chooses to heal the leper, he does so by touching him, something people would not do for fear that they might contract the disease. But Jesus touches this leper, and the leper is immediately cleansed.

Jesus's touching the leper has invited some to read this story in a sentimental fashion—like Jesus, we need to be ready to reach out and touch someone. It is not a bad thing to reach out and touch someone, but there is nothing sentimental about what happened in this encounter between Jesus and the leper, for what Jesus did for this leper was a deed of power that only he could do. Matthew tells us that Jesus had begun to heal as part of his ministry in Galilee (Matt. 4:23), but now the power manifest in his healing ministry will attract the attention of those threatened by the display of such power.

Jesus cures the leper because the leper asks him to do so. Jesus does not perform cures to attract attention. Therefore, he commands the leper to tell no one what he has done, but to show the priests he has been cured. Jesus expects the leper to keep the law of Lev. 14 requiring that he be examined by the priests before he is allowed back into society. That the leper is not to tell anyone what Jesus has done suggests the difficulty that Jesus's healing ministry presents. Jesus cannot help but display the power that is his, but those who would follow him only because he is a person of power will fail to understand the kind of Lord he is. The controversies that the healings occasion force those he heals (and us) to recognize that following this leader will not be easy.

When Jesus enters Capernaum, a town with a Greek name, a centurion, an officer in the Roman army, comes to him requesting that Jesus heal his servant. Like the leper, this non-Israelite addresses Jesus as Lord. Unlike the leper he does not kneel, but he clearly recognizes Jesus as a person of power and authority. He is able to do so because he is also a person of power and authority. Even so, the Roman officer refuses Jesus's willingness to visit his home and heal the servant, because he does not think he is worthy to have Jesus under his roof. This Gentile may respect the Jewish prohibition against entering homes of Gentiles, but "not worthy" may also indicate that he knows his life and profession are antithetical to Jesus's life and work. The centurion rather asks Jesus to speak the word of healing, believing that his servant will be healed. Again it seems that an outsider is better able to recognize Jesus than those who think they know what the Lord of Israel should look like and how he should act.

Jesus, amazed by the centurion's declaration, confesses that nowhere in Israel has he found such faith. The faith that Jesus commends in this man seems to be his recognition that Jesus can do what he asks. Such an understanding of faith renders problematic those accounts of faith in which faith is assumed to be intrinsic to the human condition, that is, faith understood as a subjective quality that gives life meaning. Even accounts of faith in which faith is identified with the need to have some general purpose in life are far too sophisticated. The faith that Jesus praises, exemplified by the centurion, is that which trusts that Jesus is who he says he is and that he can do what he says he can do.

It is this faith, moreover, that Jesus says will be found in those who will come from the east and west to dine in the kingdom of heaven with Abraham, Isaac, and Jacob, while their heirs will be thrown into darkness. This is the fulfillment of Isaiah's prophecy that the nations will stream to the Lord's house established on the highest mountain. All peoples will be drawn to that house because there they will be taught the ways of God:

> For out of Zion shall go forth instruction,
> and the word of the LORD from Jerusalem.
> He shall judge between the nations,
> and shall arbitrate for many peoples;
> they shall beat their swords into plowshares,
> and their spears into pruning hooks;
> nations shall not lift up sword against nation,
> neither shall they learn war any more. (Isa. 2:3–4)

Jesus declares that the fulfillment of this prophecy, which is also found in Mic. 4:1–8, has begun in this centurion's faith. The prophets have foretold that the nations are to be gathered to worship at the temple and that the nations, by observing the law, will learn to live in peace. That Jesus finds the faith of Israel in this centurion, a man of war, should not surprise us. Who better than those who know war to recognize the one who is peace? The apocalyptic language of outer darkness (Matt. 22:13) in which there will be gnashing of teeth (24:51) suggests, moreover, that much is at stake in how we do or do not respond to Jesus.

Later that evening, after Jesus has cured Peter's mother-in-law, many possessed by demons are brought to him, and he casts out the spirits with a word and cures all who are sick. Yet the exercise of the power of healing is not without cost. Matthew directs our attention to Isa. 53:4, in which we are told that the Messiah will bear our infirmities and carry our diseases. Jesus is able to do so because he is at once like and unlike us. The power he displays is the power to receive our infirmities, to suffer as we suffer, without that suffering becoming, as it is so often for us, a perverse form of violence and control that we exercise against God, ourselves, and our neighbors.

The church rightly learned to read Isa. 53 through the life of Jesus. Indeed, as we learn in the gospel of Luke, on the road to Emmaus the resurrected Jesus instructed two of his followers how to read the scripture. His companions report that the tomb is empty, but they are nonetheless leaving Jerusalem. It seems that they still do not understand that "the Messiah should suffer these things and then enter into his glory" (Luke 24:26). So Jesus, "beginning with Moses and all the prophets," helps them understand that this king comes as the one destined to be "numbered with the transgressors" bearing our sins so that we can live free of sin (Isa. 53:12). Matthew's gospel witnesses to the lesson that Jesus taught on the road to Emmaus.

Some are beginning to recognize that Jesus is different, and they desire to partake of that difference. A scribe comes claiming that he is ready to follow Jesus wherever Jesus might go, but Jesus rebuffs him because Jesus has "no place to go." The scribe, as might be expected of a scribe, has identified Jesus as "teacher," but he has not understood that this teacher teaches a wisdom forcing us to abandon what we take to be home. "Foxes have holes, and birds who have nests; but the Son of Man has nowhere to lay his head," Jesus replies. You cannot stay home and follow Jesus.

This title, "Son of Man," more than his being called Lord by the leper and centurion, tempts many to speculate about the role that Jesus may have understood himself to be fulfilling. The title certainly has precedent in Ezekiel (2:1, 3, 6) and Daniel (7:13), suggesting that the Son of Man is the agent of God's final judgment. Jesus is the herald of the kingdom, but what it means for him to be the herald cannot be determined from the title "Son of Man." This title in Ezekiel and Daniel signals the beginning of an apocalyptic time, but that time is present in Jesus. Jesus accepts the identification of himself as the Son of Man, but one characterized by humiliation and suffering. Jesus as the one who inaugurates the new age reveals the triumphant return of the Son of Man to be unlike any victory we can imagine (Matt. 17:12; 20:18, 28; 26:2, 24). It will never be easy for the disciples or for us to learn how to be with this one who would establish the kingdom by being crucified.

Another "disciple" approaches Jesus, asking if he might interrupt his journey with Jesus in order to bury his father. Elijah allows Elisha to return to his family before following him (1 Kgs. 19:19–21), but Jesus demands that this disciple leave his family behind: "Follow me, and let the dead bury their own dead" (Matt. 8:22). To be a disciple of Jesus, it seems, requires such dedication because what Jesus is and does means that "normal" is reconstituted. This one who would be a disciple of Jesus stands in the presence of life itself, yet remains captured by death, wanting to bury the dead. Jesus, who will die on our behalf, requires that those who would follow him not let death determine their relationship to the living.

After his encounter with the scribe and would-be disciple, Jesus retreats to a boat. This is not without significance—on a boat there is no place to escape. The disciples soon find themselves in a windstorm that threatens to swamp the boat, but Jesus, like Jonah before him (Jonah 1:4–6), is asleep. The disciples fear for their lives, so they wake Jesus, believing that he can act on their behalf. Jesus rebukes them, not because they wake him, but because they are afraid. Why should they be afraid? They have called him "Lord." What do they think that means? Their faith, unlike that of the centurion, is "little." To be of little faith will turn out to be an ongoing characteristic of the disciples' relationship to Jesus (Matt. 14:31). But it seems that little faith is better than no faith. The disciples are at least in the boat with him. They, moreover, recognize him as the one capable of saving them. They ask, "Lord, save us!" Jesus rebukes the wind and sea, and the sea becomes calm. The one capable of healing the sick and forgiving sinners is the same one with the power to command the wind and waves. We would not expect less of the one who was with the Father "in the beginning."

The disciples are amazed that Jesus is able to command the wind. Irony is seldom associated with the gospels, but Matthew's report of the disciples' question—"what sort of man is this, that even the winds and the sea obey him?"—is ironic. We know, of course, what sort of man this is because we know how the story will end. We, therefore, are tempted to assume a position of superiority to that of the disciples. But that is a form of pride we must learn to discipline if we are to be witnesses to the "sort of man" this man is. Matthew uses irony to teach us, the church, not to turn our recognition of Jesus's triumph into a status.

Like the disciples it is necessary for the church to recognize that we too are of little faith. The church, like the disciples' boat, is the ark of safety in a storm-tossed sea. Our temptation is to try to row to shore to escape the storm, but when we do so we fail to witness to the one who is peace. The church's safety comes through the confession of our sinfulness, which is nowhere more apparent than our refusal to live in accordance with who this man, Jesus, says he is. It is only through the confession of sin that the church becomes for the world what the world cannot be for itself. Even to discover how little our faith may be requires the willingness to follow Jesus as he confronts the demons.

The demons know who Jesus is. Jesus comes to the other side of the sea, to the country of the Gadarenes, and he is confronted by two fierce demoniacs. They recognize him to be the Son of God, the same description bestowed on him by the Spirit at his baptism. Demons recognize the Son because they—more than we—are able to recognize who threatens them. Demons draw their existence from death and are, therefore, able to recognize the one who is life. They fear that Jesus has come before the appointed time, but they discover that the appointed time is now. The disciples fear Jesus's absence as he sleeps in the boat; the demons fear his presence.

Faced by Jesus the demons ask him to cast them into a herd of swine. Using the word the centurion had asked him to speak, "go," Jesus sends the demons into a herd of swine, who rush to drown themselves in the sea. The demons obey. What else can evil do once it loses its parasitical hold on that which is good? The demons' self-destruction is indicative of sin, for sin cannot help but lead to our self-destruction because sin is quite literally to try to be what we are not.

The swineherders report Jesus's exorcism of the demoniacs and the loss of the swineherd to the nearby town. The whole town, a town that may be constituted by Gentiles because they have pigs, comes out to meet Jesus. We might assume that he would at least be received as someone of power. He has driven out the demons from the demoniacs. But as soon as they see him, they beg him to leave their neighborhood. It seems that outsiders are often as unwilling as the people of Israel to receive someone capable of ridding their lives of demons. If we have to choose between a life we know, even a life possessed by demons and ruled by death, and a life of uncertainty to which Jesus calls us, a life that may well expose us to dangers in Jesus's name, we too may ask Jesus to leave our neighborhood.

We should not be surprised, therefore, that Jesus complies with their wish that he leave them to their own devices. In the Sermon on the Mount he told us not to judge, he told us not to toss pearls before swine, so he does not force himself on those who are not ready to receive the gospel. The habits of the world are hard to break. What Jesus offers cannot help but change our lives, challenging our habits derived from our love and fear of death. Like those who ask Jesus to leave their neighborhood:

> We would rather be ruined than changed,
> We would rather die in our dread
> Than climb the cross of the moment
> And let our illusions die.
>
> —W. H. Auden, "The Age of Anxiety"

Jesus does what he is asked to do, then returns to the boat and goes to his own home town. One might think that home would be a place where he might be welcome and even understood. Yet we know from Jesus's response to the scribe that Jesus has "nowhere to lay his head." It is, therefore, not surprising that the story of Jesus's return to home is the beginning of opposition to him that will finally result in his crucifixion. Jesus has no safe place to be because he is the one who cannot help but challenge those who assume safety is to be preferred to truth.

Jesus arrives home and is immediately encountered by some people carrying a paralyzed man on a bed. The leper and the centurion came to Jesus, but those carrying the paralyzed man seem to have simply "run into" Jesus.

But they believed, like the leper and the centurion, that Jesus had the power to cure the one they carried. Jesus literally "saw their faith" in the load they carried.

Again, that he could see their faith helps us understand what it means to be pulled into the movement, the kingdom, inaugurated by Jesus. We are not told that the paralytic had faith, but only that those who carried him had faith. The faith of others, it seems, can save us. Jesus sees the faith of those who carry this paralyzed man, and their faith is sufficient for him. Intercessory prayer is a grace we are given that we may hold one another up before God.

Jesus responds in an extraordinary manner: "Take heart, son; your sins are forgiven." For someone paralyzed to be told that his or her sins are forgiven does not seem to get to the problem. However, Jesus does not make a strong distinction between sin and sickness. That he forgives the paralyzed man's sins does not imply that Jesus thinks his paralysis the result of sin or punishment for sin. Rather, Jesus simply acts as one ready to forgive sins as well as heal the body. Both sickness and sin are evils.[1] Neither should be part of God's good creation. Jesus has come to restore creation; healing the sick, exorcising demons, and forgiving sins are all acts of restoration.

Some of the scribes understand that Jesus is exercising an authority they cannot help but think is idolatrous. Only God can forgive sins. Yet Jesus has forgiven this man's sins. The scribes clearly think, but do not say, that this is blasphemy. They are, of course, right—if this is not the Son of God it is blasphemy. Jesus recognizes their unwillingness to say what they are thinking; he sees the evil in their hearts and challenges them: "Which is easier, to say, 'Your sins are forgiven,' or to say, 'Stand up and walk'?" (Matt. 9:5). Jesus does not wait for an answer, but tells the paralytic to stand up and carry his bed home.

Jesus cures the paralytic because he is the Son of Man, the suffering servant that heralds the new age, and, therefore, he has the "authority on earth to forgive sins." "On earth" binds heaven and earth. The heavenly Son of Man is on earth. The crowds are appropriately filled with awe, but they fail to understand what they have seen. They glorify God for having given such authority to human beings. They fail to understand that Jesus is not exercising the authority possible for human beings, but rather he is exercising the authority that only he can exercise because he is *the* human being.

There is such a thing as Christian humanism, but too often celebration of the humanism of the incarnation underwrites the assumption that Jesus exemplifies a general human possibility. But Jesus is not the exemplification of humanity. He is this man and no other. Indeed he is the only true human

---

1. Hart eloquently argues that sickness and death are evil, that they should not exist, that they are not God's will. As he puts it, "As for comfort, when we seek it, I can imagine none greater then the happy knowledge that when I see the death of a child, I do not see God but the face of his enemy" (2005, 103–5).

being. The humanity of Christ, Karl Barth rightly insists, does not exist prior to its union with the Logos:

> Those who want to see revelation in the idea of humanity as such are grasping at something that in itself is not just meaningless but nonexistent. So are those who seek revelation in Jesus as a human individual. They are all necessarily groping in the dark. This idea, the idea of humanity, and this individual who incorporates it, cannot for a single moment be abstracted from their assumption into the person of the Logos. The divine subject who unites himself with them makes them revelation. The human nature of Christ has no personhood of its own. It is *anhypostatos*—the formula in which the description culminates. Or, more positively, it is *enhypostatos*. It has personhood, subsistence, reality, one in its union with the Logos of God. . . . The one whom Mary bore was not an other or a second; he was nothing apart from being God's Son. He was in human nature, but this human nature was real only in the person of God's Son. (Barth 1990, 157)

Barth uses the technical categories of Protestant scholasticism to make clear what has been apparent in Matthew's gospel from the beginning, that is, that no other human being, no other story, can be substituted for the life of this man Jesus. Jesus is not the exemplification of a "Christ figure." The character of the gospel reflects the character of the revelation that Jesus is. We can know Jesus only through the narratives provided by Matthew, Mark, Luke, and John and performed by the church. However, like those who witnessed Jesus's healing of the paralytic, our temptation is to explain Jesus as demonstrating the power inherent but untapped or even perverted in something called humanity. But Jesus is able to save us not only because he is fully like us, but also because he is completely different than us. He is the eschatological savior making possible a renewed humanity impossible without his life. He had to live out all that Matthew tells of his life if our salvation is not in doubt.

That Jesus's humanity is his alone does not mean he is not, as Paul suggests in Rom. 5:12–21, the second Adam. It was Adam's sin that led to the condemnation of all, but it was Christ's righteousness that justifies all. Yet as Barth maintains, the parallel between Adam and Christ is best understood to be a parallel between Christ and Adam: "For Paul Jesus Christ takes the first place as the original, and Adam the second place as 'the figure of him that was to come' (Rom. 5:14), the prophetic type of Jesus Christ" (1936–77, 4.1.510–11). Adam is the name that makes the history of the world a whole, but for such a history to be known depends on the name Jesus.

That Jesus is what he does and says is the reason that he can be recognized by those who seem unlikely recruits for the mission he has been sent to accomplish. Jesus walks by Matthew, a tax collector, and says, "Follow me." Remarkably Matthew does exactly that. As is so often the case, we want to know more. What did Matthew think he was doing? Did he feel guilty about being a tax collector? Was there emptiness in his life that he saw Jesus filling? But such questions should be resisted. All we need to know is that Matthew followed him—a following that makes sense only if Jesus is the one with the authority to forgive sins.

Not only does Jesus call a person engaged in a questionable activity, he eats with tax collectors and sinners. For the first time in the gospel the Pharisees speak, asking how Jesus could be willing to eat with the unclean. It is not as if the Pharisees are asking a question irrelevant to Jesus's ministry. Jesus is concerned, as the Pharisees are, with how to maintain holiness in a world in which the people of God are not in control. The Pharisees rightly think that they should try to live avoiding anything that would make them impure and, thus, incapable of worshiping God. Jesus is not unsympathetic with their attempt to live true to the law.

The Pharisees' desire to live holy lives is right, but the critical issue is the grounds of holiness. The Pharisees, therefore, ask Jesus's disciples why Jesus, by eating with sinners, defies what they think is required by the law. They seem hesitant to ask Jesus directly, but he hears their challenge and in response makes clear his difference with the Pharisees. He has come to the sick not to the well; it is the sick who need mercy. It seems that holiness begins with the recognition that we are not well.

We are told in Hos. 6:6 what God expects of those who would be his people:

> For I desire steadfast love and not sacrifice,
> the knowledge of God rather than burnt offerings.

Yet we know that a sacrifice will be made that will be the end of sacrifice. Thus in Heb. 10:5–7 we are told that when Christ came into the world he said:

> Sacrifices and offering you have not desired,
> but a body you have prepared for me;
> in burnt offerings and sin offerings
> you have taken no pleasure.
> Then I said, "See, God, I have come to do your will, O God"
> (in the scroll of the book it is written of me).

So a sacrifice will be made, "a single sacrifice" (Heb. 10:12) to perfect "for all time those who are sanctified" (10:14). Sacrifice was the way that Israel sought sanctification and holiness to expiate for its sins. But those sacrifices are no longer necessary because the one has come, the very Son of God, who alone is capable of becoming the offering for sin. Now mercy is the form that sacrifice must take, and mercy constitutes the holiness that separates those called from the world to follow Jesus. Christ's cross is the perfect sacrifice that reveals the purpose of the law, but in fact his whole life, his calling of Matthew and his eating with sinners, is mercy. Here we see why the merciful are blessed (Matt. 5:7).

The Pharisees have no need of this physician because their illness is to believe that they are well. Jesus has come to rescue sinners. In response to the Pharisees he observes that the kingdom he has brought is constituted by those able to acknowledge their sins. In the Sermon on the Mount he told us that he has come to fulfill the law and the prophets (Matt. 5:17), but that fulfillment comes through his power to forgive sin. Speculation concerning whether Jesus knew that he was the Messiah is not necessary in the light of Jesus's call to sinners. Jesus is what he does. He has come (10:34–35; 20:28) to give his life so that we can live the life for which we were created.

The confusion concerning holiness, the separation from the world that mercy requires, is made explicit when the disciples of John the Baptist question why Jesus's disciples do not fast. John's disciples identify their fasting with the Pharisees, who also fast. Jesus's response is clear; the reason his disciples do not fast is because of him. They do not need to mourn, because they follow the one who has brought into being the new age marked by the creation of a new people begun in his disciples. The disciples are in the presence of life freed from the dread of death. In time he will be taken away, he will be crucified, and then they will have reason to fast. But not now; during his ministry, the disciples must enjoy the good gift he is. Now the new is present, and the new reconfigures death-determined time.

"Suddenly," as he was saying these things, a representative of Israel, a leader of the synagogue, comes to Jesus and, like the leper, kneels before him. He uses no title of address, but he displays the faith of the leper and the centurion. He simply says that if Jesus will come to his house he knows that Jesus can raise his daughter from the dead. Jesus and his disciples follow him to his home, but before they arrive, a woman who has been hemorrhaging for twelve years, believing she would be healed, touches his cloak. We cannot help but wonder how Matthew knows she has been suffering for twelve years—or why he thinks it important to tell us, but such details help us to sense the desperate situation of this woman. Her condition means that she was isolated because she was always unclean. That she touched Jesus was, therefore, an extraordinary and desperate act. Again Jesus credits her faith, a faith that is confident that Jesus is who he says he is, and pronounces her cured. It is not faith in general that cures her, but her faith that Jesus has the power to cure. She is at once cured and her isolation ended.

Jesus arrives at the leader of the synagogue's house and sends away the mourners, telling them that the girl is not dead but sleeping. The mourners mock his diagnosis, but it turns out to be true. It seems odd that Matthew thinks it important to tell us a story in which Jesus does no more than wake a sleeping young girl. He even tells us that a report of Jesus waking the leader of the synagogue's daughter spread throughout the district. We have no way to know why such a story might have such significance, but it is interesting to observe that Jesus refuses to make this situation worse than it was to manifest his power. One would like to think the story was spread throughout the district because this story makes clear that Jesus is no charlatan. Jesus tells the truth. The girl was only sleeping.

Jesus never tarries. Like foxes and birds, he is always on the move. The kingdom is a movement that requires him to go to those to whom he has been sent. That he must go to those in need indicates that the gospel is not and cannot be a set of beliefs. The gospel is this man, and this man must encounter actual men and women in order to call them into the community of the new age. Evangelism is people meeting and coming to know people. As we shall soon see, the disciples will be sent out to the people of Israel. There can be no substitute for the sending of people. A church that is not a missionary church is not a church. The book of Acts witnesses to the necessity for disciples of Christ to, like Jesus himself, be on the move.

Jesus's constant movement enables those in need, the blind and the mute, to have access to him. Two blind men follow him crying for mercy. How those who are blind are able to follow him is not clear, but then that is true for all of us whose vision of him is often cloudy. They ask not to be healed, but for mercy. Moreover they call Jesus "the son of David." We learned from the first verse of Matthew's gospel that this is the son of David, but here this title affirms that this kingship is charged with providing mercy and healing. This is the David of Ps. 72:12–14:

> For he delivers the needy when they call,
>   the poor and those who have no helper.
> He has pity on the weak and the needy,
>   and saves the lives of the needy.
> From oppression and violence he redeems their life;
>   and precious is their blood in his sight.

Jesus does not respond immediately to the blind men, but they follow him into the house. Jesus asks them if they believe that he is able to do what they desire, and they answer, "Yes, Lord." Like the leper, he touches their eyes, and their sight is restored. Jesus "sternly" charges them to tell no one what he has done. But they spread the news throughout the district. The reason Jesus may have charged them not to tell others what he has done is illuminated by his healing of a mute who was possessed by a demon. The mute, like the paralytic, is brought to him, and Jesus casts out the demon. The mute's speech is restored, and though we are not told what he says, we know the crowds are amazed. Indeed, they begin to say that Israel had never seen anything like what this man Jesus was doing. But the crowd's amazement only invites growing opposition to Jesus's mission.

The Pharisees respond to Jesus's healing of those possessed by demons by observing that only demons can cast out demons. They then begin the campaign against Jesus by accusing him of being a representative of Satan himself (Matt. 12:22–32). Jesus's charge to those he has cured to say nothing about what he has done may reflect his concern that he not be so misunderstood. He must be and do what he has been sent to be and do, but he does not want to be rejected for what he is not. Those who fear him will be willing to use any calumny and falsehood to discredit his ministry. Yet the die is set. We must move forward in preparation to witness the agony Jesus will undergo.

Jesus does not let the gathering opposition stop his mission. He goes through the cities and villages, teaching in the synagogues, proclaiming the good news, and curing every disease. He is surrounded by the crowds, and he has compassion for them because they are like sheep without a shepherd. In a wonderful moment Jesus, confronted with such need, asks the disciples to pray that God will send helpers. The mission of the church has begun. The disciples' prayer is answered, and the answer turns out to be them.

MATTHEW 10

The Sending

Jesus summons the disciples and gives them authority over unclean spirits and the power to cure illness. We learn the names of the twelve apostles, beginning with the first called, Simon, who will be called Peter, and ending with Judas Iscariot, who will betray Jesus. We know little about the individual disciples, but we know that they are not a distinguished group. They are people of "little faith," but they are who Jesus has called. We will learn more about some of them, particularly Peter and Judas, but the more we learn does not increase our confidence in them. In quite different ways Peter and Judas will both betray Jesus.

That Matthew tells us Judas will betray Jesus indicates that the dramatic tension of the gospel does not involve "what is going to happen to Jesus." Matthew reports the opposition to Jesus but the gospel writer assumes that the basic outline of the story is known. How Matthew tells the story of Jesus indicates that "knowing the story" is not sufficient to make one a faithful disciple. We must learn how we, like the disciples, would be tempted to betray Jesus and from that lesson discover what it means to be a faithful church.

Accordingly, the undistinguished character of the disciples is a sign of hope for us who inherit their task, for it is surely right that the church understands itself to stand in the tradition of the apostles. To be an apostle is to be a messenger of and witness to Jesus. It is not accidental that Jesus calls the disciples to preach, as he and John the Baptist had, that "the kingdom of heaven has come near." It is not accidental that he charges the apostles to "cure the sick, raise the dead, cleanse the lepers, cast out demons." He asks them and us to do what he has done. We must, however, see before we can do; accordingly the church depends on a line of witnesses through the centuries that exemplify what Jesus taught his disciples to do.

Christianity is not a philosophy that can be learned separate from those who embody it. If the truth that is Christ were a truth that could be known "in principle" then we would not need apostles. But the way the gospel is known is by one person being for another person the story of Christ. Jesus summons the disciples to him, and, so summoned, they become for us the witnesses who make it possible for us to be messengers of the kingdom. The disciples are not impressive people, but then, neither are we. Their mission, as well as our own, is not to call attention to ourselves but to Jesus and the kingdom.

That there are twelve disciples means, moreover, that this new community stands in fundamental continuity with the people of Israel. Israel was constituted by twelve tribes, and Jesus calls twelve disciples. The twelve disciples are charged to go only to Israel rather than to the Gentiles and the Samaritans. Jesus has been sent to "the lost sheep of the house of Israel" to fulfill the prophecy that Israel is God's beloved, called to be a light to the nations. We have seen that some Gentiles are ready to respond to Jesus's call, believing that the kingdom is present through Jesus's life and work. The Gentiles who respond to his call for repentance are grafted into God's promise to Israel. But Israel is not to be left behind—Jesus has come to call her to repentance. Accordingly, Jesus sends the disciples to the people of Israel to insure that they will not be lost amid the nations. Only after Jesus's resurrection will the disciples be sent to all the nations (Matt. 28:19).

Jesus gives his apostles very detailed instructions. They are not to receive any money for their work; they are to travel light, with little money and clothes; they are to stay only in towns in which they have been received; and they are to bestow the peace of God on those who provide hospitality. But they are not to tarry with those who will not provide hospitality or are unwilling to listen to them. We see exemplified what it means for the apostles, these messengers, not to judge. They do not need to judge because they have become God's judgment on those who refuse to welcome them or listen to them. That they are God's judgment is surely the reason that Jesus will need to prepare them to face persecution.

The apostles are charged to abandon those who are "unworthy," that is, those who reject their message. We must be careful, however, for such judgment can easily become a formula for self-righteousness. We may be tempted to believe that if our witness is rejected, those who refuse to listen are perverse. But the gospel we are charged to proclaim requires that before any judgment is made about those to whom we witness, we must first ask if we have been adequate witnesses. The gospel is not the gospel until it has been received. Accordingly, rejection may be a sign that the gospel has not been faithfully embodied. The character of the one witnessing must be consistent with that for which they are witnessing. The disciples are sent with strict rules concerning how their message is to be exemplified.

Jesus's command that the disciples travel light, for example, is necessary to manifest that they have nothing to commend other than Jesus himself. To be a follower of Jesus has not made them wealthy, powerful, or secure. They are charged to have nothing at their disposal other than the authority that they have been given by Jesus. As a result nothing is allowed to get in the way of the witness they make to the gospel. They cannot promise that Jesus will make his followers well-off, worry free, successful, or any other worldly good. Rather, the promise is life in the kingdom of God, a kingdom no longer determined by the power of death.

We should not be surprised, therefore, that monasticism has always remained one of the most effective forms of Christian witness, for monks and nuns must learn to travel light, to offer and receive hospitality, to trust one another for the very ability to live. Monasticism was not, of course, necessarily founded as a form of witness to those not Christian, but the attractive character of monastic life makes monks and nuns witnesses to strangers almost in spite of themselves, for the joy that radiates from truthful worship of God proves to be an irresistible witness to those who have not yet been confronted by Jesus's summons. All people are created for such joy.

Jesus's instructions for the disciples' mission, however, remain true for any understanding of Christian evangelism. Too often concern for the status of the church tempts some to employ desperate measures to insure that the church will remain socially significant or at least have a majority of the population. But the church is not called to be significant or large. The church is called to be apostolic. Faithfulness, not numbers or status, should be the characteristic that shapes the witness of the church. Indeed it may well be the case in our time that God is unburdening the church so that we can again travel light.

The disciples must, like Jesus, remain on the move. If they are rejected they must, as Paul does in Acts, move to the next house or town. The kingdom, it seems, grows through rejection. Success is not a sign of faithfulness. And yet, Jesus tells the disciples that their rejection by a town will entail judgment not unlike the judgment of Sodom and Gomorrah. The men of Sodom and Gomorrah betrayed hospitality by subjecting Lot, his wife, and his daughters to treachery, and God destroyed them. The kingdom unleashed by Jesus is the kingdom of hospitality. To reject him and those who represent him is to call down judgment on ourselves.

Jesus, therefore, prepares his apostles for rejection and persecution. They are sheep sent into the midst of wolves, but that does not mean that they are called to be stupid. Rather, they are to be as wise as serpents and innocent as doves. Wisdom and innocence are not often paired. To have wisdom often requires the loss of innocence, but the innocence that the apostles are to embody, like the Beatitudes commending the poor, meek, and mournful, is not something achieved through effort. Rather, innocence names the unavoidable vulnerability of those sent into the world who will challenge the worldly powers with the weapons of the Spirit.

Stalin famously asked how many divisions the pope had—a fair question indicating the assumption by many that history is made by the violent. Yet the church has endured without an army. Christians have often had the equivalent of an army underwriting the use of violence by those not officially identified by the church. Yet it remains the case that Christian witness—if a witness to the kingdom made present in Christ—is most transparent in those who will not kill. The church denies its apostolicity when it employs coercion to further the witness of Christ's peace.

Jesus tells the disciples—no doubt anticipating later treatment of him—that the synagogue leaders will drag the apostles before governing authorities in order to have them beaten. When this happens, they are not to worry about what they will say, but rather truthful speech will be given to them by the Spirit. To be told not to prepare speeches in their defense is surely an extraordinary demand, but one that reflects Jesus's training the disciples to confront the powers in a manner that the violence of governors and kings is challenged. Governors and kings understand those who would violently overthrow them. What they cannot face is the power of a people who refuse to fear them because they rightly fear God. The fear of God makes truthful speech possible. The speech given by the Spirit is the speech made possible by the very vulnerability that the witness to the kingdom requires. No force is more powerful against oppression than truthful speech.

The kingdom brought by Jesus, the kingdom that the disciples are charged to preach, has come near; it is the kingdom that is the alternative to all the kingdoms created by death. Jesus tells his disciples that, just as Mic. 7:6–7 predicted, brother will kill brother, fathers will betray children, and children will seek to destroy their parents; and all those so captured by the kingdom of death will hate the disciples who witness to the name of Jesus. These are quite extraordinary results for preaching the kingdom of God, but Jesus instructs the disciples to expect such a response. The kingdoms of death, the kingdoms that rule through violence legitimated by the fear of death, are challenged by this one who has come to put an end to the rule of death.

Jesus even says that he has come not to bring peace to the earth but a sword. Moreover, it seems that the family is the first place that the divisions occasioned by Jesus will be apparent. Not only will governors and kings hate and persecute the apostles, but the family will be fractured by loyalty to him. The separation that Jesus has come to enact is as real as the mission on which the disciples are sent. The sword he has brought, the sword that is an alternative to the peace of the world, is the sword of the cross. Bonhoeffer puts it this way:

> The cross is God's sword on this earth. It creates division. The son against the father, the daughter against the mother, the household against its head, and all

that for the sake of God's kingdom and its peace—that is the work of Christ on earth! No wonder the world accuses him, who brought the love of God to the people, of hatred toward human beings! Who dares to speak about a father's love and a mother's love to a son or daughter in such a way, if not either the destroyer of all life or the creator of a new life? Who can claim the people's love and sacrifice so exclusively, if not the enemy of humanity or the savior of humanity? Who will carry the sword into their houses, if not the devil or Christ, the Prince of Peace? God's love for the people and human love for their kind are utterly different. God's love for the people brings the cross and discipleship, but these, in turn, mean life and resurrection. "Anyone who loses his life for my sake will find it." This affirmation is given by the one who has the power over death, the Son of God, who goes to the cross and to resurrection and takes those who are his with him. (Bonhoeffer 2001, 197)

That Christians carry no sword other than the cross does not mean, however, that we are sent into the world defenseless. In the book of Hebrews we are told that the word of God is sharper than a two-edged sword, piercing the soul and laying bare all before the eyes of God (Heb. 4:12–13). Scripture is the weapon of truth that enables those who follow Jesus to disarm the powers by exposing their lies and deceit. Christians are not without defense, having been given God's word to shield us from our delusions that are the source of our violence.

Jesus, however, is clear. Attempts to secure our lives through the means offered by the world are doomed to failure. If we are to find our lives, it seems, we must be prepared to lose our lives. But this is not a general recommendation meaning that we should learn unselfishness—even unselfishness that may cost our lives—for the life we must be willing to lose is the life lost "for my sake," that is, for Jesus. Self-sacrifice, often justified in the name of family or country, can too easily be tyrannical. The language of sacrifice is often used by those in power for perverse ends. Jesus does not commend the loss of self as a good in and of itself. He demands that we follow him because he alone has the right to ask for our lives.

Too often Christianity in our time is justified as a way of life that leads to stability and order. "The family that prays together stays together"—but such sentiments cannot help but lead to an idolatry of the family. "Whoever loves father or mother more than me is not worthy of me; and whoever loves son or daughter more than me is not worthy of me" (Matt. 10:37) is a hard saying, but one that makes clear why Jesus must prepare the disciples for persecution. Our fathers and mothers, brothers and sisters, are now found among the disciples and not among the so-called blood relations. Let that be preached from the pulpits of America and see if those preachers will live free of persecution. Not a little is at stake. The violence of nations is often justified in the name of protecting our loves—our way of life. Yet it is exactly those loyalties that Jesus calls into question as he instructs his disciples.

In a book dealing with the power of the American flag to motivate people to sacrifice themselves in war, the observation is made:

> In the religiously plural society of the United States, sectarian faith is optional for citizens, as everyone knows. Americans have rarely bled, sacrificed or died for Christianity or any other sectarian faith. Americans have often bled, sacrificed and died for their country. This fact is an important clue to its religious power. Though denominations are permitted to exist in the United States, they are not permitted to kill, for their beliefs are not officially true. What is really true in any society is what is worth killing for, and what citizens may be compelled to sacrifice their lives for. (Marvin and Ingle 1999, 9)

Yet Jesus challenges those who would kill in the name of protecting their family and their nation. That he does so, moreover, is a clue for any consideration of the truth of Christian convictions. It is often thought that what Christians believe has become hard to believe because of modern science. But the fundamental challenge to the truthfulness of Christian convictions resides in Christian accommodation to loyalties not determined by Jesus. Of course Jesus will not let his followers kill; but he does demand that they be willing to die. That is why Christian truth is a necessary alternative to the truth of the United States. Often representatives of nonviolence are asked, "What would you do if . . . ?" with the dots filled in with scenarios that would require us to come to the aid of our spouse or our child who is being threatened by someone who may take their life. Such situations may actually confront those who follow Jesus, but his claim that we must learn to love him more than we love father, mother, son, or daughter means the answer to "What would you do if . . . ?" is not as obvious as is often assumed. To follow Jesus, to love Jesus, may mean that we and those we love cannot be spared death—a harsh and dreadful love, but a love disciplined by the love of this one who makes life itself possible. To be sure, if the Father is not the Father of Jesus then to contemplate the death of those we love is immoral. But the Father is the Father of Jesus and Jesus is the Son of the Father.

Jesus tells his disciples that if they are persecuted in one town they are to flee to the next. They are to do so because they will not have the time to make it "through all the towns of Israel before the Son of Man comes" (Matt. 10:23)—a stark reminder that this is apocalyptic time. The Son of Man has come, but his work, his life, will be consummated through cross and resurrection. The time in between is constituted by a patient witness.

The same remains true today, for we still live in apocalyptic time awaiting the return of the Son of Man. Jesus reminds the disciples and us that to faithfully witness to his peace there is always time to be patient. So the church, like the disciples, has the task to flee from one town to another so that the world may know there is time enough to live at peace with one another, for Jesus tells us our task is not to force the kingdom into existence, but to "endure"

(Matt. 10:22). To endure turns out to be the only way we can be witnesses to Christ's kingdom.[1]

Jesus also tells us that the disciples are not expected to be him, but rather we are to be "like the teacher." That likeness insures that we will be maligned, but being maligned can be endured because Jesus has gone before us as the pioneer of the faith. What he has told us in the dark, in secret, we can proclaim from the housetops. We can do so because he has called us to a ministry that cannot be defeated by death, for the fear of those who can kill the body is now countered by the confidence born of the fear of the one who alone determines life and death.

Christians rightly should fear, but they do not fear death: they fear the one who has made it possible to live courageously in the face of death. Thomas Aquinas calls the kind of fear produced by charity—the friendship that God establishes with us—filial fear (1981, part II-II Q. 19). God's love makes possible a confidence that drives out the fear that those who kill use to compel obedience to their will. Jesus tells his disciples, therefore, not to be afraid, because they are of more value than the sparrows. That God loves us, those he has called through his Son, more than he loves the sparrows does not mean that the sparrows are not loved as sparrows should be loved.

Jesus concludes his instructions to the disciples by assuring them that whoever welcomes them welcomes him as well as the one who has sent him. Jesus has been sent, and now he sends the disciples. Those who welcome these messengers will be rewarded as a righteous person is rightly rewarded. It seems that welcoming a prophet matters for the kind of life we will live with God. What we do and do not do affects our relationship with God. This is not unconditional acceptance. Jesus tells the disciples that whoever acknowledges him before others he will acknowledge to his Father. It is also the case that if we deny him he will deny us before the Father.

We rightly, therefore, fear betraying him. To deny him is to deny our very destiny, and there is no deeper sin than to deny the one who makes it possible for us to confess our sin. The disciples and we have been summoned by Jesus and given good work to do. In that work lies our salvation, our reward, our righteousness. Later, Jesus will tell us that if we have taken the time to feed the hungry, give water to the thirsty, visit those in prison, we will have served him (Matt. 25:31–46). In like manner, those who give "a cup of cold water to one of these little ones in the name of a disciple" (10:42) will have their reward. Indeed it may well be that one of the major tasks of the church is to welcome those called to be prophets.

Many Christians in our day have become hesitant to use the language of punishment and reward that animates these texts. This language suggests that our relation with God is subject to a crude exchange—for example, if we are

---

1. For my reflections on the significance of endurance, see Hauerwas 2000, 163–72.

good then God must reward us. Quite understandably many Christians are repelled by such a view of God. Instead of a God who punishes, they want a God who only loves us. The problem with such a view is not only that the language of reward and punishment is clearly central to what Jesus says concerning those who receive prophets, but such a view denies the good news that Jesus has summoned us to be participants in the kingdom of God. What the Father has done by sending the Son cannot be undone by our unfaithfulness, but the good news is that our faithfulness matters to the Father. Salvation is a life-and-death matter. Our response to Jesus's invitation to be part of the kingdom, to be a disciple, will determine our destiny before God. To be sure, no one follows Jesus in order to "get ours," but to follow Jesus means that we discover an "ours" that we could not have otherwise imagined. We are invited to take up the cross, and that is the "reward." Yet that reward makes possible a life freed from the fear of death and those who use our fear of death to "save" us. To be saved from the salvation offered by the world surely is what it means to be made righteous.

We do not learn how the disciples fared on the mission to Israel. Rather, we are told that after Jesus had finished instructing the disciples he went on to proclaim his message "in their cities" (Matt. 11:1), that is, in the same cities to which he had sent the disciples. That we do not learn how successful or unsuccessful the disciples may have been indicates that the task is not one determined by success. Rather, to do what we have been told to do by Jesus and to do what we have been told to do in the manner he has instructed is what is important. Our responsibility is to be faithful to the task God has given us. The result is God's doing.

MATTHEW 11–12

"Are You the One to Come?"

The gospels by their very nature are meant to be read retrospectively in light of the cross and resurrection. But retrospective moments are also internal to Matthew's gospel. For example, Matt. 8–9 reads differently after we have Jesus's sending of the disciples in Matt. 10. Matthew 8–9 exemplifies the cures and exorcisms that Jesus performs so the disciples will know what they are to do with the power Jesus conferred on them. Beginning with Matt. 11, Matthew prepares us for Peter's declaration that Jesus is "the Messiah, the Son of the living God" in Matt. 16. However, we must be careful not to rush to Peter's confession. We must attend to the stories that Matthew patiently tells of Jesus's healings and the controversies that those healings occasion in order to understand why Peter will not understand what he says when he confesses that Jesus is "the Messiah, the Son of the living God."

Matthew provides what may be thought of as organizational markers for his readers. For example, he begins Matt. 11 with the sentence: "Now when Jesus had finished instructing his twelve disciples." Matthew had previously used this sentence at the end of the Sermon on the Mount (7:28), and he will end Jesus's series of parables with the same sentence (13:53). Matthew also uses this formula in 19:1 and 26:1, making a total of five. This may be Matthew's way of relating his gospel to the five books of Moses. For Matthew, Moses prefigures Jesus by giving the law; but Jesus is greater than Moses because he now is the gift of the law.

Yet the status of Jesus is not easily recognized. Even John the Baptist sends his disciples to Jesus to ask if Jesus is the one long awaited or are they to wait for another. At the baptism of Jesus, John clearly recognizes Jesus as the Messiah.

What has happened to John that seems to have him reconsider this judgment? John is in prison but hears that Jesus is proclaiming his message in the cities of Israel, and from prison John sends his disciples to ask if Jesus is indeed the Messiah. John and Jesus both come to preach, "Repent, for the kingdom of heaven has come near"; but, if we are to judge from Jesus's condemnation of the unrepentant cities (Matt. 11:20–24), we have some indication that many remained unresponsive to John's and Jesus's calls for repentance. John, faced with failure, quite understandably sends his disciples to ask Jesus if he is the representative of the kingdom that has drawn near.

Jesus will answer John's query by again directing attention to the fruits of his ministry, that is, the blind see, the lame walk, the lepers are cleansed, the deaf hear, the dead are raised, and the poor have good news brought to them. As previously noted, these are the descriptions of the jubilee year enacted in Jesus's ministry. We know that Jesus has done all these things because we have witnessed his work throughout Galilee. But the jubilee year is not simply about individual repentance, rather it involves national renewal. Yet, from John's perspective, renewal may not seem to be occurring. After all, he is in prison, which seems a strange place to be for one who has pointed to Jesus as the one who has come to set the captives free.

John is in prison for holding Herod to the observance of the law (Matt. 14:1–11), but it is not clear that Jesus and John have the same understanding of the law. Matthew has indicated that John, like the Pharisees, thought it necessary to fast frequently (9:14–17). Jesus acknowledges that he does not require his disciples to fast, and he has even befriended tax collectors and sinners. That his disciples do not fast and that he befriends sinners have earned him a reputation for being a glutton and drunkard. Jesus's behavior may not look to John to be consonant with the repentance that he preached in the wilderness. Jesus, it seems, has some explaining to do.

Jesus answers John by calling attention to the fruits of his ministry. In response to the charge that he is a glutton and drunkard, Jesus observes that "wisdom is vindicated by her deeds" (Matt. 11:19). He, therefore, calls attention to his deeds, noting that those who take no offense at him will be blessed. Jesus has no better answer for John than to direct attention to the power unleashed through his ministry.

Yet Jesus does not call attention only to his deeds, but he also helps the crowd and John understand who John is. Jesus reminds the crowds that they did not go into the wilderness to hear someone who would comfort them by saying what they wanted to hear. John was clearly not someone who would change his message according to prevailing opinion. Nor, Jesus observes, did they go into the wilderness to see someone dressed in soft robes appropriate to living in palaces. Rather, they went to see a prophet, and prophets are not known for their softness or for being well dressed. John is a prophet, he stands in the line of prophets before him; it is no surprise, therefore, that he is in prison.

Jesus claims, moreover—and it is a claim that only he can make—that John is more than a prophet. Jesus's argument is subtle. John is more than a prophet because he is the one whom the prophet Malachi (3:1) said would come as the messenger to prepare the way for the Messiah. John, therefore, is greater than the prophets because he has the unique office to herald Israel's Messiah. He is Elijah. In Mal. 4:5 we are told that Elijah, the prophet who was received into heaven without dying, will be sent "before the great and terrible day of the LORD." John is Elijah because Jesus is the Messiah.

Yet as great as John is, he remains the least in the kingdom of heaven because John, like Moses, stands on the edge of the new age. Herods will try to defeat the kingdom heralded by John with violence, but it cannot be so overwhelmed. John the Baptist can be arrested and killed, Jesus will be crucified, but the kingdom that John proclaims comes through the peace brought by Jesus. This kingdom is not some ideal of peace that requires the use of violence for its realization. Rather, the kingdom is Jesus, the one who has the power to overcome violence through love.

Therefore, those who take "no offense" at Jesus are "blessed" (Matt. 11:6). Jesus becomes the form of the Beatitudes, inviting others to share in the kingdom of God. It seems, moreover, that those who have no stake in the current regime are more likely not to take offense at Jesus. Those without power are ready to dance with Jesus as he plays the flute. They are ready to mourn with Jesus as he despairs over Israel's unwillingness to repent. But those who sit in the marketplace, those who flourish in the everyday world of exchange, can only think John the Baptist to be mad and Jesus to be immoral.

John and Jesus have challenged the assumption that the way things are is the way they have to be. Indeed, John and Jesus claim that the way things are is an illusion. We live life, particularly if we are among those the market has rewarded, as if we are our own lords, our own creators. We respond violently to anyone who might challenge our presumption that we are in control of our existence. We do not want to be reminded that when all is said and done, we will all be dead. It is, therefore, not surprising that we, like those who think John mad and Jesus immoral, try to turn the kingdom into an ideal rather than a reality known through judgment.

The rejection of John and Jesus, moreover, is a collective project. Jesus reproaches the cities in which he has done his great deeds of power because they do not repent. He even suggests that Sodom would have repented and survived if that city had witnessed the deeds of power that Jesus has performed in Chorazin, Bethsaida, and Capernaum. But these cities, the collectivities of perverse normality, refuse to repent when faced by the judgment of God. Accordingly, the day of judgment, the day that Elijah heralds, will come on these cities, and it will be more terrible than what happened to Sodom.

Jesus's pronouncement of judgment on the cities in which he performed deeds of power makes us, contemporary Christians, profoundly uncomfortable. We want a gospel of love that insures when everything is said and done that everyone and everything is going to be okay. But we are not okay. Like the cities of Israel, we have turned our existence as Christians into a status meant to protect us from recognizing the prophets who would point us to Jesus. Of course we do not like Jesus to pronounce judgment on the cities in which he performed deeds of power, because we do not want to recognize that we too are judged. But the gospel is judgment because otherwise it would not be good news. Only through judgment are we forced to discover forms of life that can free us from our enchantment with sin and death.[1]

Jesus adds insult to injury by thanking the Father for hiding the secrets of the kingdom from the wise and intelligent but revealing them to infants. Jesus will later use children to answer the disciples' question concerning who will be the greatest in the kingdom of heaven (Matt. 18:1–5). Only by becoming like children, only by being humbled like a child, will we recognize those greatest in heaven. Intelligence and wisdom are often names for the power and violence employed to sustain our illusions of superiority.

In 1 Cor. 1:18–31 Paul tells us that God choose the cross to "destroy the wisdom of the wise." Paul directs the Corinthians' attention to their own selves, pointing out that most of them are not wise by human standards or of noble birth. They were chosen not because they are strong, but because they were, in the world's eyes, weak and foolish. Paul is not suggesting that Christians ought to try to be weak or foolish in order to show that they are Christian, but rather that their weakness or their foolishness is only fruitful as a witness to the cross. The cross, moreover, is the deepest wisdom of God.

Jesus, like Paul, is not suggesting that we try to be infants, but rather as those engrafted into the kingdom, we in fact are infants. We are just beginners, dependent on Jesus and one another for our very survival; we become a "new creation," in Paul's language. That the deaf, the mute, the blind, the poor, those rendered helpless in the face of suffering, recognize Jesus is not accidental. To be disabled does not make one a faithful follower of Christ, but it puts you in the vicinity of the kingdom. To be disabled is to be forced to have the time to recognize that Jesus is the inauguration of a new time constituted by prayer. To be disabled is to begin to understand what it means to be an infant *vis-à-vis* the kingdom brought by Jesus.

Jesus prays to the Father, thanking the Father that some have had the kingdom revealed to them. Jesus, the second person of the Trinity, prays to his Father. Prayer is at the heart of the relation between the persons of the Trinity because prayer makes present the Father, who is present to the Son through the Spirit. We are privileged, therefore, to overhear Jesus pray to the Father, revealing the intimacy that finds its most intense expression on the cross in Jesus's cry, "My God, my God, why have you forsaken me?" (Matt.

1. I am indebted to Rusty Reno for articulating the importance of judgment in this way.

27:46). Jesus prays, and his prayer draws us into the deepest mystery of the faith—the Trinity.

The prologue to the gospel of John is thought to be the expression of a high Christology. Yet we have seen that Matthew, like John, begins with the word that was in the beginning. Jesus's declaration in Matthew, moreover, that no one knows the Father except the Son, echoes John's declaration that "no one has ever seen God. It is God the only Son, who is close to the Father's heart, who has made him known" (John 1:18). Matthew, no less than John, reports that this Jesus is the Son who alone makes it possible for us to know that God is the Father. The Son will reveal the Father to those whom he chooses.

There is nothing arbitrary about Jesus's claiming that the Son alone reveals the Father, because we cannot know that God is the Father unless we know that Jesus is the Son. Some worry about the implications of Jesus's claim that he alone reveals the Father for those who are not Christian. What, they ask, might it mean for people who are members of other faiths or those who have no faith, to claim that we know the Father only through the Son? Too often such worries and questions betray a "little faith," that is, the kind of faith that is the mark of an established church made up of the wise and intelligent. If followers of Christ, however, are those who are infants from the perspective of the wise and intelligent, that is, from the perspective of those in power, they will find that they do not need an account of the status of those who are not Christians. Rather, they need only to be a people whose lives are so captured by the Son that others may find that they are also captivated by the joy that animates the lives of those claimed by Jesus.

To be a follower of Christ is to learn to dance when children play the flute. Rowan Williams reports how such a dance might look by describing the work of a young Chilean teacher in Australia who developed dance and drama with the mentally handicapped. Williams learned about the story of the Laura Hodgkinson Sunshine Home in Sydney, Australia, in a British television documentary called *Stepping Out*. The documentary begins with

> scenes showing the very first stages, as these young people in their twenties and thirties gradually learned controlled breathing, coordinated movement, learned to relax into their bodies and *live* in them. Then we saw the build-up, as costumes and masks were tried on, the music became more adventurous, the dancing more subtle; and the emergence of thirty-one-year-old Chris as the natural soloist of the group, dancing to Villa-Lobos and Puccini, portraying the death of Madame Butterfly with total conviction, at a level of ritual pathos which few professionals could manage. You watched the awkward, superficial, lumpy and vacant face of a "retarded" man turn into a tragic mask: every inch, every corner of the body answering the music with discipline, accuracy, complete engagement. And the climax, a breathtaking performance in the Sydney Opera House, no less, was greeted with a standing ovation. (Williams 1994, 72)

Williams confesses that anyone, himself included, might have watched *Stepping Out*, ready to be moved in a patronizing way by the so-called retarded trying to dance. It is hard to avoid the attitude that what one is watching is touching but pathetic. Yet Williams observes that the "only final response worth making was humble, awed delight. We'd been watching grace in every sense. We'd been watching love, the patient, humorous, grave care of the teacher, getting these people to value and admire their bodies, giving words and hugs of encouragement to each one as they prepared to perform" (1994, 72–73).

That is what it means for the Son to reveal the Father to the infants. To learn to dance to the flute means that we are so caught up in the dance that questions about those who are not part of the dance do not arise. At least they do not arise as a question of power. Rather, they arise only because we so desire to share with others the wonder of the dance. So Williams suggests that we learn to listen to the invitation:

> Sit down, all of you handicapped, lumpish, empty, afraid, and start to feel that you too are rooted in a firm, rich earth. Opposite you is someone who, it seems, doesn't need to learn. His roots are very deep, very deep indeed; he knows he is lovely and loved. Dancing is natural to him, he has no paralyzing, self-conscious dread, no self-protection to overcome. So he begins: he stretches out his arms, wide as he can. And so do you. Then he rises up, arms to the sky. And so do you. Then he takes your hand and swings you loose and leaves you to improvise the music—on your own, then combining with the others, then alone again, then with one or two, then all together, and alone again. (Williams 1994, 73–74)

This is the rest that Jesus offers to all who are weary. This is the gentleness and humility of heart he offers to all. This is the exemplification of the blessedness of the Beatitudes. Given the agony that awaits Jesus, it may seem strange that he calls this rest a yoke. Even stranger, it seems that Jesus suggests that we can and should take on his yoke and learn from him. Yet it is surely the case that we can take on his yoke, because he bore for us the yoke that only he could bear. That he did so makes possible our sharing his yoke, which is now easy. It is easy because his yoke is a welcome alternative to the burdens we carry that give no rest.

This is the answer that Jesus gives to the question asked by the disciples of John the Baptist, that is, he has revealed the Father. He is the one to come, the Messiah of Israel. The kingdom he brings is one of gentleness and humility that cannot help but reveal the violence of the world. Yet the very gentleness of the kingdom effects a judgment on those who refuse to believe that the love that moves the sun and the stars is the same love that is found in this man. We will not, therefore, be surprised then, after Jesus has plainly said who he is and what he has come to do, that everything he says and does invites controversy and resistance.

Jesus has said that he will provide rest to those heavily burdened, and therefore it is appropriate that he is immediately involved in a controversy concerning the Sabbath, the day set aside for rest. "At that time," Matthew tells us, Jesus and his disciples "went through the grainfields on the sabbath." His disciples are hungry, and they begin to pluck and eat heads of grain. The Pharisees see what the disciples are doing and challenge Jesus to justify their behavior. The disciples "at that time," the time of the Sabbath, the time of rest, from the Pharisees' perspective, are at work.

We, of course, naturally side with the disciples. We are predisposed to think in terms of "good guys" and "bad guys" when reading the New Testament. Surely the good guys are the disciples, so that their so-called working on the Sabbath must be justified. But it is important that we not be too ready to criticize the Pharisees. Sabbath, we know from Genesis, is rooted in the very character of God's creation. Sabbath is a gift, the gift of time given to sanctify time. God's invitation to Israel to participate in his rest is a gift to the world so that the world may know we are created in time for time. Abraham Heschel observes:

> There are two aspects to the Sabbath, as there are two aspects to the world. The Sabbath is meaningful to man and is meaningful to God. It stands in a relation to both, and is a sign of the covenant entered into by both. What is the sign? God has sanctified the day, and man must again and again sanctify the day, illumine the day with the light of his soul. The Sabbath is holy by the grace of God, and is still in need of all the holiness which man may lend to it. The Sabbath is meaningful to God, for without it there would be no holiness in our world of time. (Heschel 1951, 53–54)

God, moreover, commands Israel to keep the Sabbath in order to "remember that you were a slave in the land of Egypt, and the LORD your God brought you out from there with a mighty hand and an outstretched arm; therefore the LORD your God commanded you to keep the sabbath day" (Deut. 5:15). So there is an unmistakable political witness to the keeping of the Sabbath. In exile, deprived of land and temple, God reminds Israel that it has been given the Sabbath as "a sign between me and [them], so that [they] may know that I the LORD" sanctify them (Ezek. 20:21). So Sabbath, Israel's way of being oriented by God, was crucial for resisting those who would force Israel to live in a different time.

The news of the Emancipation Proclamation did not reach Texas until June 19, 1865, after the Civil War had ended and two-and-a-half years after the proclamation was issued. From that moment, African Americans in Texas regarded June 19 as a holiday, and many would travel to Galveston, where the news was first given by Union Major General Gordon Granger. Whites were resistant to this practice, but African Americans simply refused to show up for work on that day. Whites continued to work if they could, but they often were not able to work because they were dependent on African American labor.

Juneteenth, as it was called by African Americans and whites alike, became a day in which both remembered freedom from slavery.[2] So the Sabbath was for Israel, both in exile and under foreign rule.

The Pharisees' concern that Jesus's disciples seemed to be working may seem legalistic, and given the polemical context it no doubt was somewhat rigorist, but crucial issues were at stake. Jesus, moreover, honors the Pharisees' challenge by responding with arguments that they would recognize. Jesus often asks the crowds, "Have you not heard?" but he asks the Pharisees, "Have you not read?" In other words he appeals to their strength as students of the scripture.

He first directs their attention to 1 Sam. 21:1–7, in which David asks the priests to give to his hungry men bread reserved for those consecrated by abstinence to serve at the altar. David argues that his men share a common consecration and that they rightly should be fed with the bread set aside for those dedicated to the Lord. In like manner, Jesus argues that his disciples can pluck heads of grain because, like David's men, they are consecrated by their loyalty to him, the new David. Jesus is not finished with his argument, however, directing the Pharisees' attention to the necessity of priests working on the Sabbath to offer the sacrifice required by Num. 28:9–10.

Jesus provides a model for argument. He appeals to texts that he and the Pharisees regard as authoritative. Yet to read these texts well requires that the Pharisees acknowledge that they recognize Jesus to be challenging the status of the temple. Jesus makes the astounding claim that "the Son of Man is lord of the sabbath." Time will be reconfigured by Jesus's resurrection, making the seventh day the climax of the new creation begun by Jesus's conception.

The mode of Jesus's argument and his use of the scriptures make apparent to the Pharisees that they are in the presence of one whose very existence is a challenge to their world. Jesus claims to be nothing less than the one who refigures the time of creation, thus becoming the key for how scripture is to be read. Matthew's gospel is the exemplification of Jesus's life and work as the hermeneutical key for reading Israel's scripture. It is hard not to feel some sympathy for the Pharisees, whose world is being turned upside down. After all, two thousand years later we are still trying to receive Jesus's radical transformation of our world and lives.

Jesus, citing Hos. 6:6, claims that mercy, not sacrifice, should be at the center of Israel's worship. This is tested as soon as Jesus enters a synagogue and finds a man with a withered hand. "They" ask him if it is lawful to cure on the Sabbath. Matthew does not identify the "they," but it may well have been some of those who heard him say that mercy not sacrifice is the mark of Sabbath observance. If mercy is required, they ask if it is lawful to cure on the Sabbath. Again Jesus responds by offering an argument, but this time he argues using common sense. If one is allowed to rescue a sheep on the Sabbath, the only sheep that

---

2. In 1980, June 19 was finally given legal recognition as a Texas state holiday.

one possesses, from a pit into which it has fallen, how much more important is the care of a human being? He then asks the man with the withered hand to reveal his hand, the one he has kept hidden, and Jesus heals his hand.

The issues surrounding the Sabbath are too much for the Pharisees. Matthew reports that the Pharisees begin to conspire against Jesus in order to destroy him—an ominous development that will become, from this point on, one of the major themes in the story that Matthew tells. Jesus is, moreover, aware that they desire to kill him, but he does not seek to fight them. Rather, Matthew tells us that he departs, not seeking further confrontation. He withdraws but he does not abandon what he has been sent to do. Rather, he refuses to defend himself in a manner that mimics the conspiracy of the Pharisees. Jesus's only weapon against the violence of the lie is the truth that he has been given and that he is.

The crowds, however, continue to follow him; all who need to be cured, he cures. Yet, he orders them not to make himself known in order to fulfill Isaiah's prophecy (42:1–4) regarding the one who will proclaim justice to the Gentiles:

> He will not wrangle or cry aloud,
>   nor will anyone hear his voice in the streets.
> He will not break a bruised reed
>   or quench a smoldering wick
> until he brings justice to victory.
>   And in his name the Gentiles will hope. (Matt. 12:19–21)

The Pharisees rightly sense that Jesus has come to fulfill the offices at the heart of Israel's life; that is, he is nothing less than the prophet, priest, and king of Israel. Yet his fulfillment of each of these offices also forces Israel to reconsider what kind of Messiah it thought would come, for here is the king who refuses to rule by force, here is the priest who will be sacrificed, and here is the prophet who does not "wrangle or cry aloud." Moreover, his fulfillment of these offices means that hope is brought to the Gentiles, making justice possible. The great enemy of justice is cynicism and despair, but Jesus brings hope because he is the eschatological sign that our lives have been given purpose through this new creation.

Try as he might to avoid controversy, Jesus is drawn back into a dispute with the Pharisees because he heals a blind and mute demoniac. The crowds begin to speculate that anyone who can heal one so possessed must be the son of David. But the Pharisees again see this healing as an opportunity to conspire against him, thinking that only "Beelzebul, the ruler of the demons," can cast out demons. They do not say what they are thinking because they hope to make this part of the conspiracy against him, but Jesus knows his enemy well and responds to their silent accusations.

He observes that no kingdom, even the kingdom of Satan, can stand divided against itself. The Pharisees also have exorcists who cast out demons; if they are not to disavow their own exorcists, they cannot condemn Jesus's exorcisms. If the Pharisees condemn Jesus for casting out demons, they would have to apply the same test to the work of their exorcists. Therefore, Jesus argues that if they acknowledge that he has cast out demons, which they clearly seem to have done, they must also acknowledge that Jesus is able to cast out demons only because he does so through the Spirit. Accordingly, the Pharisees should recognize that the kingdom of God has drawn near if such work has been done.

That the kingdom is clearly present is obvious; Jesus argues that one cannot fight against Satan unless one has already bound the strongman. Jesus has bound the strongman, Satan, by his willing subjection to Satan in Satan's stronghold. He faced Satan in the wilderness and was subjected to the worst that Satan could do, and yet he prevailed. He has, as Isa. 49:24–25 says he would do, taken the mighty captive by refusing Satan's terms of battle. Satan's house not only can be, but has been, plundered through the work of the Holy Spirit. This means that we cannot have it both ways: we cannot serve God and mammon. We cannot fight Satan while at the same time employing Satan's understanding of the way things are.

To blaspheme against the Holy Spirit is a sin that cannot be forgiven because forgiveness does not simply mean that our sins are not held against us. Rather, forgiveness names an alternative community to the rule of Satan. Such community is present in this age as well as in the age to come. To be forgiven is to be gathered to Jesus. Not to be forgiven is to be scattered and lost in a world of the lost. Blasphemy is the denial, the refusal, to participate in the new world begun by the repentance made possible by the power bestowed by the Spirit on this man, Jesus.

It matters, therefore, what we say and do not say. Jesus turns on those who would accuse him of blasphemy, of exorcising Satan in the name of Satan, accusing them of saying one thing and being another. Good and evil trees will be known by the fruit they bear. But discerning the fruit is difficult because vipers become good at saying what they are not, thus making it difficult to distinguish good from evil. This will not be the case on the day of judgment, however, when all will be held accountable for every careless word uttered.

Words have played a crucial role in all Jesus has done and taught. He has taught us to discipline our speech when we are angry (Matt. 5:22–26); he has forbidden oaths (5:33–37); he has no use for empty prayers (6:7); he condemns hypocritical speech of judgment (7:4–5); he cannot abide false confessions of faith (7:21–22); and he disdains the use of words that clearly are meant to deny who he is (12:2).[3] The misuse of words he attributes to "our treasury." We speak falsely because of what we fear losing as well as because of what we

3. I am indebted to Carter 2003, 276 for drawing my attention to these texts.

think we must protect. Moreover, what we fear to lose and what we desire to protect is too often hidden even from ourselves.

All of this means that one of the essential tasks of the church is the "care" of words. One of the offices for the care of words is called theology. Theology is the discipline charged to help those who would speak after Christ, saying no more or no less than is required to witness to the truth he is. Truthful language can go dead, because all language requires constant care. That is why the church cannot live without the poetry of careful speech, which often takes the form of prayer, in particular, the prayers of monks, who have honed their prayers through the centuries by singing the Psalms.

But theologians are often tempted to say more than can be said. The mystery of God frustrates us, enticing us to explain what cannot be explained. Theologians are particularly vulnerable to these perversions when they live at a time in which the status of the church and the church's beliefs are questioned. Too often, the intelligent and wise think that the problematic character of the language of faith requires that they use their intellectual power to shore up what the church believes.

In such a context, a context in which I fear Christians have lived for some time, the reticence of the gospels frustrates us. We want them to say more than they can say. We use intellectual tools, historical research, to explain what, for example, Matthew must have really meant when he presented Jesus's exchange with the Pharisees concerning Beelzebul. It is assumed that if we know more about what people at Jesus's time understood by the devil we will be better able to understand what Jesus means when he says that Satan cannot cast out Satan.

There is no doubt that much can be learned from such studies, and they are not to be ignored. But the reading of Matthew practiced in this commentary tries to respect Matthew's reticence. That reticence, moreover, I believe to be a necessary discipline to train us to read the gospel when we have been stripped of treasures we thought we could not live without. To read the gospel without our reading challenging our power or our wealth as Christians is no easy task. I cannot pretend that this commentary is anything more than a beginning.

Like the scribes and the Pharisees, we desperately desire to be given a sign. Those who ask for a sign have no doubt heard that Jesus has healed the blind, made the lame walk, cleansed lepers, restored hearing to the deaf, raised the dead, brought good news to the poor, but they still desire a sign. Later they will even ask Jesus to show them "a sign from heaven" (Matt. 16:1). We should confess by the time we have reached this point in the gospel of Matthew that we cannot help but be sympathetic with the request for a sign. Jesus asks much of those who would follow him, and it does not seem unreasonable to be given some assurance. Yet, we must remember, the devil asked Jesus for signs in the desert.

It is unclear what kind of sign would satisfy the scribes and Pharisees—and us. Once a professor of philosophy supposedly said he would believe in God if the heavens opened and a magnificent figure appeared, declaring, in a very loud voice, "I am God." But that is exactly the kind of evidence that would make it impossible to follow Jesus, for the Father cannot be part of the metaphysical furniture of the universe and be found in this man. Denys Turner argues that because we cannot know the *quid est* of God, it is possible to say that the one and same person is both human and divine. Only if God is unknowable to us, Turner explains, is the Chalcedonian doctrine of Christ possible, for

> if Christ is truly "the *image* of the invisible God" . . . , then equally this same Christ is our access precisely to that invisibility itself; if Christ is, in some sort, a résumé of all the created order, that book in which some knowledge of the author can be read, then equally it is in Christ that the unknowable mystery of that author is most deeply intensified. In Christ, therefore, are united and intensified to their maximal degree both all that can be said about God and the incomprehensibility of that speech, its failure. In Christ we learn how to speak of God; but in Christ we discover that speech to be broken open into brilliant failure—a knowing-unknowing, a "brilliant darkness." (Turner 2004, 59)[4]

Jesus answers those who ask for a sign, therefore, by again directing attention to scripture, in particular the book of Jonah. Just as Jonah spent three days and nights in the belly of the sea monster, so, Jesus says, the Son of Man will spend "three days and three nights . . . in the heart of the earth." Even the resurrection, however, will be an insufficient sign for those who seek to confirm what they already know. Just as the queen of the south came to Solomon because of his wisdom, so those whom Israel had not expected will be drawn to the sign of Jonah, which will be even greater than Solomon's wisdom.

Jesus's use of Jonah anticipates his death and resurrection, but even resurrection does not guarantee our ability to rid ourselves of unclean spirits. Jesus has exorcised demons, but it seems that they leave only to seek a resting place somewhere else. Too often the demons return to their original home and multiply, so that the person in whom they dwell is even worse off than they were originally. Jesus suggests that this is what will happen to this generation to which he has come. His mission to call the people of Israel to repent can result in their being even more resistant than they are now to the work of the Spirit. A "little faith" may be sufficient to give the devil that all he needs to capture our souls.

These remarks about the unclean spirits are obscure and enigmatic. It would be a mistake to use Jesus's account of what happens to the demons who have been exorcised to develop a theory of the demonic. The demons, to be sure, are parasitic. They require a home they cannot establish. Jesus, however, is

4. The internal quotation is from Bonaventure's *Itinerarium mentis in deum.*

not asking us to reflect on the ontological status of evil, but rather he is again reminding us that we cannot try to at once serve God and mammon. Whoever is not for me is against me. And that includes his own family.

While Jesus was still speaking to the crowds, his mother and brothers were standing outside in order to speak with him. This is reported to Jesus, but he points to his disciples and claims that they are now his mother and brothers. Those who do the will of the Father are his brothers, sisters, and mother. Jesus has already challenged loyalty to family through the calling of the disciples (Matt. 4:18–22), his refusal to let the one desiring to be a disciple return to bury his father (8:18–22), and his prediction that in the coming persecutions brother will deny brother and fathers will rise up against their children and children will put their parents to death (10:16–23, 34–39). If there was any doubt that Jesus meant what he said, his identification of his true family as the disciples makes clear that his challenge to the family is radical.

To be a disciple of Jesus is to be made part of a new community in which the family is reconstituted. We are all children, but now a community has been established in which we are all called to be parents, brothers, and sisters to and for one another. In such a community it is impossible for an "unwanted child" to be born, for the biological family has been transformed in service to the church. What is at stake is not the family, but rather those who do the will of the Father. For Jesus to take such a critical attitude toward the family could not help but put him in tension with the people of Israel. As a faithful son of Israel, Jesus was expected to marry and have a child. Yet Jesus remains single. His singleness, moreover, is a sign that God's kingdom will not grow by biological ascription. Rather, the kingdom of God grows by witness and conversion. Through such growth Christians will discover sisters and brothers we did not know we had. Such is the wonder and the threat of the kingdom brought in Christ.

MATTHEW 13

The Parable of the Kingdom

Jesus's great sermon on the parables can be read as a commentary on his claim that those who do the will of the Father are his brother, sister, and mother. You do not become a brother or sister to Christ through birth, but you become his brother and sister by learning to be his disciple. As we shall see, the parables become one of the ways in which Jesus trains his disciples to constitute this new family. In particular, he uses parables to help the disciples discern how the kingdom of heaven is established. The parables, therefore, like the Sermon on the Mount, have always been crucial for the church to imagine the kind of community that we must be in order to survive in a world that assumes that biological kinship is more determinative than our kinship with Christ. The boat on which Jesus sits to deliver his parabolic sermon on the parables is the church that the parables bring into being.

Matthew does not tell us when or why Jesus is in a house, but only that on the same day in which his disciples are accused of breaking the Sabbath Jesus leaves the house and sits beside the sea. As soon as he leaves the house a great crowd gathers around him. Indeed, the crowd was so great that Jesus must get into a boat in order to address the crowd, who stand on the beach while he sits in the boat to instruct them. We have, therefore, a situation quite similar to that in which Jesus delivered the Sermon on the Mount. When Jesus delivers the sermon, the crowd hears Jesus, but the disciples are the ones to whom Jesus directs the sermon. In a like manner, Jesus instructs the crowd through some of the parables, but he explains the parables to the disciples because they are the ones who must learn to live in the light of the world revealed by the parables.

Jesus has used parablelike comparisons earlier in his ministry. In the Sermon on the Mount, he tells us that a wise man builds his house on the rock (Matt. 7:24–27); he suggests that the new cannot easily be joined to the old by analogy with cloth and wineskins (9:14–17) and that unclean spirits are likened to those who must search for homes in waterless regions (12:43–45). But he now uses and explains his use of parables in what might almost be called a systematic fashion. In response to the disciples' question of why he speaks to the crowd in parables, Jesus gives a seemingly odd response. He quotes God's charge to Isaiah (6:8–13) to prophecy in order that "seeing they do not perceive, and hearing they do not listen, nor do they understand" (Matt. 13:13). Jesus's use of the parables is at once prophetic and apocalyptic.

The prophetic and apocalyptic character of Jesus's parables matches his person and work. That is why Jesus quotes Ps. 78:1–3, to indicate that he speaks in parables in order to reveal what was hidden from the foundation of the world. The God of Israel, the Lord who made all that is, will be found in a virgin's womb. Jesus is the parable of the Father making manifest what was present in the beginning. Our recognition of that revelation requires our transformation in order that we might see that this man, this Jesus, is God incarnate. Just as Christ's flesh, his willingness to go to the cross, at once hides and reveals God, so the parables are meant to reveal the kind of transformation necessary for those who would follow Jesus to participate in the kingdom of heaven, which is his mission to effect.

The parables, like Jesus, are apocalyptic in form. The parables use dramatic imagery that clearly indicates their apocalyptic character, but their very form witnesses to the new age begun in Jesus. The parables, like the new age, at once offer redemption and judgment commensurate to the salvation that has come. Thus we are told that at the end of the age that angels will separate the sinners from the righteous and that evildoers will be thrown into a fiery furnace, where there will be weeping and gnashing of teeth (Matt. 13:42, 49–50). This is strong language, but a reminder that Jesus has come to call us to a way of life commensurate with his reign.

The parables, therefore, are a form of instruction that is important for the proclamation of the gospel, otherwise why would Jesus call attention to his use of parables? The parables but exemplify the character of the gospel as a whole. Donald Senior observes:

> Since the beginning of chapter 11, Matthew has focused on Jesus as the revealer of God's reign and on the varying and often hostile responses to that revelation. By their nature, "parables" fit into the dynamics of both revelation and response. "Parables" are extended metaphors or comparisons designed to draw the hearer into a new awareness of reality as revealed by Jesus, yet their artful nature adds a special twist of paradox and unexpected challenge. C. H. Dodd's classic definition has captured the essential elements of the parable: "At its simplest the parable is a metaphor or simile drawn from nature or common life, arresting the hearer by

its vividness or strangeness, and leaving the mind in sufficient doubt about its precise application to tease it into active thought." It is this opaque character of the parables that made them an extension of the mystery of Jesus' own person and helps situate the parable discourse in this section of Matthew's gospel. The parables help amplify the profound Christology that suffuses Matthew's narrative, namely that, in Jesus, the reign of God has come. At the same time, the ability to penetrate the meaning of the parables and to "understand" them, or conversely, the refusal or inability to understand the parables, separates the disciples from Jesus' chronic opponents. (Senior 1998, 146–47)

Responding to the disciples' inquiry concerning his use of parables, Jesus, as he so often does, refers them to the Psalms, in particular Ps. 78. Parables are "dark sayings" that we have heard from our ancestors, but now in those same sayings full meaning can be understood. For now, the speaker of the parables and the parables spoken are one. Jesus speaks in parables so that we might become scribes for the kingdom of heaven capable of revealing the new that has been in the old (Matt. 13:52). The parables, therefore, represent Jesus's continuing instruction, an instruction faithfully followed by Matthew, to understand Jesus's fulfillment of the Old Testament. Ulrich Luz notes:

> In Jesus' parables we find, again and again, that his own works and his mission to Israel are mirrored in parabolic form, for example, in the parable of the invitation to the great feast, or that of the mustard seed. Herein lies the germ-cell for their later salvational interpretation. But we discover, again and again, that Jesus' parables are not simply meant to be theoretical. Their significance points again and again to everyday life: they ask to be lived, not to be grasped by the intellect. (Luz 1993, 91)

Luz is certainly right to suggest that the parables invite parenetic interpretation, but such readings are but the expression of the salvation they mirror.

The parable of the sower is not advice about how to plant seed, nor is the parable of the wheat and tares meant to tell farmers how to farm. Rather, the parable of the sower is about wealth (Matt. 13:22) and the parable of the wheat and tares is about impatience and the joy that is the patience Jesus makes possible. Chrysostom argues that those who would explain the parables must not do so literally, for such an approach can lead only to absurdities. The parables are not meant to reveal what we know about mustard seeds, but rather Jesus uses the parables to instruct the disciples, not only concerning why Jesus chooses to teach in parables, but also to explain what the individual parables mean. The parables must be understood, like Matthew's whole gospel, christocentrically.

Jesus uses some of the parables to instruct the crowd and all the parables to instruct the disciples. Jesus explains the parables, however, only to the disciples. Again we see that Christology and discipleship are inseparable in Jesus's ministry. The disciples will be given the gift of interpretation, but it will be a hard-won gift. When asked by Jesus if they understand all that he has taught them through the parables the disciples will answer "yes" (Matt. 13:51), but that "yes" will be understood fully only after the crucifixion and resurrection. The disciples will "see," but they will be blinded by the light. Their blindness, a blindness that the parables are designed to create, is not hopeless, however, because they will continue to follow Jesus.

The disciples are the good soil on which the seeds of the kingdom have been spread. We know that they are the good soil, because if they were not, we would not be the church of Jesus Christ. We exist because the disciples under the care of the Holy Spirit proved to be adequate witnesses. But the soil that the disciples are is fertile because the disciples are not afraid to ask Jesus to explain why he teaches in parables. The parable of the sower, Jesus explains, is to help the disciples discern what they have been given. They are being given the secrets of the kingdom through their calling to be disciples of Jesus. Those secrets, secrets open to all but known only to those who respond to Jesus's call, distinguish the new from the old age.

Accordingly, Jesus explains the parable of the sower as a description of the results that the proclamation of the kingdom will produce. Some will respond but not understand, making them peculiarly vulnerable to the "evil one." The gospel is dangerous. Like Peter, we think that we will be able to follow Jesus, but when faced with the power of Rome and the leaders of Israel it is hard to remain faithful to a crucified Lord. Peter, like so many of us, is too ready to follow Jesus. To be too ready to follow Jesus means that we fail to understand that we do not understand what kind of Messiah this is. Jesus, therefore, uses this parable to remind us that discipleship will hurt. In particular, the word cannot flourish among those who continue to be shaped by the cares of the world. Jesus has told us that we cannot serve God and mammon but it is a hard-learned lesson, even for the disciples.

The parable of the sower is not often considered by those concerned with the loss of the church's status and membership in Europe and America, but it is hard to imagine any text more relevant to the situation of churches in the West. Why we are dying seems very simple. It is hard to be a disciple and be rich. Surely, we may think, it cannot be that simple, but Jesus certainly seems to think that it is that simple. The lure of wealth and the cares of the world produced by wealth quite simply darken and choke our imaginations. As a result, the church falls prey to the deepest enemy of the gospel—sentimentality. The gospel becomes a formula for "giving our lives meaning" without judgment.

Too often those who propose strategies to recover the lost status and/or membership of the church do so hoping that people can be attracted to become members of the church without facing the demands of being a disciple of Jesus. For a time they may be "joyful," but such joy cannot survive persecution. The shallow character of many strategies for renewal is revealed just to the extent that the resulting churches cannot understand how Christians might face persecutions. This is a particular problem in America, where Christians cannot imagine how being a Christian might put them in tension with the American way of life. This is as true for Christians on the left as it is for Christians on the right. Both mistakenly assume, often in quite similar ways, that freedom is a necessary condition for discipleship.

Accordingly, I do not think it a radical suggestion that this parable rightly helps us read the situation of the church in America as Jesus's judgment on that church.[1] The church in America simply is not a soil capable of growing deep roots. It may seem odd that wealth makes it impossible to grow the word. Wealth, we assume, should create the power necessary to do much good. But wealth stills the imagination because we are not forced, as the disciples of Jesus were forced, to be an alternative to the world that only necessity can create. Possessed by possessions, we desire to act in the world, often on behalf of the poor, without having to lose our possessions.

For example, many that would follow Jesus believe that we must continue to be willing to use violence to secure the good on behalf of the defenseless. Accordingly, pacifists are regarded as irresponsible. Yet to declare oneself a pacifist is to create a dependence on others as well as a vulnerability that forces one to conceive alternatives to violence otherwise quite literally unimaginable. This means that those committed to nonviolence dare not forget that such a commitment carries implications about our possessions. Nor can it be forgotten that nonviolence and possessions are correlates of the character of the church. A church that is shrinking in membership may actually be a church in which the soil of the gospel is being prepared in which deeper roots are possible.

It is, therefore, good news that Jesus tells us that even good soil will produce quite different results (Matt. 13:8). Paul seems to comment on Jesus's suggestion in Corinthians by calling attention to the variety of gifts present in the church:

> And there are varieties of services, but the same Lord; and there are varieties of activities, but it is the same God who activates all of them in everyone. To each is given the manifestation of the Spirit for the common good. To one is given through the Spirit the utterance of wisdom, and to another the utterance of knowledge according to the same Spirit, to another faith by the same Spirit, to another gifts of healing by the one Spirit, to another the working of miracles, to another prophecy, to another the discernment of spirits, to another various

---

1. The current controversies around sex bedeviling the church lead some to despair. But Radner is surely correct to suggest that God is punishing the church and that this is good news: "Within the redemptive context of the gospel, of course, I would consider such punishment to be a chastening, and there is such a hope within it. . . . And, as much as I resist the notion, I must at least try to believe that I am meant to be a part of this chastening, that I too deserve what has come upon my people. . . . Scripture offers us much guidance on how to suffer this reality—kings and saints, prophets and commoners. We have a Lord, as well, who has lifted up the standard" (2004, 203).

kinds of tongues, to another the interpretation of tongues. All these are activated by one and the same Spirit, who allots to each one individually just as the Spirit chooses. (1 Cor. 12:5–11)

The church will not only be constituted by people of different gifts, but it seems that what is true within a church is also true of different churches. No doubt God has given peculiar gifts to the churches in the southern hemisphere that has enabled the growth of those churches. It is not for us, that is, Christians in churches of the north, to say whether their growth is an increase of a hundredfold, sixtyfold, or thirtyfold. Such judgments require time measured in centuries, for if the parables tell us anything it is that Jesus's disciples do not need to be in a hurry, because we have all the time in the world to be the church.

It is, therefore, not accidental that Jesus follows the parable of the sower with the parable of the wheat and tares. This parable has often been used to justify, in this time between the times, a compromised church. For example, Augustine's understanding of the two cities, the city of God and the city of man, is often used to explain this parable and expound upon Jesus's explanation of the parable to the disciples. The clear contrast that Augustine draws between the city of God and the city of "man," some contend, is a contrast that can be drawn only at the end of the age (Matt. 13:40) when the angels will collect and burn the weeds. There is no question, however, that Augustine said that

> in this wicked world, and in these evil times, the Church through her present humiliation is preparing for future exaltation. She is being trained by the stings of fear, the tortures of sorrow, the distresses of hardship, and the dangers of temptation; and she rejoices only in expectation, when her joy is wholesome. In this situation, many reprobates are mingled in the Church with the good, and both sorts are collected as it were in the dragnet of the gospel; and in this world, as in a sea, both kinds swim without separation, enclosed in nets until the shore is reached. (Augustine 1977, 831)

Reinhold Niebuhr understood himself to stand in the Augustinian tradition because he drew on this parable to justify the compromises that Christians should make to act responsibly in the world. Niebuhr uses the parable to condemn all forms of Christian attempts to live without sinning. According to Niebuhr, this parable does not teach that a specific form of evil does not exist, but that in history good and evil are so mixed (in particular in the church) that we try to distinguish between them only to our detriment. Niebuhr acknowledges that Christians must make provisional distinctions, but he recognizes there are no final distinctions:

> "Let both grow together until the harvest." Man is a creature and a creator. He would not be a creator if he could not overlook the human scene and be able

to establish goals beyond those of nature and to discriminate between good and evil. He must do these things. But he must remember that no matter how high his creativity may rise, he is himself involved in the flow of time, and he becomes evil at the precise point where he pretends not to be, when he pretends that his wisdom is not finite but infinite, and his virtue is not ambiguous but unambiguous. (Niebuhr 1986, 47–48)[2]

Niebuhr used his interpretation of the parable of the wheat and the tares to argue that Christians cannot and should not be committed to nonviolence. The church, for Niebuhr, only betrays itself and the world when Christians pretend they are anything more than fallible human beings; the church is a sinful institution. Accordingly, the lesson to be learned from the parable of the wheat and tares is primarily a lesson in humility. Christians must recognize that in the church and out of the church love and self-love are "mixed up in life, much more complexly than any scheme of morals recognizes. The simple words of the parable are more profound than the wisdom of all our moralists. There is a self-love that is the engine of creativity. It may not be justified ultimately for that reason, but when we look at history, we have to say it is an engine of creativity" (Niebuhr 1986, 45).

The problem with Niebuhr's understanding of the parable of the wheat and tares, a widespread interpretation to be sure, is that not only does it contradict Jesus's explanation of the parable of the sower, but such a reading is not faithful to Augustine's understanding of the two cities. Augustine does understand the church to be mixed in its composition, but that does not mean that he thinks the church is indistinguishable from the world or that Christians can or should act as non-Christians act. For example, Augustine, in the paragraph following the observation quoted above concerning the mixed character of the church, notes that Jesus chooses disciples of humble birth and without education so that if there were any greatness in them that greatness would be Christ himself acting in them. Jesus even shows forbearance to the one among them who, through evil, betrayed him, though Christ was able to use him for good. So . . .

after sowing the seed of the holy gospel, as far as it belonged to him to sow it through his bodily presence, he suffered, he died, he rose again, showing by his suffering what we ought to undergo for the cause of truth, by his resurrection what we ought to hope for in eternity, to say nothing of the deep mystery by which his blood was shed for the remission of sins. Then he spent forty days on earth in the company of his disciples, and in their sight ascended into heaven. Ten days after that he sent the Holy Spirit he had promised; and the greatest and most unmistakable sign of the Spirit's coming to those who believed was that every one of them spoke in the languages of all nations; thus signifying that

2. I am indebted to Cartwright 1988, 44–60 for first making me aware of the significance of this parable for Niebuhr.

the unity of the Catholic Church would exist among all nations and would thus speak in all languages. (Augustine 1977, 832)

Augustine quite rightly sees that the parable of the wheat and the tares is not Jesus's justification for the mixed character of the church, but that the parable is given to encourage Christians to endure in a world that will not acknowledge the kingdom that has come in Christ.[3] The parable of the wheat and tares, like all the parables, is an apocalyptic parable, but apocalyptic names the necessity of the church to be patient even with the devil.

Just as Jesus was patient with Judas, so we must be patient with those who think we must force the realization of the kingdom. Jesus's parables tell us what the kingdom is like, which means that the kingdom has come. It is not, therefore, necessary for disciples of Jesus to use violence to rid the church or the world of the enemies of the gospel. Rather, the church can wait, patiently confident that, as Augustine says, the church exists among the nations.

Niebuhr was wrong to think Augustine could be used to support his position.[4] Augustine continued to presume the eschatological character of the world inherent in Jesus's proclamation of the kingdom of heaven. The world, for Augustine, is known only because Jesus has called a church into existence. Such a perspective is foreign to Niebuhr because he understands the gospel to be an account of the human condition that can be known whether a church exists or not. The gospel, for Niebuhr, has become a knowledge that does not need a church for its intelligibility. From such a perspective, an apocalyptic like Jesus can be seen as only mad.

There is a kind of madness commensurate with being a disciple of Jesus. To see the world, to understand that the kingdom of heaven is like a mustard seed, requires a people who refuse to be hurried. The parables that follow the parable of the sower and the parable the wheat and tares serve as commentaries on the way that disciples must endure in a world that refuses to acknowledge its true nature. The kingdom of heaven is like a mustard seed or yeast because to be drawn into the kingdom of heaven is to participate in God's patience toward his creation. Jesus is teaching us to see the significance of the insignificant. Jesus, after all, at this point in his ministry is not even commanding the attention of the Roman authorities. From the perspective of those in power, Jesus is no more than a confusing prophet to a defeated people in a backwater of the Roman Empire.

3. Some may find my commendation of Augustine odd, given my non-Constantinianism. Augustine is often identified as the source of the justifications necessary to legitimate later Constantinian developments. Augustine may have been so used, but his own position is much more ambiguous. O'Donovan 2004, 61–63 rightly argues that Augustine thought justice is a virtue realized for civil governments only when the government is conducted by Christians. O'Donovan also notes that the *City of God* is not primarily a book about justice but about forgiveness.

4. Niebuhr's most considered account of Augustine is found in 1953, 119–46.

We must be careful, however, in drawing attention to the "smallness" of Jesus's beginnings, because such attention can be used to suggest that Jesus's proclamation of the nearness of the kingdom is justified because we now know its power in Western civilization. So our willingness to begin small is legitimated because we now think that everything worked out the way Jesus said it would. Accordingly, these parables are not apocalyptically understood, but rather they are interpreted as exemplification of the modern belief in progress. Such interpretations of the parables as well as justifications for "starting small," however, cannot help but distort the character of the kingdom. We dare not forget that the parables' apocalyptic character has not changed. By our fruits we will be known; the fruits remain those blessed by the Beatitudes. Whatever worldly success Christians may have had, those so-called successes have too often distracted the church from its task to be no more than a place for nesting birds.

Jesus's explanation for why he uses parables such as the sower and the wheat and the tares means that two thousand years of Christian history are not sufficient to insure Christian faithfulness or to sustain the reasonableness of Christianity. The apocalyptic character of the kingdom remains in spite of Christian so-called success. Christians must continue to live as if all hangs on our faithfulness to this man, because all does hang on the reality of the kingdom as well as our response to the kingdom that Jesus proclaimed and is.

Our response, moreover, is constitutive of the kingdom that Jesus has brought. There is a joy that the kingdom produces. It is a quite different joy than those who live on rocky ground and as a result too quickly receive the seed of the kingdom. The parable of treasure in the field and the parable of the precious pearl make clear that much is required if we are possessed by the joy of the kingdom, for it seems that the discovery of the kingdom of heaven requires the selling of all we have in order to buy the field that contains the treasure of the kingdom or the pearl of great value. The parables addressed solely to the disciples remind them that Jesus requires that they abandon their former lives to follow him. They will soon learn that much more will be asked of them as Jesus leads them on his journey to Jerusalem.

Jesus also makes clear that the disciples are fortunate to be so "netted," because the net of the kingdom, when full, will also be filled with good and bad fish. Yet the disciples have been schooled with the patience necessary to sustain the care of the kingdom by the angels. The task of the church is to be uncompromisingly patient. Jesus asks if his disciples have understood "all this," and they answer "yes." But we know that this "yes" is premature, because the disciples have just begun to understand the master of the household who brings out of his treasury both the old and the new.

That the disciples' "yes" is ironic is a lesson for us who think we can better answer Jesus's question because we now have the whole gospel. Indeed, we not only have the gospel of Matthew, but also the gospels of Mark, Luke, and

John—not to mention the letters of Paul. We also have those who have read the gospels and Paul and left us their commentaries on the New Testament. It would be a mistake to disdain these gifts, but any "yes" we may give to Jesus's question must be a "yes" of a promise rather than a result. Our continuing struggle to understand the church's relation to Judaism, the struggle of the scribe, makes clear that any "yes" we give is one of striving not accomplishment.

But what a wonderful thing it is to be made part of that striving. The parables of the kingdom of heaven make clear that the kingdom of heaven is not "up there," but rather is a kingdom that creates time and constitutes a space. The time and space that the kingdom constitutes requires that people exist in time and occupy that space. Jesus teaches us through the parables so that we might be for the world the material reality of the kingdom of heaven, for in Jesus we see and hear what many prophets and righteous people had longed to see and hear. Indeed he is *the* parable of the Father.

After delivering his parabolic sermon, Jesus leaves and goes to his hometown. Previously when he returned to Nazareth he did deeds of power. This time he begins to teach in the synagogue, and those who hear him are astonished by his wisdom as well as his deeds of power. Yet they were also perplexed, because they knew him to be the carpenter's son. They ask, is not his mother the same Mary we all know, and are not his brothers named James, Joseph, Simon, and Judas? His sisters are also present. So they ask, "Where did he get all this?" Matthew tells us, therefore, that the people of his hometown "took offense at him." Perhaps they found his teaching even more offensive than his healings.

Matthew does not tell us why they took offense at him. We know that Jesus teaches with authority, which may have offended those who thought they knew him well. It may be that they did not think he was professionally qualified to teach or perform deeds of power. It is also tempting to think that Jesus suffers from the kind of familiarity that breeds contempt. Yet Matthew does not tell us that either of these well-known mechanisms is operative. We just know that they took offense at him.

We do know, like those in his hometown, that our familiarity with Jesus can make it impossible for us to recognize him when he comes to us thirsty, a stranger, naked, or a prisoner. We are burdened by our images of Jesus, none more destructive than the Jesus who has nothing better to do than to love us, to help us love our families, and to care for those less fortunate than ourselves. In Matthew's gospel we can catch only faint glimpses of that Jesus. So the question remains for us whether we would provide hospitality to the Jesus who seems to have better things to do than satisfy our needs.

Jesus observes (also recorded in John 4:44) that "prophets are not without honor except in their own country and in their own house." Accordingly, Jesus places himself in the great line of Israel's prophets who were rejected by those whom it was their task to serve as prophets. Jesus, like Isaiah, Jeremiah, and Ezekiel, became for Israel the embodiment of prophecy. The prophet became the word spoken, making real God's redemption. Jesus is the end of prophecy because he is God's word whom the prophets have said was to come. For him to be without honor in his own country, in his own home city, therefore, is not just another rejection of an idealist. It is the rejection of the one who alone is able to save Israel.

His rejection, moreover, is providential. What often appears as a disaster in the Old Testament retrospectively is providence. Joseph tells his brothers, "God sent me before you to preserve for you a remnant on earth, and to keep alive for you many survivors. So it was not you who sent me here, but God" (Gen. 45:7–8). Jesus is rejected by his own, but that rejection allows time for the Gentiles to be brought into the covenant (Rom. 9–11). Such judgments cannot be made prospectively as if we could anticipate God's providential care, but retrospectively they can be a form of faithfulness.

Matthew tells us that Jesus "did not do many deeds of power there, because of their unbelief." It is not their unbelief that limited his deeds of power, as if they had only had more faith he could have performed deeds of power. The problem is not the subjectivity of those who were astonished in the synagogue by his teaching. Rather, he performs only a few deeds of power in his hometown because any deeds of power would only lead to further misunderstanding and rejection. Matthew makes clear that it is Jesus's fate to be misunderstood and rejected. Even so, Jesus desires to be understood and accepted in his hometown—even in Jerusalem.

MATTHEW 14–15

John's Death, Jesus's Miracles, and Controversies

Matthew suddenly injects into the story he is telling about Jesus the story of the death of John the Baptist. The story of John's death is a mininovel that helps us understand the kind of world into which Jesus has come and to which he is an alternative. It is the only story in the gospel where Jesus does not appear, and that is why it is so important. The story of the murder of John is a story of the world of power, sex, and intrigue. It is a story about our world—the one Jesus challenges, the one for which he is the alternative.

Matthew simply tells us that "at that time" Herod, the ruler, began to hear reports about Jesus. Matthew does not think it important to tell us much about who this Herod is. We know it is not the Herod who had killed the children around Bethlehem, because that Herod died, making possible Joseph's return with the family from Egypt. This Herod is the son of the Herod who ruled at the time of Jesus's birth. By calling him "the ruler," Matthew suggests that this Herod has even less power than his father, but yet a power sufficient to arrest John the Baptist. Like his father he is well schooled in the politics of death.

Herod has arrested John because John had condemned Herod's plan to marry Herodias, the wife of Philip, Herod's brother. In Lev. 18:6 and 20:21 it is forbidden for a brother to marry his brother's wife because such a marriage is considered incestuous. John had come to call Israel to repentance, to obey the law, and it is clear that he thought those in power were not excluded from the demands of the kingdom that has come near. Herod, however, was clearly not amused by John's calling him into account and had John arrested. Matthew tells us that Herod would have preferred to put John to death, but he feared the crowd because they regarded John as a prophet. Later Herod, on hearing news about Jesus, even suspects that Jesus might be John who has risen from the dead. His suspicion suggests that Herod may believe that John is a prophet.

That Herod fears the crowd indicates the character of his rule, but such is the case for most who claim to rule on our behalf. Many in positions of power act as if their power is absolute, but they fear that they lack the ability to sustain the power they have. Herod exists in an unreal world created by and for those who occupy positions meant to sustain the illusion that they are accountable only to their own desires. That world is exemplified by Herod's birthday party in which the dance by the daughter of Herodias so pleases Herod that he promises by an oath to give her whatever she might ask. Influenced by her mother, she asks for the head of John the Baptist. Herod may have been afraid of killing John, but Herodias clearly wanted John dead.

Matthew reports that Herod was anything but happy with Herodias's daughter's request. Yet Herod had given his oath and is afraid that if he does not do what he has promised he will lose the regard of the guests at his birthday celebration. So Herod commands that John's head be brought on a platter and given to the girl. In a few powerful sentences Matthew has described the insecurity of those in power who depend on the presumption of those around them; that is, they must act in a manner that assures those they rule as well as themselves that they possess the power they pretend to possess. The powerful lack the power to be powerful, which means that they live lives of destructive desperation. That desperation, moreover, often results in others paying the price for their insecurity.

Jesus stands in stark contrast to Herod. He too is a ruler. He too is surrounded by those attracted to his power. But his rule is one in which he has been given the authority by the Father to ask of those who would follow him to sacrifice all, just as he sacrifices himself. The exercise of his power never betrays any insecurity, but rather he rules as one sure of what he has been sent to do. He is king, but he does not kill; he makes us alive by inviting us to join him in his kingdom of peace. That he represents such a rule means that those who rule as Herod rules cannot help but sense that Jesus is a threat to their pretensions of power.

John is dead. His disciples, however, have not abandoned him. They come for his body and bury him. They go to Jesus to tell him what has happened. On hearing of John's death, Jesus, just as he had after hearing of John's arrest (Matt. 4:12), withdraws by boat to a deserted place to be by himself. Yet he cannot escape the crowds who follow him from the surrounding towns. After the feeding of the five thousand, Jesus will also seek to be alone in order to pray. Matthew does not suggest why Jesus seeks to be alone at these times, but John's death is an indication of the struggle before him. We know that in Gethsemane Jesus will pray that the cup he has been given might pass from him (26:39). It is not unreasonable to believe that the agony of Gethsemane is present in Jesus's attempt to be alone in prayer.

Jesus, however, sees the crowd who has followed him as he returns to shore. He has compassion on the crowd and cures those who are sick. Much is often made of Jesus's compassion for the crowd, but too often generalized accounts of compassion are unjustifiably attributed to Jesus. That Jesus has compassion on the crowd is best understood in contrast to Herod's banquet. Jesus provides food for those without food solely because they are hungry. Herod provides food for those who are not without food as a demonstration of his power. Jesus feeds the five thousand because he has compassion for them. His feeding, therefore, is an alternative politics to the politics of envy and greed that the Herods of this world cannot avoid.

There is, therefore, a Christian way to feed the hungry that can be distinguished from those who feed the hungry for purposes beyond the feeding itself. Jesus has compassion on the crowd, so his desire to feed them comes solely from his love of them. Accordingly, those who would be his disciples need to learn how to feed the hungry in a manner that charity does not become a way to gain power over those who are fed. There is a violent and nonviolent way to feed the hungry.

Jesus knows how to feed the hungry, because he is the Son of God who, like Moses, fed his complaining people in the wilderness (Exod. 16). Like Moses, Jesus will feed the crowd that has followed him to this deserted place. The disciples ask him to send the crowd away because they recognize that there is no place for them to be fed this far away from the towns and villages. But Jesus says that the people who have accompanied him do not have to go away. Instead, he charges the disciples to feed them. The disciples protest that they do not have sufficient food to feed the multitude. Indeed, they have only five loaves and two fish. Jesus orders that they bring the fish and the loaves to him; he blesses them, breaks the loaves, and gives them to the disciples to distribute to the crowd. All eat and are filled, and twelve baskets of food are left over.

The feeding of the five thousand, which is a significantly higher number when the women and children are included, recapitulates God's care of Israel in the wilderness. The details of the feeding, moreover, suggest that food and scripture are inseparable. The five loaves of bread correspond to the five books of Moses, and the two fish represent the law and the prophets. Food and scripture are rightly tied together, because there can be no strict separation between body and soul. The words of scripture are the words of life, every bit as essential for our ability to live as bread and fish.

The feeding of the five thousand, however, not only directs our attention to the feeding of the people of Israel in the wilderness, but to Jesus's feeding of his disciples with his body and blood (Matt. 26:26–29). Jesus breaks the bread, anticipating that his body will be broken. Jesus feeds the five thousand with bread and fish provided by the disciples, but he will become for us the bread itself. Just as the bread that fed the five thousand will be more than was needed, requiring that the remainder be gathered into twelve baskets for the renewal of Israel, so Jesus's body will never be exhausted for those called to be his new Israel.

Matthew wants us to know that Jesus feeds more than five thousand because the women and the children were not counted. That women and children are not counted may indicate they had less status than men, but such is not the case in the new Israel constituted by Jesus's body and blood. Jesus does not count those he feeds—he does something far more important: he feeds them.

Jesus miraculously feeds more than five thousand with five loaves and two fish. Even more miraculously, he continues to feed his church with his body and blood, giving us life. His miracles challenge the way we see the world, but it is not just his miracles that constitute that challenge. His life itself is the challenge. His miracles cannot be separated from the work he has been sent to do. It is not his miracles that make it hard to believe in him. What makes it hard to believe in him is our unwillingness to give up our prideful presumption that we are our own creators.

Those of us who dwell in the time called modernity do not easily recognize miracles because we have lost any sense of the miracle of life. Wendell Berry suggests that we cannot recognize the miracle of life because we use the wrong language to speak of the world and its creatures. We use the analytic language that gives power to experts and fails to designate what is being described. As a result, the world has been reclassified from creature to machine, making us strangers to our own lives. Berry concludes that "humans cannot significantly reduce or mitigate the dangers inherent in their use of life by accumulating more information or better theories or by achieving greater predictability or more caution in their scientific and industrial work. To treat life as less than a miracle is to give up on it" (2000, 10).

Matthew tells us that immediately after Jesus has fed the crowd "he made the disciples get into the boat and go on ahead [of him] to the other side." He dismisses the crowds and goes, like Moses went up the mountain to ask the Lord to forgive the people for their idolatry (Exod. 32:30–34), up the mountain to pray. He was alone most of the night, but toward morning he comes to the disciples, whose boat is far from land and is being battered by the waves. When the disciples see him walking on water they are terrified. People do not walk on water. And so they grasp for any explanation that would return their world to normality—he must be a ghost.

Jesus responds to their cry of fear and after identifying himself tells them not to be afraid. Just as God names himself to Moses in the burning bush, Jesus identifies himself as "I am." This is the "I am" of Ps. 77:19, the "I am" who provides a way through the sea, a path through the mighty waters, leaving footprints unseen. Peter asks Jesus to command him to meet him on the water, and Jesus does so with the single word, "Come." Peter walks toward Jesus but notices the strong wind and begins to sink. He begs Jesus to save him. Peter does not begin to sink and then become frightened, but he becomes frightened and so he begins to sink. Losing sight of Jesus means that Peter, like all of us, cannot help but become frightened, which means we cannot survive. Jesus, as he has so often done, stretches out his hand and saves him.

Peter is often criticized for being impulsive, for having "little faith," and for doubting, but such criticism should not overlook that he asks Jesus to command him to come to him. Peter begins his journey across the water toward Jesus with the recognition that this is not something he can do on his own initiative. He asks Jesus to command him to come, recognizing that he has no ability to come to Jesus unless his ability to come to Jesus comes from Jesus. Peter's faith is little, but he at least is beginning to recognize that faith is obedience.

We are, of course, sympathetic with Peter because we too doubt. We doubt because, like Peter, we are frightened. Our fears are not governed by our fear of God, because we fear, like Herod, the opinions of others more than we fear God. As a result, we sink beneath the weight of our desires, hoping others will think us normal. But followers of Jesus, those who refuse to live in a world devoid of miracle, cannot be normal. We worship, as the disciples did, this Jesus whom they now recognize to be the Son of God.

Soon Jesus will rename Simon as Peter and declare that "on this rock" Jesus's church will be built, making this story ripe with ecclesiological implications. The church is the ark of the kingdom, but often the church finds herself far from shore and threatened by strong winds and waves. Those in the boat often fail to understand that they are meant to be far from shore and that to be threatened by a storm is not unusual. If the church is faithful she will always be far from the shore. Some, moreover, will be commanded to leave even the safety of the boat to walk on water.

Their task, however, is to witness to the one who has commanded them to leave the boat. Neither those who remain in the boat nor those whom Jesus commands to leave the boat are meant to call attention to themselves. They are to call attention to Jesus. Too often the contemporary church has offered the world explanations of "it is a ghost," rather than witness to the one who must reshape any explanation we might give.

A church that challenges the powers of this world is not a church that will need to explain Jesus. Such a church needs only to worship Jesus. To worship Jesus means that the fear we experience from being so far from land in a trackless sea, buffeted by winds and waves, will not dominate our lives. Fear dominates our lives when we assume that our task is to survive death or to save the church. Our task, however, is not to survive, but to be faithful witnesses. Fear cannot dominate our lives if we have good work to do. "Good work to do" is but another name for worship.

We have known since his baptism that Jesus is God's beloved Son (Matt. 3:17): the devil taunted Jesus to prove he is the Son of God (4:3, 6), the Gadarene demoniacs identified Jesus as the Son of God (8:29), and Jesus said he is the Son (11:27). Now the disciples confess that he is the Son of God, but even more significant, they worship him. Earlier, when Jesus had stilled the storm that had threatened to swamp their boat, the disciples wondered what sort of man could command the sea and winds to obey him. Now they have come to recognize that this Jesus is who he has said he is, and "they worshiped him." The disciples are learning, but what they confess with their lips will take time to reside in their hearts.

Jesus and the disciples go to the land of Gennesaret, and he is recognized. The word spreads throughout the region that Jesus has come. People begin bringing the sick to him and beg him to let them only touch his cloak, believing that even a touch will cure them. All who touch him are cured. Yet his notoriety attracts the attention of the Pharisees and scribes, who came from Jerusalem to challenge his work. They follow their earlier strategy of asking about the behavior of his disciples (Matt. 12:1–8) rather than about what Jesus does and does not do. So now they ask why his disciples do not wash their hands before they eat.

In Lev. 15:11, there is an admonition that anyone whose hands have been defiled must purify them by washing them in water before their hands are used in ritual. But the Pharisees and scribes identify this "law" as the tradition of the elders because it is by no means clear that Leviticus required everyone, not just the priest, to wash their hands before they eat. Jesus, however, recognizes that the question is but a ruse, so he responds with a counterargument that exposes how the Pharisees and scribes use the tradition of the elders to evade the law.

The commands are clear: honor your father and your mother, and whoever speaks evil of father and mother must die. But Jesus observes that the Pharisees and scribes have learned how to avoid honoring their mothers and fathers. Instead of supporting their parents, some try to avoid supporting needy parents by claiming they have given everything to God. However, they continue to use all that they have allegedly given to God for their own benefit.

Jesus turns the tables on his accusers by accusing them of manipulating the law through tradition for their own benefit. Quoting Isa. 29:13 Jesus charges the Pharisees and scribes of hypocrisy because they try to honor God with their words and by the manipulation of the law, but by doing so they fail to worship God, for to worship God rightly we cannot distinguish who we are from what we do. In order to drive his point home Jesus calls the crowd to him to tell them that it is not what goes into the mouth that defiles, but what comes out. It is not so much a question of whether the disciples' hands have been washed, but whether they lead faithful lives.

The disciples are concerned that Jesus's reply to the Pharisees as well as his address to the crowd has offended the Pharisees. The disciples, those who have just worshiped Jesus as the Son of God, are concerned that he has offended those who represent religious legitimacy. For some reason the disciples seem to think they need to be diplomats, but Jesus is no diplomat when he deals with hypocrites. Indeed, he says that the Pharisees and their followers, the blind leading the blind, are best left alone because they will self-destruct.

Peter asks Jesus to explain this "parable," even though it is by no means clear that it is a parable. Just as he had when he forbade the taking of oaths (Matt. 5:33), Jesus observes that speech often betrays the emptiness of our hearts, for out of our hearts, hearts often unknown to ourselves, come "murder, adultery, fornication, theft, false witness, slander." These are what defile much more than what we eat with unwashed hands. Jesus's reply to his disciples suggests that the Pharisees have placed the emphasis on the minutiae of the law, indeed they may be like Eve, adding to the law while ignoring the weighty matters.

Jesus's exchange with the Pharisees, scribes, and his disciples is prismatic of many of the controversies before the church in our time. Many who desire churches to take a more open attitude toward homosexuals do so because they think that what people do with their lives sexually is not that significant. Moreover, they can rightly point to gay people who lead morally admirable lives. Accordingly, they cannot help but view those who oppose inclusion of gay people in the church as "Pharisaic."

The problem with such analogies, however, is how arguments like those concerning homosexuality fail to see the interconnectedness of our lives. Jesus condemns adultery and fornication. He does so because he has called us to live lives of faithfulness and trust. To be faithful and to trust one another means that we must be truthful and avoid slander. No aspect of our lives can be isolated, having no relation to other aspects of our lives as well as the lives of our brothers and sisters. Sex cannot be a private matter for those who would live as disciples of Christ. That sex must be public does not determine the status of gay people in the church, but rather it suggests the kind of community that must exist in which the kind of argument and conflict required for the up-building of community can happen. Jesus makes clear that prohibitions against murder, adultery, fornication, theft, false witness, and slander cannot be separated from the habits necessary to sustain a community capable of forming people of virtue.

It matters, of course, who is included in the community that has arguments about what is and is not defiling. The question of who is to be included in the people whom Jesus is calling into existence is raised by Jesus's leaving the controversy with the Pharisees and scribes to go to the district of Tyre and Sidon. These are not Israelite cities, so it is not surprising that he encounters a Canaanite woman who identifies him as the son of David, begging him to exorcise the demon that is tormenting her daughter. Jesus, however, unlike in his encounter with the centurion (Matt. 8:5–13), remains silent. The disciples beg him to send her away because she continues to shout at them. Harshly (at least his reply seems harsh to us), Jesus tells her that he was "sent only to the lost sheep of the house of Israel." Jesus had told the disciples to go only to the cities of Israel, but this is the first time he says he has been sent to the lost sheep of Israel. And yet we have seen from the beginning that those who are not Israelites have been cured and instructed by him. Outsiders recognize, unlike many of the people of Israel, that he can do what no other person can do.

He is even recognized by a Canaanite. That Canaanites still exist, given Israel's war against them, is remarkable. This time, however, Israel's Joshua does not kill but heals the Canaanite's child. Just as remarkable is that this Canaanite is a woman, a woman capable of recognizing that this is the son of David. She refuses to be deterred by his silence and continues to beg him for help. Jesus answers in an even more derisive fashion, using the Israelite derogatory name for Gentiles, to tell her that food intended for children should not be given to dogs. Yet this woman, this extraordinary woman, observes that even the dogs are allowed to eat the crumbs that fall from their master's table.

Jesus, as he commended the faith of the centurion, praises this woman's "great" faith. There is nothing "little" about her badgering of Jesus. Faith, it seems, is exemplified by our willingness to beg. Accordingly, Jesus, as he did for the centurion's servant, declares that that for which she asks will be done, and her daughter is instantly healed. This woman, this unknown Canaanite woman, not only becomes for us Gentiles the forerunner of our faith, but her reply to Jesus teaches us how to speak. It is not accidental that we are taught to pray before we receive the body and blood of Christ:

> We do not presume to come to this thy Table, O merciful Lord, trusting in our own righteousness, but in thy manifold and great mercies. We are not worthy so much as to gather up the crumbs under thy Table. But thou art the same Lord whose property is always to have mercy. Grant us therefore, gracious Lord, so to eat the flesh of thy dear Son Jesus Christ, and to drink his blood, that we may evermore dwell in him, and he is us. Amen.

Jesus leaves Tyre and Sidon and passes along the Sea of Galilee. He seems to be in the vicinity of where his ministry began. He may even be close to where he delivered the Sermon on the Mount because Matthew tells us he went up the mountain, sat down, and again the crowds came to him bringing the lame, maimed, blind, mute, and many others. This time on the mountain he does not deliver a sermon, but rather he cures all who are brought to him. The crowd is amazed to see the mute speaking, the maimed whole, and the lame walking. They praise the God of Israel, recognizing that the long-expected kingdom has drawn near in this man's work.

They stay with Jesus three days on the mountain, which means they ran out of food. Jesus has compassion on them, observing to the disciples that if he sent them away some might faint on the way for lack of food. Jesus is the Messiah from heaven, but we can clearly recognize that he is one of us because he is quite well aware of our daily need for food. He has, after all, already taught us to pray for our daily bread. The disciples, however, protest that there is nowhere in the desert in which they may obtain enough bread to feed such a multitude. These are the same disciples that were with Jesus when he fed the five thousand, yet they continue not to understand who this Jesus is or what he can do.

This time they tell him they have seven loaves and a few small fish. He orders the crowd to sit, he gives thanks, breaks the bread, gives it to the disciples to give to the crowd. Four thousand, not counting women and children, eat and are filled. Moreover, just as when he fed the five thousand, food was left, this time sufficient to fill seven baskets. This feeding, like the feeding of the five thousand, anticipates his feeding of the disciples at Passover. This time, however, we are told that he gave thanks before he broke the bread just as he does before the meal with the disciples. To eat with Jesus is to be made part, to participate, in the continuing Eucharist of his kingdom.

Some may wonder why Matthew tells us about the feeding of the four thousand. Have we not learned all we need to know by his feeding of the five thousand? Or why does Matthew continue to tell us that Jesus heals the lame, maimed, blind, and mute? Moreover, the reports of Jesus's disputes with the Pharisees and scribes may begin to seem repetitive. But Matthew repeats stories because, under the guidance of the Holy Spirit, Matthew knows we will need all the stories we can get.

The details, like the details throughout Matthew's gospel, of the feeding of the four thousand can occasion reflection that is fruitful for the church. For example, the seven loafs of bread and the two fish have often been interpreted as the seven virtues we need to live as Christians. The two fish are, of course, the law and the gospel. It may be objected that there is nothing in the text to suggest that Jesus is using the seven fish to represent our need for courage, temperance, justice, practical wisdom, faith, hope, and charity, but neither is such a reading excluded by the text. Such readings are always possible. The crucial issue is whether such a construal builds up the body of the church.

Earlier I objected to those who would restrict forgiveness of enemies or the prohibition against oaths to the "private," because the distinction between the public and private is not in the text. But the feeding of the four thousand with seven loaves of bread does not mention the virtues. The difference between these two ways of reading the text, however, is that the former reading has no justification within the whole gospel of Matthew. In contrast the virtues can be found throughout Matthew because courage, temperance, justice, and practical wisdom are constituent habits of discipleship. Yet their content is transformed by the theological virtues of faith, hope, and charity. Such virtues, moreover, are required for a faithful reading of the feeding of the four thousand.

MATTHEW 16

"You Are the Messiah"

For many the demand to follow Jesus to be a disciple is too burdensome. Instead they want to know more about Jesus. So the Pharisees and Sadducees, like the devil, come to Jesus to test him. Just as the devil tried to tempt Jesus, so the Pharisees and Sadducees ask him to show them a sign from heaven that might prove he is favored by God. They want a conclusive demonstration of his status. Yet just as Jesus had resisted the devil, he refuses to do what the Pharisees and Sadducees ask.

This is the first time we have seen the Sadducees since they and the Pharisees had come to the Jordan to be baptized by John. The Pharisees and Sadducees were not natural allies, but their opposition to Jesus unites them. In their different ways they represent the religious establishment, that is, those who have a stake in maintaining the status quo. That they wish to test Jesus is their way of calling into question the authority he exercises, which had never before been seen in Israel. Their request for a sign, therefore, is anything but innocent.

Jesus answers them, observing that they know how to read the sky to anticipate the weather, but they do not know how to interpret the signs of the times. In short, he suggests that they would not be able to read a sign from heaven even if such a sign were given. Their request for a sign is an indication that they are an adulterous and evil generation. They are adulterous because though they pretend to be married to the law, their lives betray what they say they believe. That a whole generation can be evil is a hard but true observation about how we can contribute to our mutual corruptions.

The gospel of John is a gospel of signs. For example, Jesus raises Lazarus from the dead—a sign that would, we assume, compel belief. Yet we are told that while some believed others went to the Pharisees to warn them about Jesus (John 11:45–46). John's understanding of signs is a commentary on Jesus's response to the request of the Pharisees and Sadducees for a sign. They want a sign that can confirm Jesus's status without a sign requiring their lives to be changed. Yet the signs to which John's gospel directs our attention are like prophetic "sign-acts" that are intelligible only to the degree they call Israel to be faithful. Jesus refuses the request of the Pharisees and Sadducees because of their inability to see that the value of any sign is how the sign points to him.

In truth, it is not easy to know how to read "the signs of the times," but such a reading is required of those who would follow Jesus. Too often, however, Christians believe that we know how to read the signs of the times by reading the *New York Times*. But to so read the signs of the times is to be captured by the assumption that the way things are is the way things have to be. Pharisees and Sadducees read the daily newspapers and adjust. Followers of Jesus must read the same papers to show why Jesus offers an alternative reading of the times than that offered by the *New York Times*. Faced with such a daunting task, followers of Jesus can begin to sympathize with the Pharisees and Sadducees.

Rightly reading the signs of the times requires a church capable of standing against the legitimating stories of the day. American Christians often think that if we had been confronted with someone like Hitler we would have been able to recognize that he was evil. Yet in many ways, the church in Germany was a church more theologically articulate than the American church has ever been; still the German church failed to know how to adequately challenge the rise of Hitler. It failed because Christians in Germany assumed that they were German Christians just as American Christians assume that they are American Christians. Churches that are nationally identified will seldom be able to faithfully read the signs of the time. Jesus's condemnation of the Pharisees and Sadducees for their inability to read the signs of the times, that is, to recognize all that has been and all that is still to be must now be read under the sign of Jonah, remains a challenge for us.

Jesus has previously criticized the Pharisees for their failure to do what they profess. Indeed Jesus will soon recommend to the crowd that they should do what those who "sit on Moses' seat" teach, but "do not do as they do, for they do not practice what they teach" (Matt. 23:2–3). Jesus demands, as we have seen from his Sermon on the Mount, lives of integrity. To see the truth, to recognize the signs of the kingdom, requires that we be rightly formed by the virtues acquired by following Jesus. To know the truth requires the acquisition of the habits of truthfulness. Knowledge and virtue are inseparable.

Jesus's refusal to give the Pharisees and Sadducees a sign has profound implications for how Christians understand truth. We believe that the truth of the gospel cannot be separated from the kind of lives required for the recognition of that truth. Because we are aware of the inadequacy of our faithfulness to Christ, we are tempted to separate the truth of what we believe from the way we live. But Jesus refuses to allow us to abstract our knowing from our living. The gospel is not information; it is a way of life.

Wendell Berry's judgment that "the dominant story of our age is that of adultery and divorce" is, therefore, sobering for those who wish to follow Jesus:

> This is true both literally and figuratively: The dominant *tendency* of our age is the breaking of faith and the making of divisions among things that once were joined. This story obviously must be told by somebody. . . . But how has it been told, and how ought it be told? . . . The story can be told in a way that clarifies, that makes imaginable and compassionable, the suffering and the costs; or it can be told in a way that seems to grant an easy permission and absolution to adultery and divorce. (Berry 2000, 133–34)

We should not be surprised, therefore, that many of us in this adulterous age, like the Pharisees and Sadducees, ask Jesus for a sign from heaven. We want a sign that can be recognized without the necessity of our lives being turned upside down. But Jesus refuses to give us a sign other than the sign of Jonah. That sign is the sign of death and the defeat of death. Jonah was swallowed by the fish and lived in the darkness of the belly of the fish for three days. The fish was unable to digest Jonah, vomiting him out as God's reluctant prophet. Jesus too will be subject to death, but death, like the fish that ate Jonah, will be unable to digest the very Lord of death who faithfully does the Father's will.

Jesus had previously used Jonah to intimate his crucifixion (Matt. 12:38–42), but Jesus now suggests that the Pharisees and Sadducees will be unable to recognize the sign of his resurrection, for that sign, like the very sign of his birth, is one from heaven that requires that our lives be transformed if we are to see the world redeemed by a cross. It is impossible to follow Jesus and still cling, as the Pharisees and Sadducees do, to a world of lies and violence designed to hide our sin from us.

Jesus leaves the Pharisees and Sadducees, only to encounter the disciples who had forgotten to bring with them any bread to eat. Fresh from his encounter with the Pharisees and Sadducees, Jesus warns the disciples to beware of the yeast of the Pharisees and Sadducees. The disciples, particularly as we know from the gospel of John, do not readily pick up on an allusion. The disciples' tendency in John, in response to Jesus's declarations that "I am the bread of life" (John 6:35) or "I am the resurrection and the life" (11:25), as well as Jesus's warning against the yeast of the Pharisees and Sadducees in Matthew, is to assume that Jesus is trying to give them advice about food or life. They think, therefore, that Jesus is concerned that they have brought no bread with them. The disciples, like many of us, have no ear for language. They try to understand what Jesus says to them in terms of the old age, but their desperation to control the world in which they find themselves results in their failure to grasp the challenge of what Jesus says to them.

Jesus, aware of their confusion, confronts them because of their "little faith." Their faith is little, it seems, because they have not yet understood how following Jesus must change how we speak and hear. Jesus reminds them that they have seen him feed the five thousand and the four thousand with a little bread and a few fish. They even saw the leftover food after the crowds were fed. How could they not understand that when he referred to the yeast of the Pharisees and Sadducees he was not talking about bread, but the teaching of the Pharisees and Sadducees? Matthew tells us that the disciples then understood he was warning them against the Pharisees and Sadducees, but they will still have much to learn, for now Jesus begins to teach them what it means to follow him, namely, they must follow him to Jerusalem, where he will be killed.

Beginning in Matt. 11, Matthew has us follow Jesus through the cities and land of Israel, making us witnesses to Jesus's healings, miracles, teaching, and the controversies that his work produces. We now come to the climax of that part of our journey with Jesus as he enters the district of Caesarea Philippi. Caesarea Philippi, as its name suggests, is a city on the border between Israel and the Gentile world. It is here that Jesus asks his disciples, "Who do people say that the Son of Man is?"

The disciples respond by stating some say John the Baptist, some Elijah, and still others Jeremiah or one of the prophets. These responses have the common presumption, a presumption that is not clearly wrong, that Jesus stands in the prophetic tradition. His disciples, therefore, report the opinions of those who are part of the traditions of Israel. It is particularly interesting that some identify him with Jeremiah, for soon he will turn toward Jerusalem, expressing the same sorrow that Jeremiah enacted as the prophet of Jerusalem's destruction.

Jesus receives the disciples' reports, but then asks, "But who do you say that I am?" Some worry that when Jesus uses the identification "Son of Man," as he does when he first asks the disciples who people say that he is, he is referring to the Son of Man in the third person. Yet Jesus's subsequent question to the disciples leaves no doubt that when he asks about the Son of Man he is asking about himself. Jesus's question is, moreover, directed at the disciples because they are the ones he has called, they are the ones to whom he has explained the parables, and they are the ones who have seen him still the waves and walk on water. Simon answers, "You are the Messiah, the Son of the living God." The disciples had identified Jesus as the Son of God as he returned to their boat with Simon, but now for the first time a disciple recognizes that Jesus is the Messiah, the one Israel long expected, the one who alone has the power to free Israel from its enemies. Jesus commends Simon, the son of Jonah, who recognizes that he is the Messiah—a king, but one not easily recognized. Jesus declares Simon, like those described in the Beatitudes, "blessed."

At his baptism the voice from heaven identified Jesus as "my Son, the Beloved, with whom I am well pleased" (Matt. 3:17). At this time, the voice of the Son declares that Peter is blessed because flesh and blood could not reveal to him that Jesus is the Messiah, but only his Father in heaven. Simon knows what he does only because it has been revealed to him. It is important, however, that Peter's knowledge that Jesus is the Messiah not be used to develop a general theory of revelation. Simon does not learn that Jesus is the Messiah by some intuitive or mystical mode of knowing. Rather, Simon learns that Jesus is the Messiah because he obeyed Jesus's command to be his disciple.

Jesus is the revelation of God. There is no other revelation of God than Jesus. The gospel of Matthew is not revelation. Rather, Simon and Matthew are witnesses to the revelation of Jesus. Indeed they are witnesses that cannot be replaced. Without Simon and Matthew, without the scriptures, we would not know Jesus. But witnesses are not revelation, rather they point to that to which they witness. Simon and Matthew may be said to participate in that to which they witness, but their participation is possible only because Jesus is the Messiah, the Son of God.

Simon's recognition of Jesus changes who Simon is. Accordingly, Jesus gives Simon a new name, Peter, the rock. He tells him that "on this rock" he will build his church. Peter becomes the first among the disciples, not because he is the first called or because he is the most impressive, but because he has identified Jesus as the Messiah. His new status, however, does not suggest that the role of the other disciples is lessened. Rather, Peter's task is to serve so that none of the gifts of the church will be lost.

It has been said that Jesus came proclaiming the kingdom of heaven but instead we got the church. This understanding of the gospels often assumes that Jesus came proclaiming a new age soon to arrive, but when that arrival was delayed, his followers created an institution that Jesus never envisaged. Yet from the beginning the apocalyptic character of Jesus's proclamation has been apparent. The nearness of the kingdom requires that he gather a people to him who have the ability to live according to the new age established through his birth, life, death, and resurrection. Mary is the firstborn of that new creation. Peter is her servant.

By making Peter the rock on which the church will be built, Jesus indicates that the church will need to be so built because hell itself will try to destroy what Jesus has established. It is not Peter's task to make the church safe and secure or to try to insure its existence. Rather, it is Peter's task to keep the church true to its mission, which is to witness to the Messiah. That witness is called to be holy, requiring our willingness to confront one another if we think we have been sinned against (Matt. 18:15). The church can be a church of peace only by engaging in the practices of confession, penance, and reconciliation as an alternative to violence.

The keys that have been entrusted to Peter are the keys given to the church through which the church is made ever vulnerable to God's judgment. Peter does not stand apart from the disciples, nor does he stand apart from the church. Rather, Peter stands within the church, charged with keeping the church true to its witness to Jesus. Witness, moreover, becomes the source of the unity between Christians.

"You are Peter, and on this rock I will build my church" is obviously the text associated with the special status of the bishop of Rome. More has been written on Matt. 16:18 than any text in the Bible. That so much has been written about this passage betrays the responsibility that Jesus has given Peter. Peter's task is not to call attention to himself, but to witness to the Messiah. Yet it is also true that the papacy cannot be ignored when we encounter Jesus's identification of Peter as the rock on whom he will build his church. The later significance of Peter is no less important than the church's discovery of the doctrine of the incarnation for helping us read the gospels.

Peter has been given the office of unity, established through time and across space, to provide the church with the means for us to contend with one another so that the gates of hades will not prevail against us. Peter was not called to "keep the peace," but rather to insure that the church has the conflicts necessary for its holiness. Without the existence of such a church there will be no salvation. Peter is the name necessary to remind Christians that there has been and is a witness, across time and space, who has never failed to direct the church and the world to the reality that Jesus is the Messiah, the Christ. The question should never be whether Jesus established Peter to so serve the church, but where and how that service is to be recognized.

It is surely the case that the church, as well as Peter, fails to be what it has been called to be when Christians betray their unity, betray their call to holiness, by killing one another—for the kingdom that Jesus has brought is a kingdom of peace, of reconciliation (Matt. 5:21–26), creating in the world an alternative for the world. Peter's task is to call Christians, just as Jesus called his disciples, to be faithful citizens of a church that sustains its existence without an army.

After renaming Simon the rock on which Jesus will build his church, Jesus sternly charges the disciples not to tell anyone that he is the Messiah. He does so because of what he reveals next; that is, he must go to Jerusalem, undergo great suffering at the hands of the elders, chief priests, and scribes, be killed, and be resurrected on the third day. Jesus had told the disciples previously that they would be required to take up the cross and follow him (Matt. 10:38), but now he makes clear that his reference to the cross is no metaphor. Jesus plainly says that no one can know what it means for Jesus to be the Messiah unless that one is willing to accompany him to Jerusalem and the fate that awaits him there. Jesus does not ask us to believe in him; rather he asks his disciples to follow him—even unto death.

Peter, however, is not ready and does not believe that the disciples are ready to follow Jesus to his death. Peter, presuming his new status, takes Jesus aside and begins to rebuke him. We often assume that public relations is a modern development, but Peter assumes a role quite similar to those who are charged with putting the best possible face on bad news. Accordingly, Peter tries to help Jesus "get on message." He does so because he takes seriously his new responsibility to be the rock on which the church is built. He seems to think his task is to insure a successful outcome for Jesus's ministry. Peter is concerned for Jesus, but he fears that Jesus's announcement of his death might also dishearten those who follow Jesus.

Therefore Peter, the rock on whom Jesus will build his church, becomes the first to rebuke and betray him. Jesus had rebuked the wind and the waves, but now Peter, full of the newfound power that Jesus has given him, rebukes Jesus. He, on whom the church is to be built, follows our ancestors Adam and Eve in presuming to know better than God what God desires. This is a sobering beginning for the church, but one to be imitated countless times throughout the church's life. The church learns from Peter that our faithfulness begins with the confession of sin. We rightly believe, because Jesus has told us to believe, that God will never abandon the church; the world will never be without faithful witnesses. But the church that has Peter as the rock on which we stand must also be able to acknowledge that too often we are the first to betray what we have been given.

Peter simply cannot believe that Jesus will be defeated by the elders and chief priests and, with the aid of Rome, be crucified. Peter has identified Jesus as the Messiah of Israel, the new David, but Jesus's prediction of defeat and death does not sound like victory to Peter. Jesus, moreover, says clearly that on the third day he will be raised, but Jesus's resurrection does nothing to reassure Peter. Resurrection, it seems, is not the kind of victory that Peter is expecting.

Jesus sternly rebukes Peter and identifies him with Satan. Peter, like the Pharisees and Sadducees, has joined the ranks of those who want Jesus to accept the world as it is. Peter, the very rock on which the church is built, now becomes a stumbling block for Jesus. Peter, like the devil (Matt. 4:3, 6), tempts Jesus to turn stones into bread or save himself from death. Jesus's accusation against Peter, that he sets his mind on human things rather than divine things, does not mean that Peter is insufficiently spiritual; Jesus is spirit, Jesus is divine. Peter's failure, in spite of his confession that Jesus is "the Messiah, the Son of the living God," is his inability to recognize that Jesus's humanity is his divinity. Augustine comments on Peter being possessed by pride, not yet "humble enough to conceive of the humble Jesus Christ as my God, nor had [Peter] learnt what lesson his human weakness was meant to teach. The lesson is that your Word, the eternal Truth, which far surpasses even the higher parts of your creation, raises up to himself all who subject themselves to him" (1961, 152).

We cannot help but be sympathetic with Peter's failure to recognize Jesus. Incarnation is not an everyday affair. Two thousand years after Peter's confession at Caesarea Philippi, the church continues to fail to recognize that this Jesus is the Son of the living God. We fail to do so because, like Peter, we want Jesus to confirm our presumption that we can understand the way the world works only if we live as if God does not exist. We do not want the everyday disrupted, but Jesus is the disruption of time necessary if we are to live faithfully in the everyday.

Jesus, therefore, tells his disciples that if they are to follow him they must take up their cross. If they seek to save their lives using the means the world offers to insure their existence, then their lives will be lost. Rather, they must be willing to lose their lives "for my sake" if they are to find life. Jesus is not telling his disciples that if they learn to live unselfishly they will live more satisfying lives. Rather, he says that any sacrifices they make must be done for his sake. The crosses they bear must be ones determined by his cross.

What Jesus asks of his disciples makes no sense if Jesus is not who he says he is. You do not ask those who follow you to follow you to a cross unless you are the Son of God. You do not ask your brothers and sisters to contemplate the death of those they love if you are not the Messiah. You do not make Peter the rock on whom the church is built if you are not the one who has inaugurated the new age. But Jesus is all this and more, requiring his disciples to live lives not determined by death.

Yet what Jesus asks of his disciples is not new. From the time he calls them to follow him they were beginning to lose their lives. At this dramatic moment at Caesarea Philippi, however, Jesus makes clear to them what has been the case from the beginning. He has led them through the cities and villages of Israel, but now he will turn toward Jerusalem to face those who conspire to kill him. He clearly indicates the journey on which they are about to embark. He does not coerce them to follow him. They follow him willingly but they will abandon him at the end.

Jesus concludes this extraordinary exchange with his disciples with a clear statement of the apocalyptic character of the time in which they stand. The Son of Man, the just judge who alone has the right to judge, has come. Jesus will face and endure death, but his death is judgment on the world constituted by the fear of death. This is no delayed kingdom, but rather the kingdom has come. This is the recreation of time that requires a reinterpretation of all time. That some standing before Jesus will not taste death before they see the Son of Man come is the confirmation of Matthew's claim at the beginning of the gospel that this is the "beginning" of the new age. We, therefore, rightly claim, "Christ has died, Christ has risen, Christ will come again."

MATTHEW 17

The Transfiguration

The Son of Man has come. We see his glory in the transfiguration. Six days after the dramatic exchanges at Caesarea Philippi, Jesus takes Peter, James, and John up a high mountain. There he is transfigured, his face shining like the sun and his clothes dazzling white. Moses and Elijah appear with him and engage him in conversation. Peter, overwhelmed, suggests that they build three dwellings for Jesus, Moses, and Elijah, but while Peter is still speaking a cloud overshadows them and from the cloud a voice speaks, "This is my Son, the Beloved; with him I am well pleased; listen to him!"

An extraordinary event! Jesus has just told his disciples that he must go to Jerusalem to be defeated by the elders and chief priests and be killed. But here on this mountain we are privileged to witness his glorification. This is the glory of the Father who submits the Son to death. This is the one who commands the wind and the waves, who drives out demons, who cures the blind, mute, and lame; this is the one who justly judges, but this is also the one who becomes subject to death on our behalf.

"Six days later" harkens to creation itself. Jesus's transfiguration is the seventh day, the day God rested, bringing to completion the work of the previous six days. That day of rest is the day of perfect activity in which we are invited to enjoy God in perfect concord. Is it any wonder that the Sabbath is a day of brightness in which Jesus shines with the brightness of the sun? That same brightness, moreover, anticipates the new heaven and new earth seen by John in the book of Revelation. The end anticipates the beginning, consummating the glory present in creation. Jesus is transfigured, and we begin to see the glory of the God whose home is among mortals, who will dwell in us, and make us his people, wiping away every tear; and death will be no more (Rev. 21:1–4).

Peter, James, and John witness the glory commensurate to the triumph of the Son of Man coming into his kingdom. Is it any wonder that they fell to the ground overcome by fear? Who is ready to behold the glory of the Lord? The disciples are appropriately fearful. They, and we, rightly fear God. If we do not fear God our lives will be possessed by fears produced by our possessions. Jesus will command the disciples not to be afraid, but not to be afraid requires that we see, as they saw, no one but Jesus. To see Jesus, to follow Jesus, means that they too will be clothed in the bright white of martyrdom (Rev. 3:5) made possible because they have been washed in the blood of his cross.

At the transfiguration the disciples get a glimpse of the glory of the Son of Man—the Son who was with the Father on the seventh day and the Son who will be with the Father on the last day. John Howard Yoder observes that the confession that the Messiah has been placed by God above and not within the cosmology and culture of the world means that under his lordship the cosmos finds its true meaning and coherence. In Colossians the powers are rightly understood to be not merely defeated but reenlisted in their original purpose to praise God. In the Revelation of John the *logos*, the rationality of the universe and of history, is not only dethroned but is put to work illuminating the work of the martyrs. Yoder continues:

> To know that the Lamb who was slain was worthy to receive power not only enables his disciples to face martyrdom when they must; it also enables his disciples to go about their daily crafts and trades, to do their duties as parents and neighbors, without being driven to despair by cosmic doubt. Even before the broken world can be made whole by the Second Coming, the witnesses to the first coming—through the very fact that they proclaim Christ above the powers, the Son above the angels—are enabled to go on proleptically in the redemption of creation. Only this evangelical Christology can found a truly transformationist approach to culture. We still do not *see* that the world has been set straight. We still have no *proof* that right is right. We still have not found a bridge or a way to leap from historical uncertainty to some other more solid base that would oblige people to believe or make our own believing sure. "As it is, we do not see everything in subjection to him. But *we do see Jesus*, revealing the grace of God by tasting death for everyone" (Heb. 2:8–9). (Yoder 1984, 61)

When the disciples fall to the ground in fear after hearing the voice of the Father, Jesus touches them and tells them not to be afraid. Jesus's touch is significant. By touching them Jesus reminds them that the very one who is declared by a voice from heaven to be the Son is flesh and blood. In this man heaven and earth are joined. As a result, the earth is transformed, made bright and shining, "charged with the grandeur of God," as Hopkins wrote. The transfiguration heralds the new creation, reconstituting not only our lives but existence itself. As it is, we do not yet see that all is complete, but with the disciples we do see Jesus.

"Six days later" not only places Jesus in the seventh day of creation, but with Moses on the mountain where Moses received the instructions for the tabernacle and ark (Exod. 24:15–18). God told Moses to take Aaron, Nadab, and Abihu with him, but only Moses could come near to the Lord (24:1–2). This makes it all the more remarkable that Peter, James, and John are privileged to witness Jesus's transfiguration. Jesus will also ask Peter, James, and John to be with him in Gethsemane, but there, when he is in agony, they will find it hard to be present to him (Matt. 26:36–46). Their need to be touched will continue.

Moses, as he is often invited to do by God, enters the cloud that surrounds the mountain. That cloud is the glory of the Lord, and Moses leaves the cloud with his face shining (Exod. 34:294–35). A cloud also surrounds the disciples on the mountain, but Jesus's shining, Jesus's transfiguration, is a glory that comes before the cloud shrouds the mountain. Moses's face shines from the reflection of God's glory, and Paul tells us that the radiance on the face of Moses eventually faded (2 Cor. 3:7). But the radiance of Jesus will never fade because Jesus is God's glory. The cloud surrounds him on the mountain, the cloud of God's presence, in order for the disciples to hear God's voice. At Jesus's baptism the voice from heaven speaks and identifies Jesus as the Son, the beloved, but we do not know if anyone other than Jesus hears the voice. This time on the mount of transfiguration the disciples not only hear the voice from heaven but are told: "Listen to him!"

Jesus is joined on the mountain by Moses and Elijah, showing his inheritance as all that has been learned through the law and the prophets. God cared for Israel through the law and the prophets, for through the law and the prophets Israel was to learn how to rightly worship the one who had called it out of Egypt. Moses was instructed on the mountain how the tabernacle and ark were to be constructed appropriate for the worship of the invisible God. Jesus now transfigures Israel's life, renewing and transforming God's care of it through the law and the prophets.

Transfiguration is not and cannot be replacement. The kingdom brought by Jesus is unintelligible without God's promises to Israel. Jesus stands, just as the prophets often stood, in continuity and discontinuity with Israel's past and present. Jesus has told his disciples that he must go to Jerusalem to be handed over to those who rule Israel. Such was often the fate of Israel's prophets, but this prophet's fate is unlike any prophet ever before seen in Israel. This prophet, Jesus, is God's anointed—he personifies God's life with his people so that Israel's promise can be brought to the nations.

Peter, humbled by Jesus's previously stern condemnation, this time rightly defers to Jesus: "If you wish, I will make three dwellings here, one for you, one for Moses, and one for Elijah." Peter's suggestion, however, implies that he fails to understand that Moses and Elijah, God's good servants, now worship Jesus.

Peter wants to build booths to commemorate this great event, but Jesus's flesh is the booth of God's presence. Accordingly, Jesus cannot be, as Peter wishes, confined to a location, but rather Jesus must go to Jerusalem, and the disciples must go with him.

It is hard not to be sympathetic with Peter's suggestion that booths might be built to honor Jesus, Moses, and Elijah. Like Peter we desire to secure in place, if not tie down and domesticate, the wild spirit of God's kingdom. We do not wish to face anew the challenge of God's presence. We would like to make the success of the past our own without having to have the courage of those who followed Jesus into the unknown. Yet the church dies or is unfaithful when the achievements of the past are used to ignore the Father's command to "listen to him."

In the second letter of Peter, Peter appeals to the transfiguration to make clear to his audience that his message is not based on "cleverly devised myths." He was an eyewitness to Christ's glory, hearing the voice of the Father declare, "This is my Son, my Beloved, with whom I am well pleased" (2 Pet. 1:16–18). Accordingly, Peter encourages those to whom he writes to support this "faith with goodness, and goodness with knowledge, and knowledge with self-control, and self-control with endurance, and endurance with godliness, and godliness with mutual affection, and mutual affection with love" (1:5–7). Peter names for us the characteristics necessary if we are to faithfully "listen to him."

As they descend, Jesus tells the disciples that they are to tell no one about the vision they have seen on the mountain until after the Son of Man has been raised from the dead. The disciples ask, given the teachings of the scribes that Elijah must come first, why they should remain silent. Have they not just seen Elijah talking with Jesus? Jesus responds, stating that indeed Elijah had come, but he was not recognized. Instead they, meaning those in power, did to Elijah whatever they pleased. In like manner, he tells them, the Son of Man, the one whose transfiguration they have just witnessed, will also suffer at the hands of the unrighteous. The disciples then understand, just as Jesus had told them previously (Matt. 11:14), that John the Baptist was Elijah returned.

The disciples may finally be starting to grasp what Jesus has told them about his own fate, which in turn is helping them understand what it meant for John, in his role as Elijah, to restore all things. "To restore all things" does not mean everything is going to work out the way we want it to work out. Rather, Israel's restoration entails a complete reorientation of all things, including our definitions of power. The kingdom inaugurated in the Messiah's presence restores what was lost by calling into existence a people capable of living as an alternative to the world. That such a people can exist may seem to some precious little evidence that the kingdom heralded by Elijah and John has come, but that is exactly why it is crucial (as Yoder suggests) that we do see Jesus.

Again Jesus encounters a crowd. This time a man steps from the crowd, kneels before him, and asks him to have mercy on his son, who suffers from fits so dire he often falls into fire and water. The man explains that he had brought his son to Jesus's disciples, but they could not cure him. Jesus responds with disgust, wondering how long he will have to put up with such a faithless and perverse generation. He had previously expressed his disgust with this generation because of their desire for a sign. This time he directs his criticism against the disciples because they associate the power that Jesus gave them to exorcise demons with providing such a sign. This misuse of power made it impossible for them to cure the man's son.

Jesus asks that boy be brought to him; he rebukes the demon, and the boy is instantly cured. The disciples come to him in private to ask why they could not cast out the demon. Jesus addresses them, as he has in the past, as those possessing "little faith." Their faith is small because they have not understood that faithfulness to Jesus is not the faith that gives them power to impress with a sign. The power to exorcise demons is the faith of a mustard seed. That faith, as he told them in the parable of the mustard seed (Matt. 13:31), can produce great trees and even move mountains.

Jesus tells them again, as they gather in Galilee, that the Son of Man will be betrayed, killed, and yet on the third day will be raised. And, as Peter predicted, the disciples are greatly distressed by this news. Their inability to understand that Jesus will be betrayed and die is connected with their inability to cast out the demon that subjected this boy to such terrible fits. They continue to expect Jesus to triumph in a manner that will be a sign for the world. "Raised on the third day" does not yet sound like such a triumph; much less does "raised on a cross" sound like victory. Yet that is the victory encapsulated in a mustard seed—able to move mountains.

The kind of victory that Jesus represents is apparent when he reaches Capernaum, where we know he lived for a time (Matt. 4:13) and where Peter lived (8:14). Collectors of the temple tax approach Peter to ask if Peter's teacher pays the tax. It seems that the strategy continues to try to get at Jesus through his disciples, but it may simply be the case that Peter is known in Capernaum. Jesus and Peter, like all Jewish men, were expected to pay a yearly tax to support the temple. Peter answers "yes," though it is by no means clear that Jesus has paid the tax.

After they arrive home, Jesus engages Peter in a fascinating dialogue about his answer to the collectors of the tax. He asks Peter if the kings of the earth take tribute from their children or from others. Peter answers that kings do not tax their children but others. Jesus observes that the children are, therefore, free from taxes, which means that he and Peter do not have to pay the temple tax. They do not because they are God's children, and only God has the right to tax his creatures. This position will have radical implications when Jesus is later asked about taxes collected by the emperor.

But this is a tax to sustain the temple in Jerusalem. Jesus says to Peter that, in order not to offend those who collect the tax as well as those who pay it, Peter the fisherman should go to the sea, catch a fish, and in its mouth find a coin sufficient to pay the temple tax for the two of them. Peter's skill as a fisherman is now enlisted in an unusual way for the kingdom. Peter and the disciples will be fishers of men and women for the kingdom, and it is significant that they bring to that task their everyday skills. Jesus, who will be charged with predicting the destruction of the temple (Matt. 24:1–2; 26:60–62), obtains the funds by chance in order to support the temple. The way the money to pay the tax is obtained is a display of God's abundance. His payment is what the faith of a mustard seed looks like.

Christians rightly desire to do great things in service to God and in service to the world. But too often Christians think such service must insure the desired outcome. We simply do not believe that we can risk fishing for a fish with a coin in its mouth. Yet no account of the Christian desire to live at peace with our neighbor, who may be also be our enemy, is intelligible if Christians no longer trust that God can and will help us catch fish with coins in their mouths. No account of Christian nonviolence is intelligible that does not require, as well as depend on, miracle. Christian discipleship entails our trusting that God has given and will continue to give all that we need to be faithful.

MATTHEW 18

The Church

Peter has identified Jesus as the Messiah. Jesus has now twice (Matt. 16:21; 17:22) told the disciples that he must go to Jerusalem to suffer, die, and on the third day be resurrected. On the way to Jerusalem he will tell the disciples again that he will be condemned to death, handed over to Gentiles, flogged, crucified, and raised on the third day (20:19). These announcements initiate questions and discussions among the disciples that are at once surprising yet crucial for their formation. After the transfiguration of Jesus and before his entry into Jerusalem, Jesus instructs his disciples in a manner so that they can begin to understand the kind of people they must be in light of his crucifixion and resurrection.

Matthew tells us that "at that time" the disciples come to Jesus and ask who is the greatest in the kingdom of heaven. That is a surprising question given Jesus's announcement that he is on his way to death. If you are following someone soon to die, why worry about who is the greatest in the kingdom of heaven? Anticipating his death, are the disciples beginning to wonder who will lead them after he is gone? Matthew does not tell us. All we know is that the disciples raise the question about who is the greatest and that soon the mother of the sons of Zebedee will want to know where her sons fit into the hierarchy that she assumes is necessary to the kingdom Jesus has brought.

To answer the disciples' question, Jesus calls into their presence a child. He tells the disciples that unless they become like children they will not enter the kingdom of heaven. Children can invite us to speculate concerning the characteristics that make them exemplars of the kingdom Jesus has brought. Often, for example, children are assumed to have an innocence that adults lack. This kind of speculation, however, can result in sentimental versions of Jesus's work that betray the hardness of the kingdom. There is nothing sentimental about the demands that Jesus places on those able to receive this child.

Jesus quite clearly identifies what the child represents: unless we become as humble as a child we cannot participate in the kingdom. It seems that in issues of hierarchy "the greatest in the kingdom" is to be determined by those who are willing, those who take the time, to receive a child. A child has no acquired status; he or she is totally dependent on others. Mary bore the Messiah, but she first and foremost proved to be hospitable to a child whose existence she could not have anticipated.

Jesus, Mary's child, tells us that children are henceforth to be welcomed in his name. In a world so dark that it would kill children, Jesus tells his disciples that they must instead receive children. In a world that thinks it has no time for children, Jesus calls his followers to be people of patience, taking the time to welcome children, to have and raise them. This is possible because the kingdom has already been accomplished; time is reconfigured.

Accordingly, Jesus tells his disciples that if anyone would put a "stumbling block" (and do not forget that Jesus identified Peter as a stumbling block in Matt. 16:23) before these little ones, they would be better off drowned. The "little ones" are children, surely, but they are also anyone humble enough to follow Jesus. Jesus has called his disciples not from the elites, but from those without status. Those so called are, like any of us, tempted to turn the gift of discipleship into a status. Status seekers ask, "Who is to be the greatest in the kingdom of heaven?" But that question itself is a stumbling block suggesting the need for a status that the kingdom does not invite.

Jesus, however, is realistic. He tells the disciples that occasions for stumbling blocks are bound to come. The kingdom has come, and he has called his disciples, but he anticipates that the disciples cannot break the habits of the world. The disciples, like we ourselves, are insecure, needing to know "where we are in the world." Our everyday speech habits reflect our attempt to have the other acknowledge our status. Samuel Wells observes (2004, 88–89), for example, that our conversations often are like a seesaw in which we bring ourselves up and the other down. He provides the following example, highlighting the status transactions in brackets:

A: What do you like to read, when you get the time? [Raises B, by suggesting B is busy and thus high status.]

B: More recently I have generally gone for the later works of Tolstoy. [Raises self, by accepting shortage of time, choosing author of notoriously lengthy books, and implying a wide knowledge of his and other works.]

A: Ah! I remember *War and Peace* vividly from my childhood. [Raises self and crushes B by suggesting B's high culture was already assimilated by

A in childhood.] My parents let me stay up to watch the series on television. [Crushes self and raises B once more.]

Such an exchange makes clear that to become one of these little ones without pretense is no small thing. Just as one finds it hard "to try to be humble," so it is not easy to be a follower of this humble Jesus. Peter rebukes Jesus because he fears Jesus will be humiliated, but without humiliation few of us will ever find the way to be one of Jesus's little ones. Humiliation is the name rightly given to the recognition of our sin. Children, because they depend on others for their very existence, cannot help but live by humility. The task for disciples of Jesus is to learn how to break back into the humility from which we began as children of God.

Humility, like all the virtues, comes as a gift made possible by being part of a community that has, quite literally, no use for pretense. Pretense can be defeated only when a people have such good work to do that they have no time for the games of status. Such work is no better exemplified than the l'Arche movement begun by Jean Vanier. L'Arche is the community in which some learn to live with those whom the world calls mentally handicapped. Those who live with the mentally handicapped want to help them grow, but according to Vanier, before

> "doing for them," we want to "be with them." The particular suffering of the person who is mentally handicapped, as of all marginal people, is a feeling of being excluded, worthless and unloved. It is through everyday life in community and the love that must be incarnate in this, that handicapped people can begin to discover that they have a value, that they are loved and so lovable. (Vanier 1979, 3)[1]

Such a community both makes time and takes time. Life in l'Arche is slow because, as Vanier observes, growth toward love and wisdom is slow. Accordingly Vanier suggests that those in such a community must be friends of time, learning that many things will resolve themselves if given time. It can be a mistake to try, in the interest of clarity and truth, to come to a resolution of conflict too quickly. We cannot pretend that problems do not exist in l'Arche homes, but neither should confrontation or divisions try to be resolved immediately. We must, as Vanier suggests, be "friends of time" (1979, 80).

Jesus's response to his disciples' question concerning who is the greatest makes clear that their question is a denial of the kind of community he is calling into

---

1. Vanier later claims that the focal point of fidelity at l'Arche is to live with "handicapped people in the spirit of the Gospel and the Beatitudes. 'To live with' is different from 'to do for.' It doesn't simply mean eating at the same table and sleeping under the same roof. It means that we create relationships of gratuity, truth, and interdependence, that we listen to the handicapped people, that we recognize and marvel at their gifts" (1979, 106).

existence. A people who have the patience to be with little ones must also be able to exorcise those aspects of the body that cause the little ones to stumble. In 1 Cor. 12, Paul writes what can be considered a commentary on Jesus's suggestion that a foot that causes us to stumble should be cut off:

> Just as the body is one and has many members, and all the members of the body, though many, are one body, so it is with Christ. For in the one Spirit we were all baptized into one body—Jews or Greeks, slaves or free—and we were all made to drink of one Spirit.
>
> Indeed, the body does not consist of one member but many. If the foot would say, "Because I am not a hand, I do not belong to the body," that would not make it any less a part of the body. . . . But as it is, God arranged the members in the body, each one of them, as he chose. If all were a single member, where would the body be? As it is, there are many members, yet one body. (1 Cor. 12:12–20)

Paul tries to teach the people of Corinth that they need one another in order to be whole. Jesus teaches his disciples that at times they may well discover it is better for the church to "cut off" a hand or a foot if such members make it impossible to grasp or walk. Again Jesus uses dramatic imagery to help the disciples understand that how they live together is crucial for the salvation that has come through his ministry. Yet just as they must deal with hands, feet, and eyes that cause them to stumble, they must also be unwilling to lose any of the little ones who may become lost from the flock.

In Ezek. 34:11–19 the Lord God promises to search for his sheep, rescuing them from places where they have been scattered on days when it is dark and the clouds are thick. The sheep will be brought from the nations to be fed on the mountains of Israel in good pastures. The Lord God declares that "I myself will be the shepherd of my sheep, and I will make them lie down, says the LORD God. I will seek the lost, and I will bring back the strayed, and I will bind up the injured, and I will strengthen the weak, but the fat and the strong I will destroy. I will feed them with justice."

Jesus has been the good shepherd, but now he tells the disciples that they must be shepherds for one another. Jesus has been the shepherd who has left the ninety-nine to go in search of the one who has gone astray. So like him they must seek the one lost because it is the will of the Father in heaven that not one of these little ones should be lost. Nothing is more important than to take the time to care for the one who is lost. To seek the lost is what will define the disciples' ministry—to seek out those who will let themselves be found.

The parable of the lost sheep and Jesus's prioritizing of little ones is not about the modern presumption of equal dignity. Rather, both indicate the Father's preferential love of the lost. Wells writes about a Sunday at St. Elizabeth's Church in Norwich, in which the people were in a struggle for survival. At St. Elizabeth's the Eucharist was celebrated every Sunday with every member present—infants, children, young people and adults. Before the Eucharist, however, it was the custom for the person presiding to kneel on the floor to present a scripture passage using wooden figures arranged on a piece of felt on the floor. The presider would keep his eyes on the figures, handling them gently, hoping to make the telling of the story a meditation by the congregation. Wells reports:

> On one occasion the presentation concerned the Good Shepherd. Bringing together themes from Psalm 23, Luke 15 and John 10, the presentation displayed the safe sheepfold, the good pasture, the refreshing water and the places of danger where the sheep could get lost. The members of the congregation shared their experience of the church and the neighborhood, and whether each felt life was safe, good, refreshing or dangerous. One child said for him the church was like the refreshing water, because home was a place of danger. One adult said church was a place of danger, because once she and another had been pelted with stones as they left the service. Finally attention fell upon the sheep themselves, which were made out of different kinds of wood. "I wonder if it makes any difference that the sheep are different colors," said the storyteller. Immediately one of the older children responded adamantly, "It makes no difference at all—we should treat them all the same." There was a long pause. No response was forthcoming from the 30 or so members present. At last there was a quiet voice from a 6-year-old child near the back. Pointing at the wooden figure with a sheep across his shoulders, she said, "Because they all have the same shepherd." (Wells 2006, 171)

The parable of the lost sheep is not about us; it is about God's unrelenting love of Israel and those called to be disciples of God's son. The people called by Jesus cannot help but refuse any logic that would suggest some should be sacrificed for the good of the greatest number. Jesus's ministry, his patience with his disciples, embodies God's fierce desire to have the little ones cared for. Just as God refuses to lose sight of them, neither can we lose them to our sight.

So that we will not be lost to one another, Jesus gives the disciples instructions for being a community of the lost, of the little ones, capable of caring for one another. He tells us how we can avoid becoming stumbling blocks. If we believe that another member of the church has sinned against us, we are to go alone to that member and point out the fault to him or her. Jesus does not say we might think about going to the member if we think we have been wronged. Rather, he tells us we are obligated to go and confront the person whom we believe has sinned against us.

The first reaction, a normal reaction, to Jesus's instruction is to think that this procedure is far too extreme for most of our petty conflicts. I may become angry at someone, but if I wait I may discover I will get over it. Who wants to appear to others as one who is too easily offended? However, these responses inadequately understand the kind of community that Jesus thinks necessary if we are not to be stumbling blocks for the little ones. Furthermore, the little ones often include ourselves, and the lost sheep is often our brother or sister sitting next to us in the pew. A community capable of protecting the little ones, a community who cares for the lost sheep, is a community that cannot afford to overlook one another's sins because doing so keeps the community from embodying the life of grace determined by God's forgiveness through the sacrifice of his Son.

The sin that another member commits is not just a sin against the person injured; rather it is a sin against the whole church. In Lev. 19:17–18 the Lord tells Moses to tell Israel, "You shall not hate in your heart anyone of your kin; you shall reprove your neighbor, or you will incur guilt yourself. You shall not take vengeance or bear a grudge against any of your people, but you shall love your neighbor as yourself: I am the LORD." Failure to confront the brother or sister whom we think has sinned against us is not simply a recommendation of how we are to work out our disputes and disagreements, but rather an indication of the kind of community that Jesus has called into existence. This is a people who are to love one another so intensely that they refuse to risk the loss of the one who has gone astray—or the loss of ourselves in harboring resentments.

Thus Jesus tells his disciples that if the one whom they believe has sinned against them does not listen to them then they are to take with them one or two others so all that is said can be confirmed. If the member still refuses to listen it must be told to the whole church. If the offender still refuses to listen even to the church, then they are to be treated as a tax collector or Gentile, that is, as someone who is no longer privileged to be a participant in the community of those called by Jesus. Jesus clearly implies, just as he had with the analogy of our hands and feet, that his new people must excommunicate.

Some may well find this inconsistent with his teaching that we are to love our enemies (Matt. 5:43–48), that we are to do to others as we would have them do to us (7:12), and that we are to love our neighbors as ourselves (22:39). Yet excommunication is an act of love. Excommunication is not to throw someone out of the church, but rather an attempt to help them see that they have become a stumbling block and are, therefore, already out of the church. Excommunication is a call to come home by undergoing the appropriate penance.[2]

The procedure outlined by Jesus in Matt. 18 is how and what it means for his disciples to be at peace with one another. Jesus assumes that those who follow him will wrong one another and, subsequently, they will be caught in what may seem irresolvable conflict. The question is not whether such conflict can be eliminated, but how his followers are to deal with conflict. He assumes that conflict is not to be ignored or denied, but rather conflict, which may involve sins, is to be forced into the open. Christian discipleship requires confrontation

2. For the best critique we have of therapeutic accounts of forgiveness as well as "the craft of forgiveness," see Jones 1995, 3–70, 207–40.

because the peace that Jesus has established is not simply the absence of violence. The peace of Christ is nonviolent precisely because it is based on truth and truth-telling. Just as love without truth cannot help but be accursed, so peace between the brothers and sisters of Jesus must be without illusion.

Yet we must confess that truth is about the last thing most of us want to know about ourselves. We may say that the truth saves, but in fact we know that any truth, particularly the truth that is Jesus, is as disturbing as it is fulfilling. That is why Jesus insists that those who would follow him cannot let sins go unchallenged. If we fail to challenge one another in our sins, we in fact abandon one another to our sin. We show how little we love our brother and sister by our refusal to engage in the hard work of reconciliation.

Peter, the stumbling block, understands the implications of what Jesus requires. He asks, "If another member of the church sins against me, how often should I forgive? As many as seven times?" We cannot help but be sympathetic with Peter's question, because it simply seems contrary to good sense to offer unlimited forgiveness. What kind of community would be sustained on the presumption that forgiveness is always to be offered?

Peter's question presupposes that he is the one who has been sinned against. He assumes that he is in the position of power against the one who has wronged him. But Jesus's reply reminds Peter that he is to learn to be the forgiven. Jesus tells him not seven times, but "seventy-seven times." There is no limit to the forgiveness offered by the Father through the Son. If there were a limit to the Father's forgiveness, then Peter would no longer be a disciple. The demand that Christians learn to forgive one another presupposes that we are a people who have first been forgiven.

"Seventy-seven times" echoes Lev. 25:8 and the establishment of the jubilee year. The forgiveness to be exercised in the church is possible because the jubilee has come in Jesus. Accordingly, the forgiveness that marks the church is a politics that offers an alternative to the politics based on envy, hatred, and revenge. This is the politics that Jesus taught when teaching us to pray by asking that our debts be forgiven as we forgive our debtors. The new age has begun unleashing into the world a new people, a new politics called church determined by the forgiveness wrought in this man Jesus.

The political character of Jesus's response to Peter is made clear by Jesus's parable of the servant who, having been forgiven his debt by his king, refuses to forgive a fellow servant his debt. The king of the unforgiving servant, on being informed about his servant's behavior, has him tortured until he would pay his debt. And so, we are told, our "heavenly Father will also do to every one of you, if you do not forgive your brother or sister from your heart." We must remember, if we are to be peacemakers capable of confronting one another with our sins, that we have first been forgiven and we are, therefore, members of a community of the forgiven.

As the parable makes clear, the forgiveness that makes peace possible is not without judgment. The question is not whether we are to hold one another accountable, but what is the basis for doing so and how is that to be done. To be sinned against or to know that we have sinned requires that we have the habits of speech that make it possible to know what it is to be a sinner. On only this basis do we have the capacity to avoid arbitrariness of judgment that results from the assumption we must be our own creator. That is why it is so important that the church continually attend to the language necessary to name sin as sin. Lying, adultery, stealing are not just wrong or just mistakes. They are sin.

Throughout his ministry Jesus teaches us what it means to be a disciple. Our task is to learn how to be for one another exemplifications of what he has taught. This includes our ability to speak the truth in love, which is made possible only by our having no sin to hide. Jesus is now on his way to Jerusalem. Along the way he will continue to instruct the disciples on matters dealing with divorce, possessions, and hierarchy. We should not be surprised that he does so, because he has called into existence a community capable of living truthful and, thus, reconciled lives.[3]

---

3. Some of the above paragraphs are taken with revision from Hauerwas 2001, 89–100.

MATTHEW 19–20

Marriage, Wealth, and Power

As Jesus travels toward Jerusalem, large crowds follow him into Judea, and he cures them there. Jesus has never been free of those who would challenge him, but now he is in Judea, which means that he cannot escape controversy. The Pharisees come to him to test him because they assume that Jesus bears the burden of proof.

The first confrontation begins as the Pharisees ask Jesus whether it is lawful for a man to divorce his wife for any cause. The question presumes that divorce is a given; divorce is the sole prerogative of the man—the only question is whether a man may divorce his wife for any cause whatsoever. Throughout the Torah, Moses instructs the people that while a man may divorce his wife, he may not marry a divorced woman. This is brought out to the extreme in Deut. 24:1–4, where it is commanded that a man who divorces his wife because "he finds something objectionable about her" may not even remarry that same woman if she has taken another husband after the first, regardless of whether the second dies or divorces her. To do so would be "abhorrent to the LORD." Jeremiah later uses this image from Deuteronomy to describe Israel's relationship with God—after turning to false gods, how could God take Israel back?

The Pharisees' question tries to force Jesus to accept their worldview, but Jesus refuses to accept the presuppositions on which their question is based. Instead, he refers them back to the beginning, that is, to God's creation, in which we were created "male and female" (Gen. 1:26–27; 2:18–24). God recognized that it was not good for Adam to be alone, so he took a rib from Adam and made that rib into a woman, a woman that Adam recognizes to be flesh of his flesh. That recognition, moreover, is why "a man shall leave his father and mother and be joined to his wife, and the two shall become one flesh." Jesus, the one present with the Father at creation, then adds, "Therefore what God has joined together, let no one separate."

Jesus's comment on what it means for us to have been created male and female follows from Mal. 2:14–16:

> The LORD was a witness between you and the wife of your youth, to whom you have been faithless, though she is your companion and your wife by covenant. Did not one God make her? Both flesh and spirit are his. And what does the one God desire? Godly offspring. So look to yourselves, and do not let anyone be faithless to the wife of his youth. For I hate divorce, says the LORD, the God of Israel, and covering one's garment with violence, says the LORD of hosts. So take heed to yourselves and do not be faithless.

God created male and female and in doing so created the relation of husband and wife, later reflecting God's calling of Israel to be his bride. God even requires the prophet Hosea to marry a "wife of whoredom" as a sign of Israel's unfaithfulness and God's unrelenting faithfulness. Jesus, therefore, reminds the Pharisees that marriage is not just about marriage, but it is about the very character of Israel's faithfulness to the one who has been faithful to it. Marriage, and the question of divorce, cannot be abstracted from the purpose of marriage for the people of God.

The grammar of the Pharisee's question to Jesus is very similar to discussions about marriage and sex by contemporary Christians. We ask about "any cause" before we know what we are talking about. We ask about homosexuality before we know what or how we should think about marriage. To begin the conversation this way, however, is a deep mistake. Jesus's response to the Pharisees reminds us that we cannot think about marriage abstracted from the kind of community that the church must be in which people can be called to marriage without being a stumbling block to the little ones.

Jesus begins with the creation, indicating that marriage is part of God's gift to all people. Yet the discovery that marriage is given so that we might also know what it means to be faithful is a knowledge gained, and it may be known in other ways, from God's calling of Israel to be for the world a light to the nations. Marriage is given to all people but discerning the *telos* of marriage comes through God's gifts to Israel. God has made it possible for all people to desire to be fruitful, but that desire can become demonic if our children are not received into a community that has learned we live by gift.

By nature we are called to desire one another as male and female. By grace that desire is made life giving. Marriage can be a remedy for the sin of lust, but Augustine rightly maintained that even before Adam and Eve fell they would have had sexual intercourse. How else could they have fulfilled God's command that they be fruitful and multiply? (Gen. 1:28). According to Augustine, Adam and Eve would have had sexual intercourse even if they had not fallen but their sexual relations would have been free from lust; only after the fall did it become impossible for our sexual relations to be free of distortion caused by our pride and greed.[1] Jesus's appeal to God's creative purpose to try to bring the Pharisees back to the story is necessary if we are to understand and practice rightly the gift of one another in marriage.

Yet the Pharisees are not satisfied to be reminded by Jesus of the purpose of marriage. They ask why then, if God has prohibited divorce, does he allow for a certificate of divorce in Deut. 24? Jesus responds that Moses did so only because of the hardness of Israel's heart. Jesus forbids divorce, except in instances of unchastity, and whoever marries another after divorce commits adultery. This prohibition was also given earlier in the Sermon on the Mount (Matt. 5:31–32).

Jesus's prohibition of divorce and remarriage in this context, however, throws new light on the "except for unchastity" clause. We simply have no way in the abstract to specify what might constitute unchastity. But we can now see that the attempt to use Jesus's exception to provide a way to avoid Jesus's prohibition of divorce imitates the Pharisee's question to him about "any cause." Questions about marriage that begin with trying to specify what "except for unchastity" might mean are too often Pharisaic attempts to separate marriage from its purpose given in creation for the up-building of God's people.

Jesus's answer to the Pharisees is one that does not require them to leave their frame of reference. His answer is faithful to all that Israel has been called to be. However, the disciples, who understand the radical implications of Jesus's answer to the Pharisees, particularly for men, ask if it would be better not to marry at all. Jesus does not try to dissuade them that they have drawn the right conclusion. Instead he frankly says that while not all can accept this teaching, some are gifted to be eunuchs for the kingdom of heaven. We must not forget that Jesus is a "eunuch." Accordingly, not all called to be his disciples will find it necessary to be married or have children.

Jesus's commendation of those who for the sake of the kingdom have become eunuchs is a direct affront to Israel. Anyone whose testicles are crushed or whose penis is cut off is not to be admitted to the assembly of the Lord (Deut. 23:1) and is also excluded from priestly service (Lev. 21:20). No doubt

---

1. Augustine observes that just as artisans engage in physical tasks that go beyond their natural powers through the development of training so "why should we not believe that the sexual organs could have been obedient servants of mankind, at the bidding of the will, in the same way as the other, if there had been no lust, which came as the retribution for the sin of disobedience?" (1977, 585). Augustine realizes that many cannot imagine that in paradise Adam and Eve might have had such control over their sexual organs, so he gives some examples of people who can do extraordinary things with their body: some people can move their ears, some can bring their scalp over their forehead, some can swallow an incredible number of articles and then bring them up from the diaphragm in perfect condition, some can imitate the cries of birds and beasts, and some can even "produce at will such musical sounds from their behind (without any stink) that they seem to be singing from that region" (1977, 588).

there are a number of explanations for these attitudes toward eunuchs in Israel. Eunuchs were often associated with forms of worship that Israel regarded as idolatry and with behavior that was immoral. But at the heart of the concern with eunuchs was Israel's refusal to let those who persecuted it prevent it from having children. Malachi is clear that God wants "godly offspring."

Yet Jesus, the Messiah of Israel, says to the disciples that those who have received the gift of celibacy constitute the very character of the kingdom of heaven. To be called to be a eunuch for the kingdom of heaven is, perhaps, the most decisive mark of this community of the new age. Followers of Jesus do not need to marry or have children to be followers of Jesus, because the kingdom does not grow by biological ascription, but through witness and conversion.

That we are created male and female is a great gift. That God has meant females and males to be attracted to one another, to become one flesh through sexual intercourse, and to have children, is a great gift. Yet some worry that that the terms "male" and "female" can only underwrite perverse forms of being male and female in which the female is the perpetual loser. Some worry that marriage and the family can and do underwrite hidden forms of manipulative power relations that are destructive for all involved. Some, therefore, recommend that Christians avoid male and female categorizations as well as any attempt to justify marriage and the family.

Paul's recommendation in Eph. 5:21–33 that we are to be subject to one another is considered by many to be particularly problematic: "Wives, be subject to your husbands as you are to the Lord. For the husband is the head of the wife just as Christ is the head of the church, the body of which he is the Savior. Just as the church is subject to Christ, so also wives ought to be, in everything, to their husbands." Yet Paul's command that husbands love their wives as Christ loved the church should be a challenge to gender stereotypes that assume we know what it means to be male or female separate from Christ and the church.

Origen observes that the God who created humanity in the beginning according to his image created the savior male and the church female, bestowing on both the same humanity according to his image. The Lord, becoming man, left the Father on account of his bride, the church. Origen also observes that our savior also left his mother so that he might be our brother and sister (Manlio 2002, 89). Whatever cultural assumptions may be in play concerning what determines a male and a female cannot help but be challenged by a people who believe that they have, male and female alike, been made part of the people of the new age.

Jesus's answer to the disciples, however, does not mean that it is a good thing not to marry. Rather, marriage is given a new dignity because those who follow Jesus no longer have to marry to avoid being, like Adam, alone. Marriage is not a necessity, but now a calling for the up-building of the body of Christ. A community is created by its faithfulness to the gifts given in Christ.

Its constituents are thereby entrusted with the ability to make promises of lifelong fidelity. As Paul writes, "'For this reason a man will leave his father and mother and be joined to his wife, and the two will become one flesh.' This is a great mystery, and I am applying it to Christ and the church. Each of you, however, should love his wife as himself, and a wife should respect her husband" (Eph. 5:31–32).

Jesus affirms the dignity of marriage by laying his hands on, as well as praying for, the little children who are brought to him. The disciples rebuke those who bring children to him, but Jesus insists that the children be allowed to come to him. Just as he had earlier focused the disciples' attention on a child in response to the question of who is the greatest in the kingdom of heaven (Matt. 18:1–5), he again identifies these children as those to whom the kingdom of heaven belong.

The juxtaposition of Jesus's commendation of those who have been given the gift not to marry and his identification of children as those to whom the kingdom of heaven belongs illumines the apocalyptic character of his ministry. Apocalyptic is the revelation of what has been hidden but is now revealed through the beginning a of new age. Such an announcement is dramatic and overwhelming, but the kingdom that has drawn near makes possible the transformation of the everyday. Jesus is apocalyptic, making it possible for some not to marry, while at the same time making it possible for the church to take the time that children require, to make room for them. Apocalyptic is the disruption of time necessary to make the normal extraordinary.

The church's sexual ethic, moreover, can be understood only against this background. The church will be and is composed of the single and the married. Both are called to a life of faithfulness. Both are called to the vocation of parenting so that all children will rightly be brought up in the faith. All are called to be friends, defying the loneliness that threatens anyone not married. Such loneliness is particularly a threat in societies in which we are told we must be independent of all relationships other than the ones we have chosen. Marriage in such a society, moreover, can become too significant, just to the extent that marriage names our only hedge against loneliness. As a result too many people discover that rather than living their life alone they end up living their life alone with someone.

It therefore becomes crucial that such a people are able to distinguish between friendship and marriage, so that what is appropriate in one will not be confused with what is appropriate in the other. Too often calls for recognition of relationships between people of the same sex confuses marriage with friendship. In a culture as confused as the one in which we now find ourselves, however, remembering that our task as Christians is to provide a safe place for children is a good way to begin to think about what it means to be married or single.

Moral confusion is not, however, a condition peculiar to our time. Matthew tells us that a young man came to Jesus and asked him, "Teacher, what good deed must I do to have eternal life?" In his encyclical *Veritatis splendor*, Pope John Paul II praises the man who asks this question because the pope suggests that the young man rightly senses that there is an essential connection between the moral good and the fulfillment of our destiny (1994, 88). Jesus responds to his questioner, "Why do you ask me about what is good? There is only one who is good," thereby directing the questioner to the source from which any answer must come—to God.

Of course there are problems with how the question is put. Jesus is addressed as "teacher" rather than the one who is the source of what is good. Moreover, the question asks about what "good deeds" must be done to have eternal life. The questioner does not seem to have understood Jesus's constant criticism of those who do the deeds commanded by the law, but do them in a manner only to win approval from others. Yet the questioner is serious because he does ask about eternal life. Jesus, therefore, responds that if the questioner wishes to enter into life, he must keep the commandments.

In defense of his question, the young man asks Jesus which of the commandments he should keep. Jesus responds by enumerating the commandments often identified as the second table of the Ten Commandments: "You shall not murder; You shall not commit adultery; You shall not steal; You shall not bear false witness; Honor your father and mother." Jesus joins Lev. 19:18 to these others: "You shall love your neighbor as yourself." The one who has come to be instructed by Jesus claims that he has kept all of these commandments, but asks what he still lacks.

That the one seeking eternal life asks what he still lacks indicates that he has not really "kept the commandments." How can he be rich and faithful to the commandments? Karl Barth observes that this young man who seeks eternal life does not understand how important Jesus's selection and combination of the commands are:

> The well-known command of God is set before the rich man in its external aspect—the aspect from which it can be seen that it involves a concrete doing or not doing. It is not as if there were not included in these forms the command to love and fear God above all things, the prohibition of making or worshipping the images of God, the command to keep holy His name and His Sabbath—just as the commandments of the "first table" do not exclude but include the concrete forms of the God of the "second." In the New Testament sense it is not possible either to love one's neighbour without first loving God, or to love God without then loving one's neighbour. We can and must say, indeed, that in this unity of the command of God there is reflected the mystery of the person of Jesus Christ—the unity of the eternal Word with our flesh, of the Son of God with the Son of David and the Son of Mary. (Barth 1936–77, 2.2.616)

Jesus, as Barth indicates, knows well what the rich man lacks. What he lacks is what he has. Jesus says to him: "If you wish to be perfect, go, sell all your possessions, and give the money to the poor, and then you will have treasure in heaven; then come, and follow me." But when the young man hears this he leaves, grieving because he had many possessions. Barth suggests that the two requirements Jesus places before this young man—that he should sell what he has and thus become free for God and that he should give his money to the poor and therefore become free for his neighbor—"both derive their meaning and force from this final demand, that he should come and follow Jesus. To follow Jesus is the practice of this twofold freedom to the extent that life in the following of Jesus is the life of that covenant partner of God who as such is so completely bound to his neighbor" (1936–77, 2.2.622).

John Paul II echoes Barth when he observes that "following Christ is thus the essential and primordial foundation of Christian morality: just as the people of Israel followed God who led them through the desert toward the promised land (Exod. 13:21), so every disciple must follow Jesus, toward whom he is drawn by the Father himself (John 6:44)" (John Paul II 1994, 98–99). To follow Jesus does not mean that the law is left behind, but rather what the law has always required is now fulfilled. Yet it also means that there is no abstract ethic to be known separate from what it means to follow Jesus.

After the young man goes away, Jesus makes it clear to his disciples what has happened, namely, that to be rich and to enter the kingdom of heaven is not easily done. Indeed Jesus suggests that it is easier for a camel to go through the eye of a needle than for a rich person to enter the kingdom of God. The disciples then ask a question that quite rightly presumes that some of us possess more than others: "Then who can be saved?" Matthew tells us that Jesus did what we are seldom told he does, namely, he "looked at them" and said that for those bound to die it is impossible, "but for God all things are possible."

Our temptation is to think that Jesus's reply is intended to "let us off the hook." Being rich is a problem, we may think, but God will take care of us, the rich, the only way God can. Yet such a response fails to let the full weight of Jesus's observation about wealth have the effect it should. We cannot serve God and mammon (Matt. 6:24). Jesus's reply challenges not only our wealth, but our very conception of salvation. To be saved, to be made a member of the church through baptism, means that our lives are no longer our own. We are made vulnerable to one another in a manner such that what is ours can no longer be free of the claims of others. As hard as it may be to believe, Jesus makes clear that salvation entails our being made vulnerable through the loss of our possessions.

The story of Ananias and Sapphira in Acts 5 makes clear that Jesus means what he says. Ananias and Sapphira are members of the church. They sell a piece of property, but they kept some of the proceeds for themselves, refusing to tell the church all that they had made from selling their property. When

Ananias brings some of the money to the church, Peter challenges Ananias for lying to the church. In response to Peter's accusation, Ananias drops dead, soon to be followed by Sapphira who undergoes the same sequence of events. Note well: it is our possessions that encourage us to lie, making impossible the trust necessary to be Jesus's disciples. To be saved, to be part of the body of Christ, is to participate in a people who make truthful speech with one another not only possible but necessary.

With Jesus, however, Peter responds in a defensive manner. He reminds Jesus that he and the disciples have left all to follow him. Jesus does not contradict Peter's self-evaluation. He does not because, as Barth observes,

> what distinguishes the disciples of Jesus from the rich man, and gives them the advantage over him, what differentiates the obedient from the disobedient, is the fact that they may be witnesses to this divine possibility. They have actually left all and followed Jesus. How did this happen? It happened as they made use of that which they possessed as little as he, but which was at their disposal as the gift and present of God. It happened as they recognised, claimed and appropriated that which they lacked no less than he, but which was available for them in Jesus. (Barth 1936–77, 2.2.625)

Jesus then makes explicit that his disciples, because they have followed Jesus, will sit on twelve thrones as judges of the twelve tribes of Israel. They are fit to be judges of the tribes of Israel because they have left family and fields to follow the one who is the fulfillment of God's promise to Israel. They will, therefore, receive more than they have given, inheriting eternal life. They are the last to be called, but they will be the first in the new age brought by Jesus. That the last will be first suggests what an extraordinary transformation, an overturning, Jesus represents.

Israel is often compared to a vineyard by the prophets:

> Let me sing for my beloved
>   my love-song concerning his vineyard:
> My beloved had a vineyard
>   on a very fertile hill.
> He dug it and cleared it of stones,
>   and planted it with choice vines;
> he built a watchtower in the midst of it,
>   and he hewed out a wine vat in it;
> he expected it to yield grapes,
>   but it yielded wild grapes. (Isa. 5:1–2)

Israel and Judah are explicitly identified as God's pleasant planting in which God "expected justice, / but saw bloodshed; / righteousness, / but heard a cry!" (Isa. 5:7). It is not surprising, therefore, that Jesus next tells a parable of a vineyard to illumine what it means for the first to be last and the last first, for it is a parable of God's justice—the kind of justice that the disciples will execute from the twelve thrones on which they sit to judge the tribes of Israel. These thrones, threatening thrones of judgment, are nonetheless the thrones of Israel. God's judgment of Israel demonstrates God's unrelenting love for his people.

"For the kingdom of heaven," Jesus says, is like a landowner who hired some laborers for his vineyard early in the morning, some later in the morning, some at noon, some at midday, and some late in the day. All the laborers he hired would have had no work if he had not hired them to work in his vineyard. Those first hired agreed to work for the usual daily wage. At the end of the day the owner told his manager to call the laborers so that they might be paid. The manager was told to begin payment with the last hired and end with the first hired. He was to pay each the agreed-on daily wage.

When the first hired came to receive their wage, they assumed that they would be paid more, but they received the same as those hired at the end of the day. They grumbled at being so paid, pointing out they had worked longer and during the heat of the day. The landowner, however, responded by calling those first hired "friends," indicating that he had done no wrong to them because he paid them according to their original agreement. The landowner observes that he can do as he will because he gives what belongs to him. Accordingly, the first hired should not be envious of the last hired because of the landowner's generosity. Through this parable Jesus makes it unmistakably clear what it means for the last to be first and the first to be last.

Commentators on the parable emphasize the impartiality of God's grace implied by the landowner's mode of payment. But it is not impartiality that characterizes God's grace in this parable, but rather the sheer abundance of God's grace. God's love cannot be used up, making possible the wide diversity characteristic of those whom Jesus calls. In the parable of the sower, Jesus tells us that the seed that fell on good soil would have different yields, suggesting that the gifts of God would create difference for the glory of the kingdom. So it is quite right that this parable, emphasizing different contributions to the work of the kingdom, challenges the assumption that those of us who think we are followers of Jesus are among the first hired. We must remember that the church also includes those hired at the end of the day.

It is particularly important for Gentile Christians to remember that as heirs of the promise to Israel we are the last hired. The decisive commentary on Jesus's parable of the vineyard is Paul's understanding of God's faithfulness to Israel developed in Rom. 9–11. Paul writes to Gentile Christians to insist that God's promise to Israel remains in effect. Israel has stumbled on the stumbling block that is Jesus, but it has done so that salvation may come to the Gentiles (11:11–12). Accordingly, no account of the church, of those last hired, can ever be intelligible without the story of Israel, and those who are the inheritors of that story, the Jews.

Christians under the illusion created by Constantinianism forget that we are dependent on God's continuing care of the Jews.[2] To be the last hired, therefore, means that those who would be disciples of Jesus cannot forget that God's generosity makes it incumbent on us to remember that Israel's story is our story. Israel has faithfully told the story of its unfaithfulness in its scripture, which is now our Old Testament. That story is also the church's story illuminating the ways we have betrayed the one who has grafted us into Israel's "cultivated olive tree" (Rom. 11:24).

The parable of the vineyard is no doubt about the abundance of God's grace, but crucial for the parable is that the owner told his manager to pay the last hired first. If he had begun paying those hired first they would not have known that all were being paid at the same rate. God's grace is the grace of truth refusing to hide from us the character of our envy of those whom we think undeserving. The parable of the vineyard exemplifies God's justice—a justice disciplined by the truth.

That truth, moreover, Jesus again makes clear to the disciples as he tells them for a third time that they are on their way to Jerusalem where the Son of Man will be handed over to the chief priests and scribes, condemned to death, mocked, flogged, and crucified by the Gentiles, only to be raised on the third day. Such is the fate of the owner of the vineyard. This is God's justice necessary for any recompense for all—whether hired first or last. This is the overturning that the kingdom of heaven effects.

Again, however, the radical character of the new age begun in Christ provokes a question, a very human question, concerning status. The mother of James and John, the sons of Zebedee, comes to Jesus with her sons, asking a favor of him. She asks Jesus to declare that these two sons will be allowed to sit on his right and left hand in the kingdom. Her request presumes that Jesus had a special regard for James and John because they were among the first called and he took them with him to the mount of transfiguration. Their mother, moreover, clearly assumes that—as was suggested by Jesus when he said that

2. No one makes this clearer than Bader-Saye, who argues that "if the church is understood as that body of people grafted into and thus carrying forward of Israel's conventional politics (alongside the Jews), then this means we can no longer read the New Testament as superseding the social concerns of the Old Testament. We cannot divide the Christian community from the explicitly political identity of Israel. The church, as much as the Jews, exists within the one covenant of God, which leaves no arena of life unaccounted for, including politics. This means that attending to Israel as a way to rethink ecclesiology will mean resisting the depoliticizing of the church. Such depoliticizing of ecclesiology has both internal and external roots. Internally, the church has lost its political witness because of its inadequate understanding of election, which sought to leave the Jews and their materiality behind. Externally, the churches in the West have been depoliticized by accepting their place in a modern liberal polity that renders them largely irrelevant to the public square" (1999, 2–3). It may seem strange to call the depoliticized church a continuing form of Constantinianism, but that is exactly what it is in our time, namely, the creation of a privatized Christianity in service to the modern nation-state.

the disciples would sit on the thrones of Israel—to sit at Jesus's right and left will be positions of power.

Jesus tells her and her sons that they cannot know for what they ask. Addressing the sons directly, he asks them if they are able to drink his cup, the cup he has just described will be his in Jerusalem, and they naively respond, "We are able." This is the same James and John that Jesus will take with him to Gethsemane where Jesus will pray and ask the Father to let the cup pass from him (Matt. 26:36–46). James and John's declaration that they are able to bear the cup that Jesus must drink is clearly revealed as bravado. They cannot even stay awake with Jesus in Gethsemane.

Yet Jesus tells them that they will indeed drink of his cup. He will share his cup with them at Passover (Matt. 26:26–29), and that sharing means that they will share in his death. James, we know from Acts 12:2, will be killed by King Herod. Though they will share Jesus's cup in ways they cannot yet imagine, Jesus tells them that it is not his to grant who will sit at his right and left, but those places are prepared by his Father. All things have been given to the Son, but the Son defers to the Father the fate of those who are his own.

When the other ten disciples hear Jesus's response to James and John, they are angry at the two brothers. But Jesus calls them to him and explains that they are thinking the way the rulers of this world think, who lord their power over those whom they rule. The rulers of this world, of the Gentiles, are tyrants, but that is not the way it is to be with them. Rather, they are to be servants of one another, which means that any who would be first must become like a slave, for that is how the Son of Man has come to them. Jesus has come to serve rather than to be served, giving his life as a ransom for many.

This is the climax of Jesus's instructions for how the church is to be ordered in light of his cross and resurrection. The church is to be the exemplification of his life, giving life to the world. If the church is ordered and governed by our serving one another, the church becomes for the world an alternative to tyranny. It is, therefore, not accidental that Barth quoted Matt. 20:25–26 in the Barmen Declaration, challenging the Nazi attempt to appoint a state official to govern the church:

> The various offices in the Church do not establish a dominion of some over the others; on the contrary, they are for the exercise of the ministry entrusted to and enjoined upon the whole congregation.
> We reject the false doctrine, as though the Church, apart from this ministry, could and were permitted to give to itself, or allow to be given to it, special leaders vested with ruling powers. (quoted from Cochrane 1962, 241)

The cup that Jesus drinks is the cup that cannot help but challenge any politics that depends on rulers who, in the name of being our servants, become our lords. Romans 13 is often cited to justify Christian support of state coercion, but those who do so often fail to read Paul's advice just prior to Rom. 13 that Christians should

> bless those who persecute you; bless and do not curse them. Rejoice with those who rejoice, weep with those who weep. Live in harmony with one another; do not be haughty, but associate with the lowly; do not claim to be wiser than you are. Do not repay anyone evil for evil, but take thought for what is noble in the sight of all. If it is possible, so far as it depends on you, live peaceably with all. Beloved, never avenge yourselves, but leave room for the wrath of God; for it is written, "Vengeance is mine, I will repay, says the Lord." No, "If your enemies are hungry, feed them; if they are thirsty, give them something to drink; for by doing this you will heap burning coals on their heads." Do not be overcome by evil, but overcome evil with good. (Rom. 12:14–21)

It is possible to live this way only if we have learned to be servants of one another and, therefore, refuse to rule as the Gentiles do. What may seem like a matter of internal church politics is, as Paul indicates in Romans, a profound political challenge to the powers that be. John Howard Yoder suggests that in Romans and Matthew, Jesus and Paul assume that those who lord over us are a fact of life. Jesus does not affirm that fact of life as the work of providence or as a divine institution.[3] Of course, those who act as our tyrants will also claim to be exercising their power on our behalf, but that does not legitimate their tyranny.

Yoder argues that Jesus's call for disciples to become servants creates a different political alternative represented in Christian discipleship: "It will not be so among you." The disciples are not to try to take over and rule as the Gentiles do. Rather, they are to do something else. They are to be an alternative community to those who think that government depends on coercion and violence. By being a countersociety, moreover, the church offers the world a politics otherwise unavailable. Without the existence of a church so formed, there would be no one to challenge or even recognize, as was recognized at Barmen, a state becoming evil.[4]

Some may think this a far too political reading of Jesus's response to his disciples' concern about the status of James and John, but the political character of Jesus's ministry will become unavoidable as we move with him to Jerusalem. He has not come to be served, but to serve. But the world will not have a savior determined so to transform our habits of rule. His life will certainly be given as a ransom, but that ransom is not only to free us individually from our sins. Rather, he has ransomed us from the very temptations he resisted in the desert,

---

3. Rom. 13 does suggest that worldly power has a role to play in securing order. But Paul does not say that Christians are, therefore, to carry the sword in order to punish evildoers. Christians can, however, expect those who do carry the sword to do so modestly.

4. See Yoder 1984, 151–71 for his reflections on Jesus's charge to his disciples.

to make possible our participation in the only politics that can save us. He has brought to an end our slavery to the politics based on the fear of death, making it possible for us to be servants to one another and the world.

Jesus continues toward Jerusalem. He leaves Jericho, and a large crowd follows him. Sitting beside the roadside are two blind men who hear Jesus passing by. They cry out to him, "Lord, have mercy on us, Son of David!" Jesus is recognized by the blind for who he is, and he does not deny that they have rightly identified him. He is the son of David on his way to his capital city, Jerusalem. The disciples tried to silence the shouting of the Canaanite woman (Matt. 15:21–28), but this time it is the crowd that orders these blind men to be silent.

Jesus refuses to let the crowd determine the situation. He stands still and calls to the men, asking what they want him to do for them. They respond, "Lord, let our eyes be opened." Moved by compassion, Jesus touches their eyes, and they immediately regain their sight. They not only regain their sight, they follow him. These men, who have not had the advantage of being healed by Jesus early in his ministry, nonetheless follow him because they have recognized him as the Lord, the son of David.

This is the last healing that Jesus will perform before he enters Jerusalem. He will cure the blind and the lame in the temple, but he will do so on his enemies' home grounds. From this time until his death, Jesus will be subject to the forces that will lead to his crucifixion. He will enter Jerusalem in triumph, he will cleanse the temple, he will be in controversies with the Sadducees, Pharisees, scribes, and priests, but his life is now subject to the representatives of the powers of death. It is the beginning of the time in which he will give himself up to those who would have no power without his willingness to submit to their fears. Now we will have to follow Jesus as he confronts the powers so that we might live free of the terror our fears create. He has done all he can to prepare his disciples for what awaits them in Jerusalem.

MATTHEW 21–22

Jerusalem and the Temple

Jesus and the disciples come near to Jerusalem, reaching Bethphage and the Mount of Olives. This will be the staging area for Jesus's triumphal entry into Jerusalem. It is a triumphal entry, but one that parodies the entry of kings and their armies. This is the entry of the one who has come to serve, but that he has come to serve makes him no less a king.

The great King David went to the Mount of Olives in grief because of Absalom's conspiracy against him (2 Sam. 15:30–31). Yet in Zech. 14:1–5 the Mount of Olives is the place where the Lord declares he will stand in order to defeat those who have gathered against Jerusalem. From that mount the Lord will become king over all the earth, forever securing Jerusalem from destruction. Jesus stands on the Mount of Olives as one in mourning for Jerusalem, but also as its priest-king destined to bring all nations to the recognition of the God of David.

Accordingly, Jesus tells two of his disciples to "go" into the village ahead of them, where they will find a donkey tied with her colt. They are to untie the donkey and colt and bring them to Jesus. If anyone asks what they are doing, they are to say that "the Lord needs them," and they will be sent with the donkey and colt back to Jesus. Jesus identifies himself as the Lord, but one that will ride on an ass, a creature not normally associated with what it means to be a king. Victors in battle do not ride into their capital cities riding on asses, but rather they ride on fearsome horses. But this king does not and will not triumph through force of arms.

Jesus rides on a donkey, Matthew tells us, because in Zech. 9:9 the ruler of God's people will come so mounted:

> Rejoice greatly, O daughter Zion!
> 　Shout aloud, O daughter Jerusalem!
> Lo, your king comes to you;
> 　triumphant and victorious is he,
> humble and riding on a donkey,
> 　on a colt, the foal of a donkey.

The disciples did what Jesus had told them to do. The donkey and colt were where Jesus said they would be. They bring the beasts to Jesus, putting their cloaks on them for him to sit on. Jesus enters Jerusalem—an entry long prepared by Ps. 118, a psalm in which Israel is surrounded by the nations that threatened its very life only to be saved by the Lord, a psalm of victory of Israel's Lord, a psalm in which the gate of the Lord is opened so that the righteous may enter and proceed to the very horns of the altar. Jesus enters Jerusalem, enacting this psalm so that Israel, an Israel currently under the rule of a foreign power, may see the victory of its God.

A crowd, a very large crowd, welcomes Jesus to Jerusalem by spreading their cloaks on the road and cutting branches from the trees to prepare his way. They praise him, using the words of Ps. 118:

> Hosanna to the Son of David!
> 　Blessed is the one who comes in the name of the Lord!
> Hosanna in the highest heaven!

This crowd, however, does not include everyone in Jerusalem. Matthew tells us that the city is in turmoil. Many ask, "Who is this?" The crowds, the same crowds who welcomed him, answer that "this is the prophet Jesus from Nazareth in Galilee." They are not wrong to name Jesus a prophet. Jesus has identified himself as a prophet when he observed that prophets are not without honor except in their own country (Matt. 13:57–58). Jesus knows, moreover, that Jerusalem is a city that kills its prophets (23:37); yet he accepts the description of being a prophet. However, those who describe him as a prophet must learn that he is not only a prophet but also a priest and a king.

Jesus's triumphant entry into Jerusalem is an unmistakable political act. He has come to be acknowledged as king. He is the son of David, the one long expected, to free Jerusalem from foreign domination. Yet this king triumphs not through violent revolt, but by being for Israel the one able to show it that its worship of God is its freedom. He is Israel's long-expected priestly king whom the prophets said would come. His entry into Jerusalem is, therefore, rightly celebrated by those who are not in power.

Jesus enters Jerusalem and goes immediately to the temple. It is tempting for us—for people who have learned to distinguish between politics and religion—to describe his entry into Jerusalem as political and his entry into the temple as religious. But his going to the temple is perhaps even more politically significant than his triumphant entry. The temple defines Israel. The worship of God and political obedience are inseparable. The abuses surrounding the temple and Israel's political subjugation are but aspects of the same political reality.

To call Jesus's entry into Jerusalem and his cleansing of the temple politics challenges the dominant understanding of politics in modernity. We normally do not associate questions of truth and worship with politics. But I am suggesting that Jesus's drawing on the promise of God to Israel refuses to let Rome determine what counts or does not count for politics. Politics, for Jesus, is about power. But the power that Jesus exercises is that which is life-giving, drawing as it does on the very source of life itself.

Jesus has earlier in his ministry suggested that those charged to keep the Sabbath do not do so. Jesus, the prophet and king of Israel, now assumes the role of its great high priest because he alone can make the sacrifice necessary to restore the holiness that is at the heart of the life of the temple (Matt. 12:5–6). Jesus's ministry will now center on the temple, not only because the temple is the center of Israel's life, but because Jesus has come that we might truly worship the true God. Without true worship of God, there is no way to know what a true politics might be.

Jesus enters the temple, driving out those who were selling and buying. He overturns the tables and seats of those profaning the temple by making it just another place of commerce. Jesus assumes the mantle of the prophets Isaiah and Jeremiah by condemning those who buy and sell, telling them that the temple is to be a house of prayer, even for foreigners (Isa. 56:6–8), but they have, according to Jer. 7:11, turned that house into a "den of robbers." Jesus acts as the prophets have often acted, making God's word present through action. His cleansing of the temple becomes for Israel the temple cleansed.

Some use Jesus's cleansing of the temple to justify the use of violence. They speculate that Jesus must have been so angry at the money changers that he resorted to violence against them. However, to call Jesus's overturning of the tables and seats of the money changers "violence" is to stretch our language in a manner that makes discriminating between different kinds of violence impossible. At the very least, those who would use Jesus's action against the money changers to justify war need to acknowledge that Jesus did not kill the money changers. Moreover, it is significant that as soon as he drove the money changers and those who bought and sold from the temple, the blind and the lame came to him in the temple and he cured them. David had prohibited the blind and the lame from coming into his house (2 Sam. 5:8), and in Lev. 21:17 the blind and the lame were prohibited from offering sacrifices to God. Jesus truly cleansed the temple, overturning the established order by inviting into the temple those who had been excluded. The blind and the lame come to Jesus in the temple, and he heals them. He brings peace to the temple.

Jesus's enactment of the jubilee now shapes the worship of God at very center of Israel's life, that is, the temple itself. Jesus has restored the temple not only for the blind and lame, but for the poor. Those who sold doves did so because in Lev. 5:7 it was permitted for the poor to substitute doves and pigeons if they could not afford sheep. That provision became but another way for some to exploit the poor. Jesus cleanses the temple, and even the children, who had always been excluded from the temple, are heard praising Jesus in the temple, singing, "Hosanna to the Son of David." Jesus has not only cleansed the temple, he has started a revolutionary celebration. What Jesus has done is not a justification for violence, but rather he has shown how worship, the celebration of God's goodness, is itself an alternative to violence.

We have no indication that Jesus has acted in anger, but what he has done angers the chief priests and scribes. They see the amazing things he has done, they hear the children singing, and they are outraged. They are the protectors of the holiness of the temple. Jesus has unleashed praise. They cannot believe that he is willing to put up with what is being done by those who have joined him in the temple. They ask Jesus if he does not hear what the children are saying. The children are actually calling him "the Son of David." Jesus answers that he knows quite well what the children are singing. The children sing because we were told that children would sing in the presence of Israel's anointed in another of Israel's hymns of triumph:

> O LORD, our Sovereign,
>> how majestic is you name in all the earth!
> You have set your glory above the heavens.
>> Out of the mouths of babes and infants
> you have founded a bulwark because of your foes,
>> to silence the enemy and the avenger. (Ps. 8:1–2)

Jesus is the great high priest who has come to restore to Israel the right worship of Israel's God. The chief priests and scribes understand that this is about power. They will soon ask him from where he gets the authority to do what he has done. They do not understand that the son of David can do what he does: cleanse the temple by making it the place where the blind, lame, poor, and children can praise God. If Jesus is not the Messiah he is certainly acting as if he is.

He has entered Jerusalem and the temple. What has been done will not be undone. The cry of the children in the temple has alerted the authorities that Jesus is a threat to their status. Those in power know what they must do to protect themselves from one like Jesus. They will not be challenged without a fight. Jesus is aware of the conflict and does not seek to prolong the confrontation. He leaves the city for Bethany, with plans to return the following day.

The next morning Jesus returns to the city. He is hungry. He sees a fig tree by the side of the road, but he discovers only leaves—no fruit is on the tree. In Jer. 8:13, the Lord had said to Jeremiah that he wanted to gather the nations but he had found no "figs on the fig tree," and even the leaves had withered. Jesus, fresh from his confrontation with the chief priests and scribes, curses the fig tree, declaring that no fruit would ever come from it again. The tree withered, just as the scribes and chief priests had withered the temple.

The disciples were amazed, wondering how the fig tree had at once withered. Just as the disciples were amazed when Jesus stilled the wind and the waves (Matt. 8:23–27), they still cannot understand how Jesus can do what he is able to do because they have yet to grasp who he is. But again, Jesus reminds them that, unlike the chief priests and scribes, if they have faith, what was done with the fig tree is just the beginning. They will be able to throw mountains into the sea if they so ask in prayer with faith. The disciples still do not possess such faith, but they are being led by Jesus into a confrontation that means they will either have faith or be destroyed.

Jesus again enters the temple and this time begins to teach. The chief priests and the elders of the people challenge him, asking not only by what authority he has to teach, but also who gives him the right to cleanse the temple, cure the blind and lame in the temple, provide for the poor, and start a children's choir. Again this is a trick question, because if Jesus appeals to any authority other than himself he will betray who he is. So he asks a question in return, promising to answer the chief priests and elders if they will answer his question.

He asks them if the baptism of John came from heaven or was of human origin. The chief priests and elders argue among themselves, fearing that if they say that John's baptism was of human origin, the crowd who regarded John as a prophet would not approve of their reply. But if they say that John's authority is from heaven then Jesus will ask them why they did not believe John when he said the kingdom had drawn near. Caught in a dilemma of their own making, they confess they do not know from where John's authority came. Jesus, therefore, refuses to tell them by what authority he cleansed the temple, taught in the temple, and healed in the temple.

The chief priests' and elders' question has been repeated through the centuries of Christian history. Attempts to answer the question as posed inevitably result in diverse forms of Christian heresy, for the attempt to establish grounds more determinative than Jesus's life, death, and resurrection for why we should believe in him results in idolatry. If one needs a standard of truth to insure that Jesus is the Messiah, then one ought to worship that standard of truth, not Jesus. There is no place one might go to know with certainty that Jesus is who he says he is. To know that Jesus is the Son of God requires that we take up his cross and follow him. Having taken up the cross, Christians discover they have no fear of the truth, no matter from where it might come.

Jesus, however, is not through with the chief priests and elders. Indeed he is just getting started. We have seen him use parables to instruct his disciples to understand the character of the kingdom of heaven. Faced with the chief priests and scribes, he uses the parables to help them see the challenge he presents to their rule. He asks them to consider ("what do you think?") a man with a vineyard who had two sons. He asked the first son to work in the vineyard, who declined, only to later change his mind and go to the vineyard. The father went to the second son with the same request, and this son readily agreed, but did not go to the vineyard. Jesus asked the chief priests and elders which did the father's will. They were, of course, forced to answer that it was the first.

Jesus draws for them the unmistakable conclusion, that they are the second son who has failed to do the father's will. Therefore, the tax collectors and prostitutes will enter the kingdom of God before them because the tax collectors and prostitutes believed John's proclamation that the kingdom had drawn near and recognized that they must repent. The tax collectors and prostitutes had their lives changed, and so they—but not the chief priests and elders—believed in John.

Jesus offers another parable of a vineyard. A landowner planted and fenced a vineyard and dug a winepress in it and built a watchtower. He leased his vineyard and traveled to another country. At harvesttime he sent his slaves to collect his part of the produce. But the tenants beat one slave, stoned another, and killed another. He sent other slaves, and they treated them the same. Finally he sent his son, believing that the tenants could not help but respect his son. Yet the tenants killed the son, thinking that if they did so they will get his inheritance.

Jesus asks the chief priests and elders what the owner will do to these tenants when he returns. They, like David in response to Nathan, say that the owner will put these wretched tenants to a miserable death. Moreover, the owner will lease the vineyard to other tenants who will give him the fruit of the vineyard at harvesttime. Jesus explains to them the implication of the parable by asking them if they never read in scripture what is said in Ps. 118:22–23, Israel's great song of victory:

> The stone that the builders rejected
>   has become the cornerstone;
> this was the Lord's doing,
>   and it is amazing in our eyes.

Jesus has been the enactment of Ps. 118 from the time he entered Jerusalem, an enactment that now is climaxed by the claim that the stone that was rejected has become the cornerstone. Peter, after the crucifixion and resurrection, uses the same passage from the psalm when he explicitly identifies Jesus as the cornerstone in Acts 4:11 and in 1 Pet. 2:1–8. Jesus is the cornerstone for the house in which he is the sacrifice acceptable to God.

The parable of the wicked tenants can serve as an outline of Matthew's understanding of the life of Israel. God called Israel to be his vineyard fenced by the law, grounded in the land, and protected by worship of God in the temple.

God sent his prophets to call the people to faithfulness, but the people beat, stoned, and killed them. Finally God sent his very Son, but even he has been rejected. Jesus makes it clear that all that was done by the landowner of the vineyard was the Lord's doing (Matt. 21:42). Therefore, the kingdom of God will be taken away from them and given to a people who produce the fruits of the kingdom. Moreover, anyone who falls on this stone will be broken, and anyone on whom it falls will be crushed.

Jesus has left no ambiguity about how this parable is to be understood. The chief priests and the Pharisees realize that they are the "rejected." Yet they are not in any fashion ready to repent. Rather, they want to arrest Jesus, but they know that the crowds regard him as a prophet so—just as they refused to answer Jesus question concerning John the Baptist—they do not do what they would like to do because they feared the crowds. Just as Herod had John the Baptist killed because he feared losing face, so the chief priests and Pharisees fear the crowd because they know that their power depends on lies.

Jesus's use of the vineyard in these parables, as well as his cursing of the fig tree, suggests to some that Jesus is rejecting Israel as his promised people. Such a reading makes sense because we know, as is hinted throughout Matthew's gospel, that the Gentiles often understand Jesus better than his own people do. Moreover, at the end of the gospel Jesus charges the disciples to go to all the nations (Matt. 28:19). But it is also clear that the mission to the nations does not mean that God's promise to Israel has been superseded. Rather than presuming that these parables provide grounds for determining "who is in and who is out," we should rather attend to how these parables work to help those who are "out" identify themselves. The chief priests and Pharisees realized that he was speaking about them.

Jesus's denunciation of the leaders of the people of Israel will become increasing sharp, but those denunciations do not entail the rejection of the people of Israel. Jesus and the disciples are Israelites. After the resurrection the disciples will continue to worship in the temple (Acts 3:1). Jesus's cleansing of the temple is not a rejection of the significance of the temple, rather it is an indication of its importance. The God of Israel, the God worshiped in the temple, is the same God who is the father of Jesus, the Son. The people of Israel, the Jews, can never be "left behind," because if they are left behind Christians discover that we can make no sense of Jesus.

The Christian task is not to try to determine why or why not Jews cannot worship Jesus as we do. Our task is to be faithful to Jesus. Only when we are faithful to Jesus will Jews be able to tell us why they cannot follow him as we do. Unfortunately, too often Jews have had to reject Jesus because we have not faithfully followed him. It therefore becomes crucial that however the difference between Christians and Jews may be understood in one time and place, this difference not become *the* difference for all times and places. The difference, both for Christians and for Jews, must be a matter of ongoing negotiation if we are to be faithful to the God who has claimed us. God will surprise us yet.

As Christians, our task is like that of the chief priests and Pharisees: to be able to recognize ourselves in the parables. Identifying ourselves as Christians can be a form of protection from the recognition that we have become like the chief priests and Pharisees, whose assumption of responsibility for the tradition fills them with prideful presumption. Christians are tempted to rule like tyrants, believing that we possess the truth, a universal truth available without suffering. But Matthew makes clear that we cannot know the truth that is Christ without undergoing the training to be his disciple. Those undergoing such training have little time for speculative games concerning who is in and who is out.

Jesus, however, is unrelenting. He continues to confront the chief priests, elders, and Pharisees by speaking to them in parables. Jesus begins his parable with the familiar "the kingdom of heaven may be compared to a . . . ." Unlike the first parables that Jesus uses to direct the chief priests, elders, and Pharisees in locating themselves in relation to his work, this time the parable uses the formula that forces self-recognition that distinguishes them from those who would follow Jesus. He gives them a parable that will help them see where they stand in relation to the banquet that Jesus began by cleansing the temple.

A king gives a wedding banquet for his son, sending his slaves to call on those who had been invited, but they would not come. He sent other slaves to tell them that a great banquet has been prepared. But those invited made light of the invitation and went about their daily business. Some even seized the king's slaves, mistreated them, and killed them. The king was enraged and sent his troops to destroy the murderers and burn their city. Again he sent his slaves into the street, gathering all who were found there, both the good and the bad, and the wedding hall was filled. When the king came to see the guests, one man was not wearing a wedding robe. The king asked him, "friend"—the same address of the owner of the vineyard to those first hired—how did you get in without a wedding robe? The man was speechless. The king had the attendants bind him and throw him into outer darkness with weeping and gnashing of teeth. Jesus concludes that "many are called, but few are chosen."

This parable reprises Matthew's gospel. Jesus has come to feed us. He has fed the five thousand and the four thousand. The kingdom is about food and, in particular, food for the poor. But the food given by Jesus is not only to feed the hungry but to stage a banquet. This is a feast of God's abundance. Yet many seem to think that they have all they need and refuse to take the time to attend the king's banquet. They act as if they need no king, consumed as they are by their daily lives. Some, insulted by the persistence of the king's invitation, even kill his slaves. Jesus, just as he had in the parable of the wicked tenants, suggests that the way the king's slaves were treated is the way that Israel had treated God's prophets.

This is an extraordinary parable that makes for uneasy reading for those who want Jesus to underwrite a general critique of elites in the name of creating a community of unconditional acceptance. To be sure, just as the previous parables had been, this parable is meant to make those in power and the well-off uncomfortable. Most of us, particularly in the commercial republics of modernity, refuse to recognize that we are ruled by tyrants or, worse, that we have become tyrants of our own lives. We believe that we are our own lords, doing what we desire, but our desires make us unable to recognize those who rule us. We have no time for banquets prepared by the Father to celebrate Jesus's making the church his bride. We have no time for the celebration of that great thanksgiving feast in which we are "living members" of the king's "Son our Savior Jesus Christ" (*Book of Common Prayer* 1979, 365). Such a people are right to be challenged by God's hospitality to those who must live in the streets.

Yet this parable also makes clear that those who come to the banquet from the streets are expected to be clothed by the virtues bestowed on them through their baptism. If the church is to be a people capable of hospitality, it will also have to be a community of holiness. Jesus expects those called to his kingdom to bear fruit (Matt. 21:43). He has made clear in the Beatitudes how those called to his kingdom will appear. To be poor and outcast may well put one in a good position to respond to Jesus's proclamation of the kingdom, but Jesus expects the poor and downcast to live lives worthy of the Lamb who will be slain. Only a people so formed will be able to resist emperors, who always claim to rule us as our benefactors.

The Pharisees begin to understand that Jesus is no ordinary threat, and they plot to entrap him. They send their disciples to him with some of the Herodians. The latter are significant because their loyalty to Herod suggests that they willingly cooperate with the Roman authorities. The Pharisees, on the other hand, try to establish some distance between themselves and Rome. They approach Jesus using flattery—"Teacher, we know that you are sincere, and teach the way of God in accordance with truth, and show deference to no one; for you do not regard people with partiality"—as true a description as one could want. Liars can speak the truth, but when they do so, those determined to live by the truth must be on their guard.

They ask Jesus whether he thinks it is lawful to pay taxes to the emperor. It is a clever question that is meant to put Jesus in an impossible position. If Jesus says that taxes should not be paid, it would make him a rebel against Rome. If he says that taxes should be paid, he will appear to be on the side of the Herodians, collaborators with Rome, and he will not be a credible prophet. Jesus is not taken in by their flattery, not only recognizing them as hypocrites but naming them as such. He refuses to respond directly to their question but instead asks them to show the coin used for the tax.

Rome, it seems, not only required a tax, but wanted the tax paid in Roman coinage. Those who sought, like the devil, to entrap him brought the required coin to him. He asked them, "Whose head is this, and whose title?" They answered that it was the image of the emperor's head. Jesus then told them that they should give to God the things that are God's and to the emperor the things that are the emperor's. When they heard this answer, they were amazed and left him.

Unfortunately, through much of Christian history, Christians have not been amazed by this answer. Rather, they have assumed that they know what Jesus meant when he said we are to give to the emperor what is the emperor's and to God what is God's. It is assumed that Christians are a people of a double loyalty to God and the state. Christians are told that they should never let their loyalty to the state qualify their loyalty to God, but they never seem clear when and if such a conflict might actually happen. Christians are usually Herodians but lack the means to recognize themselves as such.

Jesus requests the coin, minted to pay the tax, to be given to him. He does not possess the coin. He does not carry the coin, quite possibly because the coin carries the image of Caesar. Jesus's question is meant to remind those who carry the coin of the second commandment: "You shall not make for yourself an idol, whether in the form of anything that is in heaven above, or that is on the earth beneath, or that is in the water under the earth. You shall not bow down to them or worship them" (Exod. 20:4–5). Jesus's answer that the things of God are to be given to God and not to the emperor is a reminder to those who produced the coin that the very possession of the coin makes them idolaters.

Jesus is not recommending in his response to the Pharisees that we learn to live with divided loyalties, but rather he is saying that all the idolatrous coins should be sent back to Caesar, where they belong.[1] Just as Jesus knows no distinction between politics and religion, neither does he know any distinction between politics, economics, and the worship of God. Those who have asked him whether they should pay taxes to the emperor are revealed to be the emperor's faithful servants by the money they possess. "No one can serve two masters; for a slave will either hate the one and love the other, or be devoted to the one and despise the other. You cannot serve God and wealth" (Matt. 6:24)—nor can you serve God and the emperor.

That God and the emperor cannot both be served is, moreover, not solved when the emperor is said to be the "people." The people often turn out to be more omnivorous in their desire for our loyalty than emperors. Nor is the problem of loyalty to God and Caesar solved by the separation of church and state. That separation too often results in legitimating the state to do what it wants while sequestering the church into the mythical realm of the private. Moreover, Christian accommodation to play the game dictated by Caesar's coin insures that the separation between state and church makes Christians faithful servants of states that allegedly give the church freedom.

1. I am indebted to Douglas Johnson for this way of reading Jesus's response to the Pharisees and Herodians.

For many, this account of Jesus's claim that we are to give to the emperor what is the emperor's and to God what is God's creates an insoluble problem because they do not see how followers of Jesus can then live in the world as we know it. But to recognize that we have an insoluble problem is to begin to follow Jesus. Jesus's response to the Pharisees and Herodians does create an insoluble problem, but that is what it is meant to do. You know you have a problem, at least if you are a disciple of Jesus, when you do not have a problem.

All this began because Jesus had returned to the temple to teach. In the temple he is locked in battle with each significant faction of Israel's life. Next it is the Sadducees' turn. Matthew tells us that the Sadducees say that there is no resurrection. Determined to make Jesus choose sides on the issue of whether there will be a resurrection, they present Jesus with a case that they are sure reveals the absurdity of belief in the resurrection. The Sadducees note that Moses said that if a man died childless his brother should marry his widow to raise up children for his brother so "his name may not be blotted out of Israel" (Deut. 25:5–10). The Sadducees ask who is the husband in heaven of a woman who has been married to seven brothers, each of whom have married her in order to fulfill Moses's command. The Sadducees obviously think that they have a wonderful example that makes the idea of resurrection absurd.

Jesus responds by observing that they fail to do what they claim is their strength, that is, not to go beyond what the text says. He bluntly tells them that they do not know the scriptures or the power of God. In Exod. 3:6 God identifies himself as the God of Abraham, the God of Isaac, and the God of Jacob. The Sadducees ask a question that presumes God can do nothing about childlessness, forgetting that Israel's story is made possible by God's power to raise up children in unlikely ways. God, moreover, is the God of the living and not of the dead, which means that Abraham, Isaac, and Jacob enjoy a life with God. Resurrection names God's refusal to abandon us even in death.

Jesus suggests that we cannot let our imaginations be undisciplined when we try to understand what life with God involves. For example, the case the Sadducees presented is absurd because in the resurrection we will neither marry nor be given in marriage, because we will, with the angels, have a life with God and one another where there is no aloneness to be overcome. Jesus does not say that we will or will not have some memory of our marriages in resurrection, but our histories will no doubt be radically transformed. Yet we know that the way we have lived will not be irrelevant to our resurrected life precisely because the very names of Abraham, Isaac, and Jacob matter to God.

Many think that the central religious question is whether there is an afterlife or if we have souls that are eternal. Many think that Christianity is unintelligible if one does not believe in the eternal soul, failing to remember that only God is eternal. All creation is gift, including our continuing life with God after death. That life, moreover, we believe to be sure, for as Paul tells us that "in fact Christ has been raised from the dead, the first fruits of those who have died.

For since death came through a human being, the resurrection of the dead has also come through a human being; for as all die in Adam, so all will be made alive in Christ" (1 Cor. 15:20–22).

The Christian hope is that God would have us share the life of love called Trinity. Our time, the time of our life, no doubt will be transformed by God's time. The name of that transformation is "resurrection." All we know about resurrection is what we are privileged to witness in Jesus's victory over death. There the Father, through the Son, subjected all things that gain their power from death to the Son, making it possible for us to share in that subjection through the gift of the Holy Spirit. We need to know no more about resurrection than what we have been given through the sharing of the body and blood of Christ.

When the crowd heard Jesus's response to the Sadducees, they were astonished. Jesus is still in the temple. The leaders are determined to show the crowd that he is a teacher with no authority. Prior to the intervention of the Sadducees, the Pharisees and Herodians tried flattery to force him to side for or against Caesar. One of the Pharisees, a lawyer, observing that Jesus has silenced the Sadducees, now tries to test him by asking which commandment is the greatest.

Jesus answers by quoting Deut. 6:5, the Shema of Israel. The commandment to love the Lord with all one's heart, soul, and might is prefaced by "Hear, O Israel: The LORD is our God, the LORD alone." The command to love God is a command that presumes God's love of Israel. Such a love is no vague generality, but rather is manifest in the concrete and daily care of God for his people. We know what it means to love God only because of God's love for us through the law and the prophets. This love can be harsh and dreadful, because to be loved by God is to be forced to know ourselves truthfully.

Jesus continues by quoting Lev. 19:18, that we are to love our neighbor as ourselves. On these two commandments, Jesus tells the lawyer, hang all the law and the prophets. Jesus is often interpreted as suggesting that these two commandments replace the law and the prophets, but he says that the law and the prophets "hang" on these commandments. To be sure, it will always be a matter of dispute what is entailed by "hang," but we cannot forget that this is the same Jesus who told us in the Sermon on the Mount that he had not come to abolish the law and the prophets and that not a letter of the law would pass away until all is accomplished.

The verse prior to the one Jesus quotes, Lev. 19:17, enjoins us to reprove our neighbors, but we are also told to take no vengeance or bear a grudge against our own. In the same chapter of Leviticus we are commanded not to steal, deal falsely, lie, swear falsely by God's name, defraud, revile the deaf, put a stumbling block before the blind, or render unjust judgment. To love our neighbor as ourselves does not mean that we get to decide what such love means; rather to love well is constituted by practices such as those outlined in Matt. 18:15–20, which provide an alternative to mistrust and vengeance.

To learn to love our neighbor as ourselves, moreover, means we must learn to love ourselves as God has loved us (1 John 4:11). To learn to love ourselves truthfully is not easy because we most often desire to love ourselves on our own terms. The challenge that Jesus presents by joining these commandments is to learn that one is loved by God so that one is thus able to love God and others. Such a love requires a lifetime of training in which we are given the opportunity to have our self-centeredness discovered and overwhelmed.

In the *Nicomachean Ethics*, Aristotle suggests that we must be our own best friend if we are to be friends with others. Friends, according to Aristotle, wish one another well, like to spend time with each other, and share each other's distress and enjoyments. Yet that is exactly what those who are friends with themselves do; their memories of what they have done are agreeable, having acted in such a manner that they do not regret what they have done (1999, §1166a1–30). We must therefore be friends with ourselves if we are to be capable of friendship with others.

Christians often think that Aristotle's suggestion that we should be our own best friend is antithetical to what Jesus means when he says that we should love our neighbor as ourselves. Christians, of course, do think that we must often regret what we have done, discovering that sin has often possessed us, even, or especially, when we think that we are doing our best. Yet Jesus does not say that we will learn to love our neighbor only when we have learned to love ourselves; he says that we will be able to love ourselves only when we learn to love ourselves as God loves us and our neighbor. Neither Aristotle nor Jesus knew our modern distinction between egoism and altruism. That distinction has encouraged many to assume that the love Jesus recommends is complete self-giving altruism. Jesus's combination of the two commandments, however, challenges the assumption that we know ourselves well enough to be capable of altruism. Rather, to learn to love our neighbor as ourselves requires that we learn to be befriended by God so that we will have selves sufficient for love.

God is love. The heart of the life of the church and of every Christian is love. Love, however, is not easy, but difficult and hard. Unfortunately, the emphasis on love as *the* defining characteristic of the Christian life not only resulted in the Christian accommodation to the world's standards of the good, but also made it difficult for Christians to understand what it might mean for us to face the hard demands of love. In particular, the separation of love from the one who has come to teach us what it means to be loved by God by making us disciples tempts Christians to sentimental accounts of love. As a result, accounts of Christian morality are often hard to distinguish from utilitarianism. Once Christians make love a relatively unspecified ideal, they are tempted, if not willing, to do great evils that goods may come because they have lost the skills necessary to discern good from evil.[2]

2. The problem is not just the emphasis on love, but the assumption that what makes a

Much hangs on how the law and the prophets fit with Jesus's response to the lawyer concerning which commandment is the greatest. Jesus's response has unfortunately been used to characterize the difference between Christians and Jews. Christians are alleged to represent a religion of love in contrast to Jews, who represent a religion of law. Yet Jews and Christians are first and foremost commanded by Jesus to love the "Lord our God," which means that however our differences are to be understood, we each must learn to love and obey the God who has loved us each through the law and the prophets. To be a Christian is to be called to a life of love, but that calling is a lifelong task that requires our willingness to be surprised by what love turns out to be.

Since Jesus returned to the temple, he has been under continuous questioning. He now poses a question to the Pharisees who have gathered together. He asks them whom they think the Messiah is: "Whose son is he?" They answer that the Messiah is the son of David. We know that Jesus throughout the gospel has often been identified as the son of David by those asking to be cured and by who witness those cures (Matt. 9:27; 12:23). The Pharisees seem to join the consensus that the Messiah is the son of David.

Yet Jesus directs their attention to Ps. 110:1, in which David, the great psalmist, through the Spirit begins by addressing the Messiah as Lord. If David calls the Messiah Lord, Jesus asks, then how can he be David's son? The Messiah is greater than the son of David, being the one whom David has called Lord. Jesus again proves himself to be an adept reader of scripture, using the skills of reading that the Pharisees themselves often use to reveal the limits of the Pharisees' answer.

None of the Pharisees were able to respond to Jesus's question. Nor from that time on did anyone dare to ask him more questions. The attempt to undermine Jesus's authority as a teacher by asking questions designed to entrap him or to show that he lacks legitimacy has been a failure. Those who fear him will now only intensify their conspiracy to destroy him. Jesus, however, must do what he has been sent to do, which means that he cannot avoid saying and doing what those who plot against him will use to have him killed.

Christian can be determined by what Pinches 2002, 34–58 identifies as a persistence toward monistic accounts of morality.

MATTHEW 23

Jesus on the Attack

From the time that Jesus reentered the temple to teach, he has let those who would question him set the agenda. Now, however, he begins to make clear that he has not come back to the temple only for discussion. His unrelenting concern for holiness is made clear in his uncompromising and severe attacks on the scribes and Pharisees. From the beginning Jesus has told his followers that what they teach and who they are cannot be separated. He is the sworn enemy of hypocrisy. We should be what we appear to be. The series of "woes" that Jesus pronounces on the Pharisees are, therefore, primarily directed at their hypocrisy.

Some commentators are so taken aback by the vehemence of his attack on the scribes and Pharisees that they wonder if Jesus could have actually pronounced these judgments against the scribes and Pharisees. It is often assumed that Jesus's judgmental tone and his unforgiving judgments are incompatible with the great commandment, but even more at odds with his admonition that we should love our enemies (Matt. 5:38–48). Yet as I already suggested, the love that Jesus preaches is not incompatible with judgment and, in particular, judgment on hypocrisy. Faithful love, if it is faithful, is judgment.

Jesus begins by addressing the crowds as well as his disciples. For "crowds" to be in the plural seems to suggest there are several factions in the temple. He begins with a list of indictments against the scribes and Pharisees. They "sit on Moses' seat" delivering judgments concerning the law. Jesus instructs the crowds as well as his disciples to practice what the scribes and Pharisees teach. That he does so suggests that Jesus and the Pharisees share much in common.

The problem is not what the Pharisees and scribes teach, but rather that they do not practice what they preach.

Jesus will soon develop a series of woes that seem to reject completely the scribes and Pharisees for their hypocrisy. However, we should remember that hypocrisy is morally ambiguous. The hypocrite at least keeps alive what they and we should be. Indeed, hypocrisy can be considered a moral achievement because hypocrites are just truthful enough to have the resources to condemn themselves. The severity of Jesus's judgments against the scribes and Pharisees honor those whom he judges because they are close to the kingdom. But that they are close to the kingdom makes their failure all the more disastrous for Israel.[1]

Jesus has three complaints against the scribes and Pharisees. First, they put heavy burdens on the shoulders of others, and they are unwilling to aid the ones they so burden. This is in marked contrast with Jesus's invitation to all those who are weary and carry heavy burdens to come to him because his yoke is easy and his burden light (Matt. 11:28–30). Second, they love to do their deeds in a way that will be seen by others; they have no sense of the importance of Jesus's admonition that we should be careful of practicing our piety before others (6:1). They fail to see that even if what they do is right, if it is done to be seen it becomes easily perverted. Finally, Jesus condemns the scribes and Pharisees for seeking status and prestige. They want to have the honored place at the banquets and the best seats in the synagogues. They want to be treated with respect in the marketplaces and addressed as "rabbi." In short, these are people who have learned that if you are treated as if you are important many people will assume you are important, including yourself. That is why, of course, the life of the scribes and Pharisees described by Jesus is self-destructive—for such a life leads to self-deception.

Jesus's initial denunciation of the Pharisees and scribes is but a negative image of what he commends to his disciples. He tells the disciples that they are not to call one another "rabbi," because they have only one teacher. They remain, therefore, students. Nor are they to call anyone "father," for they have only one Father in heaven. The political implications of Jesus's prohibition against the use of the title "father" should not be missed. He is denying all uses of the appellation "father" when that title is put in service by those who use the term to justify their power over others. Finally, he tells the disciples that they are not to be called instructors because they have only one instructor, the Messiah.

Jesus's commendations to his disciples as well as his condemnations of the scribes and Pharisees presume, as he has just acknowledged, that he is the Messiah. Jesus's criticism of the scribes and Pharisees is drawn from God's gift to Israel through the law and the prophets. He is not condemning the Pharisees and the scribes because they do not acknowledge that he is the Messiah.

---

1. I am indebted to Samuel Wells for this account of hypocrisy.

Rather, he is making clear that they cannot acknowledge that he is the Messiah because they do not live by the very law they advocate. He does not, for example, condemn the wearing of phylacteries and fringes. The externals are not the problem, but they become a problem when they no longer serve to shape the life of prayer.

The disciples' only advantage over the scribes and Pharisees is that they lacked the forms of resistance to Jesus that comes from status. Jesus again reminds them that they must be servants to one another, for all who exalt themselves will be humbled, and those who are humbled will be exalted in God's upside-down kingdom. This is a hard lesson to learn for crafty creatures like ourselves, capable of transforming any position, even the position of being a slave and servant, into a position of power and prestige. We desire that others regard us without the necessity that we regard them. Such is our fear of being otherwise lost in the cosmos. Jesus singles out the wiles of the scribes and Pharisees for condemnation, but the games that the scribes and Pharisees play are variations on the games we all play.

The series of woes that Jesus directs at the scribes and Pharisees make for difficult reading in light of the Christian condemnation and persecution of the Jews. That these characterizations of the scribes and Pharisees have unfairly been used to condemn all Jews as well as Judaism is a sign of Christian failure and sin. But the sin is not that Christians thought it necessary to make judgments informed by those forms of life that Jesus's condemns, but that we have failed to apply those judgments to ourselves. We cannot forget that Jesus condemns the scribes and Pharisees from a position of weakness. He has no power to act against those he condemns. Christians betray Jesus when they make judgments—like those that Jesus makes against the scribes and Pharisees—from positions of power that transform those judgments into violent and murderous actions rather than attempts to call ourselves and our brothers and sisters to a better life.

Jesus's woes are not unique in Israel's life. Rather, they are a continuation of the prophets' condemnation of the misuse of Israel's gifts. Isaiah 5 is one long harangue against those who have misused the vineyard given by the Lord. Those who make iniquitous decrees, write oppressive statutes, and turn aside the needy from justice are condemned in Isa. 10. Jeremiah 13:27 condemns the abominations and adulteries of Jerusalem, and Amos 5:18–24 famously mocks those who desire the day of the Lord. Jesus stands in a long line of God's prophets who in the name of God's gift of the law to Israel pronounce judgment on those who have betrayed Israel. Jesus is not standing outside Israel when he pronounces the woes on the Pharisees and scribes, but rather his judgments are the judgments of Israel against herself.

He begins by passing judgment on the scribes and Pharisees for the effect that their hypocrisy has on others. The kingdom of heaven is attractive and inviting, but the scribes and Pharisees prevent those so attracted from entering the kingdom because they do not live as if they have entered the kingdom. Jesus even suggests that the Pharisees are missionaries, but those they convert are made even more corrupt than the Pharisees themselves.

Jesus's next series of woes condemns the scribes and Pharisees for concentration on minutiae of the law rather than on weightier matters. For example, they try to determine the status of oaths sworn on the gold of the sanctuary as opposed to those sworn on the altar. Jesus, who has forbidden his followers to make oaths (Matt. 5:33–37), observes that an oath should be kept no matter what part of the altar or sanctuary is used to legitimate the oath. Moreover, the scribes and Pharisees worry about whether seasonings must be tithed in support of the temple as indicated in Lev. 27:30–33, yet they avoid the weightier matters of the law. Drawing on Mic. 6:8, Jesus reminds them that what the Lord requires is to do justice and to love kindness and to walk humbly with the Lord. Jesus does not say that they ought to neglect supporting the temple, but such support is not an alternative or substitute for practicing justice and mercy.

Jesus, like Jeremiah, stands in the temple to proclaim God's word. God desires to be worshiped in the temple. In Jeremiah, God promises to dwell in the temple if Israel will amend its ways, act justly with one another, not oppress the alien or widow or orphan, not shed innocent blood, and not go after other gods. If Israel assumes that it is safe because it possesses the temple, then God will cast it out (Jer. 7:1–15). Jesus's condemnation of the scribes and Pharisees echoes Jeremiah's prophetic call to Israel that its worship of God cannot be separated from justice and mercy.

The vital link between worship and justice sets the stage for Jesus's condemnation of the Pharisees and scribes for appearing clean on the outside but leading lives possessed by greed and self-indulgence. One must be what one appears to be. To be what we appear to be requires that our lives, our desires and habits, be transformed. Such a transformation cannot be accomplished by simply copying external forms of righteousness, but must come from lives shaped by truthful worship of God. To live otherwise is to live lives of self-contradiction.

Indeed, Jesus suggests that the scribes and Pharisees are like whitewashed tombs that are beautiful on the outside but are full of bones and filth. This is a reminder that to live a life of immorality is not to live as if we are dead, but quite literally to live a deadly life. Jesus calls us to life, not to death. Hidden immorality draws its power and its results from death and our fear of death. The result is to impose our fear of death on others, requiring that they acknowledge our immorality as righteousness. Deadly exchanges are necessary to keep up the appearances.

Finally, Jesus condemns the scribes and Pharisees for honoring the tombs of the prophets and decorating the graves of the righteous while believing that if they had been present they would not have shed the blood of the prophets. Jesus makes clear that they honor the prophets only because they are dead. Jesus, a prophet without honor in his own country (Matt. 13:57–58), recognizes that they are the kind of people who would kill a prophet in the name of a prophet. Jesus, like John the Baptist (3:7), identifies these killers of the dream as snakes and vipers who will not escape being sentenced to hell.

Prophetically, Jesus tells them that he will send prophets and scribes, some of whom these Pharisees and scribes will flog and kill. They will pursue those whom Jesus will send from town to town, in order to shed their blood, thus standing in the history of those who murdered all the righteous—beginning with Abel and continuing to Zechariah. Jesus tells the Pharisees and scribes that this generation will do these very things. This generation is the one determined by the coming of Jesus, the same Jesus who has told us that he will be put to death. He will not be the first to die at the hands of those determined to maintain the illusion that they represent Israel's righteousness, but he also knows he will not be the last.

This is a sobering list of failure and judgment, with descriptions of hypocrisy and failure in which we cannot help but see ourselves. It is surely the case, for example, that many of us are kept from entering the kingdom by the lives we lead as Christians. Our problem is very simple—we simply do not know how to live as a people who believe that Jesus is the resurrected Lord. The joy and freedom that should name the lives of those freed from the demons become lost amid attempts to make our difference depend on matters that do not matter. We become adept at praising the prophets of the past, having lost the ability to discern the prophets among us.

Jesus describes the scribes and the Pharisees as "blind guides." That they are blind is not unrelated to their desire to be guides. Those who would lead others often fear those they lead, and in particular they fear hurting those they lead. They think that their task is to make the life of those they lead secure. Yet a people who depend on prophets can never lead lives of safety. A people required to remember that they are a people whose forebears have murdered the righteous cannot live lives of safety. Those who would lead too often must hide from themselves what they know to be true because they think that those whom they lead cannot bear the truth. The blindness of the Pharisees and scribes is a blindness that threatens the church no less than any people. The only difference between the Pharisees and those who would lead Jesus's people is that the latter lead a people who have no reason to fear the truth.

Jesus's condemnation of the scribes and Pharisees is sobering, but we dare not overlook that the criticism Jesus makes of the scribes and Pharisees assumes that the people he is calling to be his church will need people like the Pharisees and scribes. He even says that he will send prophets and scribes to the synagogues and towns of Israel. The church will need persons called to positions that help the church avoid hypocrisy through agents of direction to keep before the church the vision of the kingdom; the church will need agents of memory to help the church read its scripture and tradition; the church will need agents of linguistic self-consciousness to guard the church from mental laziness; the church will need agents of order and due process to insure unity and encourage participation in the decisions of the church (Yoder 1984, 28–34).

Each of these agents will be tempted to hypocrisy. There is no guarantee that ensures we will live lives of integrity. Hypocrisy can be avoided only if the church is a community capable of truthful speech. If such a community is missing, then those who would lead are doomed. Jesus's condemnation of the Pharisees and scribes is severe, but his woes are also woes of sadness. Jesus's description of how those called to help Israel live faithfully have come to lead false lives is suffused with pathos. His condemnations are harsh, but what could be worse than for the Pharisees and scribes, like any of us, to get the life they think they wanted?

Jesus's lament for and against the scribes and Pharisees is climaxed by his cry of sorrow for Jerusalem. "Jerusalem, Jerusalem"—a city that has killed its prophets. "Jerusalem, Jerusalem"—the city of the temple now desolate. "Jerusalem, Jerusalem"—a city that Jesus desires to protect like a hen gathers her chicks under her wings. Yet Jesus's lament is not without hope. Jesus had entered Jerusalem enacting Ps. 118. He now leaves the temple quoting Ps. 118:26: "Blessed is the one who comes in the name of the LORD."

The next line of the psalm reads, "We bless you from the house of the LORD." Jesus is the one who has come in the name of the Lord. He will become the house of the Lord. As Jesus leaves the temple, his disciples point out the buildings that make up the temple. In spite of all that Jesus has said in and about the temple, the disciples seem intent on showing Jesus that the temple, when all is said and done, is an impressive edifice. But Jesus prophecies that the temple will be destroyed so that not one stone will be left on another. The center of Israel's life will be destroyed. A thought unthinkable, but one destined to be Israel's future.

The temple was destroyed by the Romans in AD 70. Some make much of the destruction of the temple as a confirmation of Jesus's prediction. Indeed the suggestion is made that Matthew's understanding of Jesus's ministry and life depends on the destruction of the temple. However, the fate of the temple did not lie in the hands of the Romans, but rather was to be determined by Jesus's death and resurrection. He will be accused of threatening to destroy the temple only to rebuild it in three days (Matt. 26:61). This is an accusation that is ironically true in the light of his crucifixion and resurrection. Jesus's crucifixion is the destruction of the temple; through his death and resurrection we now worship him.

MATTHEW 24–25

Enduring

Jesus has left the temple and returned to the Mount of Olives. The disciples come to him "privately," asking when the temple will be destroyed and what will be the sign of the coming age. It is appropriate that they ask these questions about time on the Mount of Olives because the Mount of Olives is identified in Zech. 14:1–5 as the mount on which the Lord will stand to save his people from the nations that have surrounded it. Zechariah describes an apocalyptic time in Israel's existence. The disciples are participating in a time they do not yet comprehend, but it is clear from Jesus's suggestion that the temple will be destroyed—an apocalyptic event that rightly makes the disciples wonder what sign will herald "your coming" and the correlative "end of the age." They still have to learn that Jesus is that sign as well as the object that the sign signifies.

Jesus does not respond directly to the disciples' questions but instead warns them against those who will come in his name claiming to be the Messiah. Jesus tells them that many will be led astray by those who claim to be the Messiah. The times will be dramatic—dominated by wars and rumors of war. Nations will rise up against nations, and the world will be threatened by famines and earthquakes in various places. The dramatic nature of the times will tempt the disciples to try to nail down the time of the end of the age, which Jesus tells them they must not try to do. False messiahs will use the expectation of the end of the age, but that is why the disciples must recognize that "the end is not yet."

Jesus had earlier condemned the Pharisees and Sadducees for asking for a sign (Matt. 16:1–4), but he now uses the disciples' question to train them to know how to wait in a world in which some presume they can read the signs of the time. Jesus tells the disciples that this is exactly what they must not do. Their task is not to anticipate the end of time, but rather their task is to learn to endure even under persecution (24:13). All the disciples need to know, all we need to know, is that a new age has begun in Christ.

Jesus tells the disciples that they will be persecuted, handed over to death, and be hated by all nations because of his name. Just as Jesus could not help but produce enemies, so the disciples will have enemies who will hate them. That they will be hated, that Christians have been and will continue to be hated, is not necessarily a sign of faithfulness; but if Christians are faithful, they will be hated. They will be hated because those who have gone to the nations in Jesus's name cannot help but produce enemies who refuse to acknowledge the challenge that Jesus's people present to any loyalty not determined by discipleship to Jesus.

Jesus, therefore, prepares his disciples to expect that many will fall away from following him in the face of the hatred that comes from the nations. They will not only fall away but some of his followers will hate and betray one another. Without the name of Jesus they are left with no alternatives but to kill or be killed. Lawlessness will reign, and love will go cold. This is a description of our fate not unlike that of Thomas Hobbes, who described human life without a sovereign as "nasty, brutish, and short." Hobbes's sovereign, however, rules by fear and violence. Jesus rules, but his rule is one that refuses to use our fear of one another to secure our obedience.

Jesus is preparing his disciples for the long haul. The end has come, but the end that has come requires that the disciples must learn to wait. Endurance is the way of the disciple between the time of Jesus and the proclamation of the good news of the kingdom throughout the world. Only when that news is proclaimed throughout the world, to all the nations, will the end come. But such a proclamation does not mean that when all people and nations have heard the name of Jesus the kingdom will come, because "to hear" the name of Jesus requires that name to be embodied in the faithfully lived lives that constitute the church. Jesus's name for such faithfulness is "endurance."

In *Broken Lights and Mended Lives*, Rowan Greer suggests that one form of the endurance that Jesus commends is monasticism. In the Middle Ages monasteries served the double function of refuges and foundations for the reordering of society:

> There is something to be said for the view that the Church began by providing deliverance from the disasters that attended the collapse of Roman rule in the West, but ended by becoming the basis for a new order of society. A pattern that can be discerned in the first centuries of the Church's existence, leading to the new order of the Christian Empire, seems to repeat itself when we examine the end of late antiquity and the birth of the new order of the Middle Ages. Is this a way of looking at our own times? And are we living in the midst of the death

of an old culture in which Christ brings us not so much an ordering of society as a deliverance from it? (Greer 1997, 206)

Greer's book, a meditation on how we are to live as Christians, assumes a positive answer to this last question. Greer directs our attention to the life of Paulinus of Pella, a minor Roman official, as an exemplification of how we must learn to live in a world coming apart, for the story of Paulinus, the story of how a fairly worldly young man lost possessions and power in the changing empire, is a story of endurance. Paulinus regards his life as God's gift, for, he says, God has reasonably chastened him "with continual misfortunes, he [God] has clearly taught me that I ought neither to love too earnestly present prosperity which I knew I might lose, nor to be greatly dismayed by adversities wherein I had found that his mercies could succor me." Greer observes: "His Christian faith did not empower Paulinus to take an active and constructive part in the events of his time, nor did it lead him to withdraw from society to the security of the monastery. But it did enable him to endure, and in that enduring there is testimony to the victory of Christ" (1997, 196).[1]

Paulinus becomes for Greer the exemplification of Augustine's account of the fall of Rome in *The City of God*. Augustine, according to Greer, rightly refuses to interpret the fall of Rome as a disaster, because Augustine does not accept the view that the Christian empire was sacred. Augustine does not narrate the future of the church in terms of Rome, but rather Rome is a character in the larger narrative of God's care of the church, which means, according to Greer, that

> the paradox of the Christian life is that the evils we suffer in our earthly pilgrimage must be taken with absolute seriousness, but so must the destiny that awaits us in the City of God. There are no victories or defeats in the present that really matter. All that counts is the final victory for the saints in the age to come. The practical implications of Augustine's view is that what matters is to endure. The Christian can be neither fully involved in society nor fully withdrawn from it . . . we can endure and so prevail. (Greer 1997, 205–6)

Some may wonder if calling attention to a figure like Paulinus does not qualify my earlier attack on Constantinianism. However, the criticism of Constantinianism does not mean that the significance of a life like Paulinus, a life that daily tried to negotiate the world as he found it, is to be denied. Rather, the question is whether a church exists constituted by disciplines that can make lives like Paulinus's possible. Paulinus was able to be Paulinus because he knew that monks existed.

Jesus does not answer the disciples' question of when the temple will be destroyed, nor has he given them an answer to their question concerning the

1. This material is a revision of Hauerwas 2000, 170–71.

sign that will signal Jesus's coming and the end of the age. Rather, Jesus tells them how they must learn to wait in this time between the times. Christians have been unable to heed Jesus's warning not to try to calculate the day and the hour he will return. Jesus plainly tells us that only the Father has such knowledge, but the temptation to be God, particularly by those who count themselves Christian, is hard to resist. Desperate to have a handle on history, Christians have used the very apocalyptic imagery that Jesus deploys to prevent attempts to determine the end of the age to do exactly what Jesus says cannot and should not be done, that is, to try to know what only the Father knows (Matt. 24:36).

Some Christians have taken Jesus's apocalyptic language literally in order to try to identify this or that war or rumor of war as the beginning of the birth pangs of the end. Unfortunately, they sometimes even identify this or that war as the war that Christians must fight to bring the age to the end. They fail to see that Jesus uses apocalyptic language, a dramatic language necessary to understand the radical transformation that the kingdom names, to announce that the kingdom has come and is present. They will hear of wars and rumors of wars, but the kingdom that Jesus has brought means that war has been brought to an end. Jesus's use of apocalyptic language, in particular that of the prophet Daniel, is not an invitation for his followers to try to predict the future, but to help his disciples learn to live in the presence of the one who has come that they might learn to live in peace in a world of war. Apocalyptic is a vehicle of prophecy that enables us to see ourselves and the world in which we live in light of God's purpose for his creation (Bauckham 2005, 6–7).

Even Christians who do not employ Jesus's apocalyptic imagery to map contemporary events nonetheless assume that Christians have a stake in trying to determine the meaning and direction of history. This is often the project of liberal Christians who continue the habits of Constantinianism. John Howard Yoder suggests, for example, that our age is obsessed by "a deep desire to make things move in the right direction. Whether a given action is right or not seems to be inseparable from the question of what effects it will cause. Thus part if not all social concern has to do with looking for the right 'handle' by which one can 'get a hold on' the course of history and move it in the right direction" (1994b, 228).[2]

Those who attempt to read "the signs of the times" in these two quite different ways have little use for one another, but ironically they share in common the belief that Jesus has answered the disciples' questions. Yet Jesus is trying to help the disciples understand how they must live when their questions should not have been asked and cannot be answered. Or put differently, Jesus is trying to help the disciples live when his life must shape any questions to be asked.

2. I am indebted to Huebner 2002 for his development of Yoder's understanding of "handling history."

The disciples, by following Jesus, must learn how to tell the false messiahs and prophets who will often produce great signs and omens—signs and omens quite different from the sign of the cross.

Both temptations—to employ Jesus's apocalyptic imagery to predict the end time or to discern the movement of history—betray the character of Jesus's training of his disciples. He is trying to teach them how they must live in the light of his coming. The dramatic character of apocalyptic language should help the disciples understand the challenge he presents to them. We, along with the disciples, make a disastrous mistake, however, if we all allow our imaginations to be possessed by the images of apocalypse rather than by the one on whom those images are meant to focus our attention—that is, Jesus.

For example, Jesus tells his disciples that when they see "the desolating sacrilege standing in the holy place" then those in Judea must flee to the mountains (Dan. 9:27; 11:31; 12:11, 1 Macc. 4:54). That time, the time of the "desolating sacrilege," Jesus makes clear, is a time of crisis that requires a readiness to leave what we are doing behind. Those on the housetop should not go down into the house to take anything from the house; those in the field should not turn back to get their coats; and those pregnant and nursing infants will be distressed. Given the crisis that such a sacrilege creates, they should even pray that the required escape not happen in winter because of the hardships that winter imposes or on a Sabbath when they are prevented from traveling.

Speculation surrounding what Jesus must have meant by "desolating sacrilege" is endless. Many assume that Jesus must be referring to some future desecration of the temple such as that perpetrated by Antiochus IV Epiphanes, who is the object of Daniel's prophetic judgment. Yet Jesus has just told his disciples that the stones of the temple will be thrown down. How can a ruined temple be desolated? Jesus is trying to help his disciples understand that it is not the temple that will be desecrated, though that will happen, but that he will be desecrated.

Jesus is the great high priest and he is the temple (Heb. 8–9). His crucifixion is the desolating sacrilege. Surely it is the death of the Son of God that is the sacrilege that desolates the cosmos. That desolation constitutes the crisis he describes. That crisis has been present since he was born and throughout his ministry. His crucifixion will deepen the crisis. That desolation, moreover, requires the readiness that his dramatic language of response suggests. The language of apocalypse is necessary to prepare the disciples for that crisis to come. As we shall see, those lessons consist in direct admonitions as well as parables to train the disciples how to wait and watch.

He tells the disciples that at that time there will be suffering that has not been known since the beginning of the world and will never be known again. It is his suffering. It is the suffering of the Son of God at human hands. The days of the world have been "cut short," making possible salvation of the elect. But days of crisis also invite vultures adept at feeding on the corpse of the old age. False messiahs will claim to do what Jesus is thought not to have done, that is, to provide great signs and omens. But those same signs and omens can only lead the elect astray.

Indeed these vultures will parody Jesus's ministry, going into the wilderness or inner rooms, suggesting that they have a secret knowledge to be shared only with the elect. Jesus warns his disciples beforehand so that they will not be mislead by these pretenders, for the very elements of the cosmos will herald the coming of the Son of Man (cf. Isa. 13:10; Ezek. 32:7):

> The sun will be darkened,
>   and the moon will not give its light;
> the stars will fall from heaven,
>   and the powers of heaven will be shaken.

On that day Daniel's vision will be fulfilled. A sign will appear in heaven, the Son of Man will come on the clouds of heaven, and he will be given dominion over all peoples, nations, and languages that they may serve him (Dan. 7:13–14). The elect will be gathered from all the nations to constitute a new people never before imagined. Jesus will appear in heaven raised high on a cross with arms outstretched to receive those called from the nations.

Jesus's use of Daniel is not an attempt to invite his disciples to "think ahead," but to discern the present. Accordingly, he directs their attention to the lesson of the fig tree whose leaves suggest summer is near. So the disciples should see "all these things" and recognize that the Messiah is near. Jesus says plainly that this generation will not pass away without all this taking place, for in him eternity has disrupted our time. Heaven and earth will pass away. They are, after all, created. But Jesus and his words will not pass away. How could they? He is the word of God.

The disciples' task is to stay awake, to be ready, exactly because they do not and cannot know the day and hour of the triumph of the Son of Man. Disciples are not in the game of prediction. Rather, they are called to be ready and prepared. Disciples, like Noah, are to build an ark even if it is not raining. The name given to that ark is church. The builders of the church will be surrounded by many who go about their lives, eating, drinking, marrying, living as if nothing has changed, even though Noah has built an ark. But the floods will come, drowning all. The only difference is that when the Son of Man comes not all will be swept away, because his coming is a quite different flood. It is the flood of his blood meant to save the lost. Some will be left judged by this just judge. Jesus is not threatening, but rather stating facts.

The disciples have been learning what it is they must do. Jesus observes that if the owner of a house had known that the thief was coming, he would have stayed awake and not let his house be robbed. Of course, the problem for most of us is that we think it quite unlikely that someone will want to break into our house. But the disciples must learn to live as those who recognize that the thief is coming and will likely come at an unexpected hour.

Apocalyptic names the time that requires waiting. It is not just any kind of waiting, but rather it is the waiting made possible by a hope made real. Jesus is that hope, and he instills the same hope in those who would follow him. It is not the hope of idealism that tires when the ideals seem unreachable. Rather, it is the hope schooled by the Father's patience to redeem the world through his Son. Without patience, those filled with hope threaten to destroy that for which they hope. Without hope, the patient threaten to leave the world as they find it. Disciples of Jesus must learn how to take the time patiently to hope in a world that thinks it has no time for either hope or patience.

Just as he had used parables earlier (Matt. 13) to help the disciples learn what the kingdom of heaven was like, Jesus now uses parables to help the disciples learn how to wait. He begins with a question: "Who then is the faithful and wise slave?" Jesus describes two slaves who have been put in charge of their master's other slaves while he is gone. As he was expected to do, one slave continues during his master's absence to give food to the other slaves. That slave is blessed because when the master returns the slave has done what he was expected to do. The master accordingly puts that slave in charge of all the master's possessions.

But a wicked slave says to himself that the master is delayed and begins to beat his fellow slaves. He drinks and eats with drunkards, no longer attending to his master's work. But the master of that slave will return when the slave does not expect him, and the master will "cut him to pieces and put him with the hypocrites, where there will be weeping and gnashing of teeth" (Matt. 24:51). That the slave will at once be cut to pieces and yet still be able to join the hypocrites should be sufficient to alert anyone that Jesus is not using this language to describe an actual state of affairs. It is interesting to reflect, however, if it is a worse fate to be cut to pieces or to have to spend one's life with the hypocrites.

Jesus does not explain this parable. Rather, he assumes that those called to be servants to one another are meant to continue to serve no matter how long it takes for the master to return. Jesus has given his disciples good work to do. No speculation about "the end of the age" can or should suggest to followers of Jesus that they no longer need to be of service to one another. Indeed, that the end has come makes such work all the more imperative as well as intelligible, for it is the work of hope and patience made possible by Jesus, the Son of Man, who has come in glory.

Jesus does not explain the parable of the two slaves, the one who works while the master is away and the other who uses the master's absence to beat his fellow slaves, but rather tells two other parables; he also provides an account of good work to illumine all three parables. The parables that follow, the parable of the ten bridesmaids and the parable of the talents, emphasize both the necessity to be watchful and the work necessary to sustain those who watch. That work, moreover, is specified. It is the work of giving food to the hungry and drink to the thirsty, welcoming the stranger, clothing the naked, caring for the sick, and visiting those in prison (Matt. 25:35–36).

In order to introduce the parable of the ten bridesmaids, Jesus uses the familiar formula, "The kingdom of heaven will be like this," only this time he says, "*Then* the kingdom of heaven will be like this." "Then" signals that he is telling the disciples how they must learn to live in the light of his death and resurrection. Ten bridesmaids took their lamps to wait for the bridegroom. Five were wise and took with them extra oil for their lamps. Five were foolish and did not prepare ahead. The bridegroom was delayed, and the bridesmaids understandably became drowsy and went to sleep. But late in the night the shout went out: "Look! Here is the bridegroom!" The bridesmaids arose and trimmed their lamps, but the foolish bridesmaids' lamps had run out of oil. They asked the five who had brought extra oil to share their oil but they were denied because if they shared their oil it would mean that none of them would have light by the time the bridegroom arrived. The foolish bridesmaids went to buy extra oil, but by the time they returned the bridegroom had come, the wedding banquet had begun, and the door was shut. The bridesmaids asked that the door be opened, but the bridegroom refused, saying that he did not know them. Jesus admonishes the disciples that they should "keep awake, therefore, for you know neither the day nor the hour."

In Isa. 54:1–8 God declares that he desires to be Israel's husband so that the nation will not be barren. Israel, we know from Jer. 31:32 and Hos. 2:1–20, was often unfaithful to God's covenant of marriage. Yet God will not abandon his bride. That bride, moreover, Paul identifies as the church (2 Cor. 11:2; Eph. 5:21–33), and in Rev. 19:7 we are even told this:

> Let us rejoice and exult
>   and give him the glory,
> for the marriage of the Lamb has come,
>   and his bride has made herself ready;
> to her it has been granted to be clothed
>   with fine linen, bright and pure.

We should not be surprised, therefore, that Jesus uses a wedding banquet as the central motif for this parable of the kingdom. Weddings, of course, are occasions of celebration, but judgment is also present as Jesus made clear in the parable of the king who invited all to the banquet to celebrate the wedding of his son (Matt. 22:11–14). The parable of the bridesmaids, therefore, is at once an invitation to a celebration and a judgment against those who are unprepared. The wise bridesmaids rightly celebrate with the delayed groom because they had prepared for a long night of waiting. The bridegroom arrived at an unexpected time. The foolish bridesmaids failed to understand that in a time when you are unsure of the time you are in it is all the more important to do what you have been taught to do. In the dark you must keep the lamps ready even if they are not able to overcome the darkness.

Some may think Jesus's parable to be quite unfair to the bridesmaids who had not prepared ahead. Those who stress compassion as *the* hallmark of what makes Christians Christian cannot help but think that the bridesmaids with the oil should have shared with those without. But if they had shared their oil when the bridegroom had come, there would have been no light. Those who follow Jesus will be expected to lead lives that make it possible for the hungry to be fed and the stranger welcomed, but the practice of charity requires a community prepared to welcome Christ as the bridegroom, for he alone makes possible hospitality to the stranger in a world where there will always be another stranger needing hospitality.

The kind of preparation that the wise bridesmaids exemplify is again evoked by Jesus in the parable of the talents. He connects the parable of the talents with that of the bridesmaids, "for it is as if a man, going on a journey," entrusted his property to three of his slaves. Jesus's "for it is as if" associates the preparation of the five bridesmaids with the money that has been entrusted to the three slaves. A man going on the trip summoned his three slaves to him and gave five talents, two talents, and one talent to them, respectively. The first two slaves used their talents in trade and doubled what they had been given. The slave who had been given one talent dug a hole in the ground and hid what he had been given.

When the man returned, the slaves who had doubled what they had been given were rewarded by being praised as "good and trustworthy." Their master not only put them in charge of many things but invited them to "enter into the joy of your master." But the slave who had received the one talent came to his master, confessing that he knew his master to be a harsh man who gathered where he had not sown or scattered seed, so he had hidden his one talent in the ground and was thereby able to return it. The master, however, was not impressed and called him a wicked and lazy slave. His master observes that if the slave knew he reaped and gathered what he had not sown, he could have at least put the money in the bank to gather interest. So he took the money from him and gave it to the slave with ten talents, for those with more will be given more, but the worthless slave is to be thrown into outer darkness.

No parable has been more misused than Jesus's parable of the talents. Once any parable is abstracted from Jesus proclamation of the kingdom, once any parable is divorced from its apocalyptic context, misreading is inevitable. Speculation begins, for example, about how much a talent might be or whether the master's observation that the money could have been put in a bank might mean that Jesus approves of taking interest. Speculative uses of the parable have even been employed to justify economic practices that are antithetical to

Jesus's clear judgment that we cannot serve God and mammon. Jesus is not using this parable to recommend that we should work hard, make all we can, to give all we can. Rather, the parable is a clear judgment against those who think they deserve what they have earned, as well as those who do not know how precious is the gift they have been given.

The slaves have not earned their five, two, and one talents. They have been given those talents. In the parable of the sower (Matt. 13:1–9), Jesus had indicated that those called to the kingdom would produce different yields. Those differences should not be the basis for envy and jealousy, because our differences are gifts given in service to one another. So are the talents given to the slaves of the man going on a journey. It is not unfair that the slaves were given different amounts. Rather, what is crucial is how they regarded what they had been given. Jesus makes clear in this parable that we can do only what we have been given.

The one who received one talent feared the giver. He did so because he assumed that the giver had given a gift that could only be lost or used up. In other words the one with one talent assumed that he or she was part of a zero-sum game. Those who assume that life is a zero-sum game think that if one person receives an honor then someone else is made poorer. So the slave with one talent feared losing what he had been given, with the result that he tried to turn the gift into a possession. In contrast, the first two slaves recognized that to try to secure the gifts they had been given means that the gifts would be lost. The joy of the wedding banquet and the joy into which the master invites his slaves that had not tried to protect what they had been given is the joy that comes from learning to receive a gift without regret.

The parable of the talents and the parable of the ten bridesmaids are commentaries on the slave who continued to work, to feed his fellow slaves, until his master returns. Each of these parables teach us how to wait patiently as those who have received the gift of being called to be a disciple of Jesus. Jesus's disciples are not called to do great things, although great things may happen. Rather, Jesus's disciples are called to do the work that Jesus has given us to do—work as simple and hard as learning to tell the truth and to love our enemies. Such work is the joy that our master invites us to share.

In the climax of Jesus's great sermon occasioned by his disciple's question concerning what sign will signal the coming of the end of the age, Jesus returns to Dan. 7:13–14. The Son of Man comes in glory, and all the angels will be with him. The nations will be gathered before him because he is a king. He is, however, a shepherd-king who will separate the sheep from the goats. He will put the sheep on his right hand and the goats on his left. To those on his right hand he will say that they are blessed by his Father and will inherit the kingdom prepared for them since the foundation of the world, for when he was hungry they gave him food, when he was thirsty they gave him drink, a stranger and they welcomed him, naked and they gave him clothing, sick and they cared for him, in prison and they visited him. The righteous, however, ask the king when did they do for him all that he has said. The king answered that just as they did any of this for the least of these who are members of his family they did it to him.

The king then addressed those on his left hand, telling them that they are accursed and will be sent to the eternal fire prepared for the devil and the devil's angels, for the king was hungry and they gave him no food, thirsty and they gave him no water, a stranger and he was not welcomed, naked and given no clothing, sick and in prison and they did not visit him. They ask, like those on the king's right hand, when they failed to do any of this for him. Again the king answered, "Truly I tell you, just as you did not do it to one of the least of these, you did not do it to me." They, moreover, will go away into eternal punishment and the righteous to eternal life.

It is significant that the righteous have not known that when they ministered, provided hospitality, and visited that they did all of this to Jesus. They have done what God would have us to do and so doing have ministered to Christ himself. All people, whether they are Christians or not, know all they need to know to care for "the least of these." The difference between followers of Jesus and those who do not know Jesus is that those who have seen Jesus no longer have any excuse to avoid "the least of these."

The disciples now have the answer to their question. Jesus is the sign of the end of the age, making possible for them to have the time, as Jesus did, to feed the hungry (Matt. 14:13–21; 15:32–39), cure the sick, comfort the comfortless (15:21–28), welcome the stranger (8:5–13), and be imprisoned and crucified between two prisoners. This is the work they have witnessed and been given as they have followed Jesus on his journey through the towns of Israel and finally to Jerusalem itself. This is the way they will learn to be watchmen for the kingdom, for by performing the work of the kingdom they will be given the gift of discernment so that they will be able to resist the temptations of the devil.

In a wonderful essay entitled "The Scandal of the Works of Mercy," Dorothy Day lists the works of mercy, codified by Thomas Aquinas, based on Matt. 25:

> The spiritual works of mercy are to admonish the sinner, to instruct the ignorant, to counsel the doubtful, to comfort the sorrowful, to bear wrongs patiently, to forgive all injuries, and to pray for the living and the dead. The corporal works are to feed the hungry, to give drink to the thirsty, to clothe the naked, to ransom the captive, to harbor the harborless, to visit the sick, and to bury the dead. (Day 2002, 103)

Her colleague, Peter Maurin, whom Day identifies as the founder of *The Catholic Worker*, was, according to Day, as much an apostle to the world as he was to the poor. He did not believe that works of mercy were a strategy to care for the poor until another and better more effective social policy could be found. He believed that works of mercy were the social policy that Jesus had given his people for the renewal of the world. According to Day, Maurin thought that in order to convince people

> it was necessary to embrace voluntary poverty, to strip yourself, which would give you the *means* to practice the works of mercy. To reach the man in the street you must go to the street. To reach the workers, you begin to study the philosophy of labor, and take up manual labor, useful labor, instead of white collar work. To be the least, to be the worker, to be poor, to take the lowest place and thus be the spark which would set afire the love of men towards each other and to God (and we can only show our love for God by our love for our fellows). These were Peter's ideas, and they are indispensable for the performing of the works of mercy. (Day 2002, 104)

Day calls this understanding of the works of mercy a scandal because it challenges the assumption that Christians are to do something for the poor by trying to create alternatives to capitalism or socialism. The problem with trying to create such alternatives is that we seduce ourselves into believing that we are working to feed the hungry, clothe the naked, give drink to the thirsty, welcome the stranger, care for the sick and those in prison without knowing anyone who is hungry, naked, thirsty, a stranger, sick, or in prison. Day and Maurin knew that attempts to create a "better world" without being a people capable of the works of mercy could not help but betray Jesus's response to his disciples' question of what sign will there be of Jesus's coming and the end of the age. The sign is that they have the time to feed the hungry, clothe the naked, give drink to the thirsty, welcome the stranger, care for the sick and those in prison.

Moreover, such work will be offensive to those in power who claim to rule as benefactors of the poor and hungry. A people shaped by the practice of the works of mercy will be a people capable of seeing through those who claim to need power to do good, but in fact just need power. Great injustice is perpetrated in the name of justice. Great evil is done because it is said that time is short and there needs to be a response to this or that crisis. Christians live after the only crisis that matters, which means that Jesus has given us all the time in the world to visit him in the prisons of this world.

MATTHEW 26

Betrayal and Arrest

Matthew signals that Jesus had finished instructing his disciples with his familiar, "When Jesus had finished saying these things," except this time he writes, "When Jesus had finished saying *all* these things." Matthew adds "all" to indicate that Jesus has come to the end of his teaching ministry and that we have been taught all we need to know to be his disciple. Jesus's life takes a drastic turn, but Matthew has been preparing us by helping us obtain the patience to follow Jesus even to the cross.

In Deuteronomy, after Moses had "finished writing down in a book the words of this law to the very end" (31:24), he sang a hymn praising God for his care of Israel in spite of its infidelity. We are told that Moses then

> came and recited all the words of this song in the hearing of the people, he and Joshua son of Nun. When Moses had finished reciting all these words to all Israel, he said to them: "Take to heart all the words that I am giving in witness against you today; give them as a command to your children, so that they may diligently observe all the words of this law. This is no trifling matter for you, but rather your very life; through it you may live long in the land that you are crossing over the Jordan to possess." (Deut. 32:44–47)

Moses's "all" and Matthew's "all" serve the same function. Just as Moses commands that we take to heart *all* of his instruction, so we are to take to heart *all* that Jesus has taught and done. We and the disciples now know all we need to know in order to follow Jesus to the cross. Matthew has patiently tried to teach us what it means to follow Jesus so that we might not abandon him at the cross. Just as Israel often betrayed the gift of the law, we and the disciples will abandon him, yet he will not abandon us.

Jesus says to his disciples that they know in two days that the Passover is coming and the Son of Man will be handed over to be crucified. Suddenly, at least it seems sudden, Jesus will be betrayed, arrested, and crucified. Events move swiftly, making us feel that time is out of control. Yet Jesus says, "The Son of Man will be handed over." Those who would kill Jesus have the illusion that they are in control, but it is the Father's will that Jesus be handed over. Jesus submits to his fate at the hands of his adversaries, but he submits to fulfill the will of his Father.

In Judges, during the time of the conquest, we are told that Israel did what was evil in the sight of the Lord and worshiped Baals and Astartes. They followed other gods and bowed down to them. God's anger was kindled against Israel, "and he gave them over to plunderers who plundered them, and he sold them into the power of their enemies all around, so that they could no longer withstand their enemies" (2:11–15). In Rom. 1, Paul says that God gave up all humanity to "the lusts of their hearts" and to "the degrading of their bodies . . . because they exchanged the truth about God for a lie" (Rom. 1:24–25). This time, however, the Father hands over the Son "to give his life a ransom for many" (Matt. 20:28).

Israel was required to remember Passover so that she would never forget that the Lord saved the firstborn of Israel from death by having the blood of a slaughtered lamb put on the lintels and doorposts of their dwellings in Egypt. The Lord passed over the doors so marked, saving the firstborn of Israel but not the firstborn of Egypt (Exod. 12). Jesus now becomes the Passover lamb for the world, marking our foreheads with his blood so that we might escape the world's reign of terror.

Yet those in power in Israel have had enough of Jesus. He had for days taught and argued with them in the temple, challenging their understanding of what it meant for Israel to be faithful. So the chief priests and elders of the people gather in the palace of high priest Caiaphas to conspire against him. They conspire to arrest Jesus by stealth and even plan to kill him. However, like Herod, they fear those whose support they needed to sustain their power. They therefore agreed not to arrest him during the Passover festival, fearing that if they tried to arrest him a riot might occur. However, those seeking to do Jesus harm are resourceful. They will return.

While Jesus is in Bethany in the house of Simon the leper, a woman came to him with an alabaster jar of costly ointment and poured it on his head while he sat at the table. Jesus is again in the presence of those considered unclean. Yet this extraordinary woman, this anonymous woman, comes to Jesus, defying any boundaries to anoint him with precious oil. Samuel anointed David to be king (1 Sam. 16:12–13), and the priest Zadok anointed Solomon to be king (1 Kgs. 1:39), and this woman anoints Jesus who is a king destined to die.

The disciples become angry and protest the woman's action, pointing out that the ointment was valuable and could have been sold and the money given to the poor. They have, after all, just heard Jesus commend those who care for the hungry, the thirsty, and the naked. But Jesus commanded them not to trouble this woman because they will always have the poor with them, but they will not always have the bodily Jesus with them. This woman has anointed Jesus's body in preparation for his death and burial.

Jesus's response to the disciples has sometimes been used to justify Christian wealth. Jesus's observation that we will always have the poor with us seems a counsel to justify ways of life that assume there is nothing we can do to eliminate poverty. Yet Christianity is a faith of the poor. This woman poured precious ointment on a poor person. The poor that we will always have with us is Jesus. It is to the poor that all extravagance is to be given. The wealth of the church is the wealth of the poor. The beauty of a cathedral is a beauty that does not exclude but in fact draws and includes the poor. The beauty of the church's liturgy, its music and its hymns, is a beauty of and for the poor. The literature of the church, its theology and philosophy, are distorted if they do not contribute to our common life, life in which the poor are central, determined by the worship of God. The church's wealth, the precious ointment poured by this woman on Jesus, is never wasted on the poor.

No doubt such an account of the church's wealth can be an invitation to self-deception and a justification of injustice. Yet "the poor you always have with you" is not a description to legitimate a lack of concern for the poor, but rather a description of a faithful church. This woman, this unnamed woman, has done for Jesus what the church must always be for the world—precious ointment poured lavishly on the poor.

Prudentius, a Christian poet and contemporary of Ambrose, celebrated the life of Saint Lawrence. Lawrence was a deacon in the church of Rome in the middle of the third century. Lawrence, the senior deacon of the church of San Lorenzo, was in charge of the "holy things," the liturgical objects such as the chalices and candlesticks, but also the treasury. The prefect of the city had heard that Christian priests offered sacrifices in vessels of gold and silver cups and asked Lawrence to place before him the wealth of the church. According to Prudentius, Lawrence replied:

> Our church is rich.
> I deny it not.
> Much wealth and gold it has
> No one in the world has more.

Accordingly, Lawrence promised to bring forth all the "precious possessions of Christ" if the prefect would give him three days to gather the church's wealth.

The prefect gave Lawrence the three days, which Lawrence used to gather the sick and the poor:

> The people he collected included a man with two eyeless sockets, a cripple with a broken knee, a one-legged man, a person with one leg shorter than the other, and others with grave infirmities. He writes down their names and lines them up at the entrance of the church. Only then does he seek out the perfect to bring him to the church. When the perfect enters the doors of the church, Lawrence points to the ragged company and says, "There are the church's riches, take them." Enraged at being mocked, the prefect orders Lawrence to be executed but adds, "I shall not let you die in a hurry." (Wilken 2003, 225–26)[1]

Lawrence exemplifies what it means for the church to always to have the poor with us. It is not the church's task to make the poor rich. Of course, rich and poor Christians alike are called to serve one another, which means that the hungry are to be fed and the naked clothed. But the church is the church of the poor, drawing from the riches discovered by people who must learn to care for one another because such care is the richness produced by following Jesus.

Jesus tells us, therefore, that wherever the good news is proclaimed in the world, what this woman did for him will be told in remembrance of her. Her anonymity is the anonymity of the poor. Her anonymity is the anonymity we all share. Our names will be lost in the mist of history. We fear being lost, but our fear is a form of unfaithfulness. She is our forbearer. We do not need to know her name or the name of the countless poor who have faithfully served Jesus, because what she and they have done is remembered by the one alone who has given us his body and blood so that we might become remembered through remembrance of him: "This is my body, which is given for you. Do this in remembrance of me. This is my blood of the new covenant, which is shed for you and for many for the forgiveness of sins. Whenever you drink it, do this for remembrance of me."

Jesus's extravagance angers the disciples. One of the twelve, Judas Iscariot, went to the chief priests and asked what they would give him to betray Jesus. Matthew does not tell us why Judas betrays Jesus. That he was given thirty pieces of silver suggests that money was not irrelevant. Indeed in the gospel of John we are told that Judas was a thief (John 12:6). We recoil at the thought that Jesus might be betrayed for something as trivial as money. But Jesus has told us that we cannot serve God and mammon. Judas, it seems, has made his choice. Evil, the darkest evil, too often comes disguised in the insignificant.

Nor do we know why the chief priests thought they needed Judas. He will be used to indicate the time when Jesus might be captured and to identify Jesus, but Judas seems to be a minor player in the drama of Jesus's crucifixion. He is given thirty shekels of silver—the same amount of the wages reported in Zech.

---

1. Prudentius reports that Lawrence was killed by being roasted on a gridiron.

11:7–17 given to the shepherd appointed in the hope that the sheep of Israel and Judah could be one. That shepherd was commanded by God to throw the silver into the treasury in the house of the Lord to indicate the inadequacy of the shepherd.

What God commanded the shepherd to do was a prophetic judgment, but Judas does what he does for no good reason. He is evil personified, doing what he does for the love of evil itself. Judas, this pathetic man, has come completely under the power of the devil. The evil that he does is done blindly, but evil by its very nature is blind. Evil cannot see what it does because if evil was able to comprehend itself it would not be evil.

Betrayal now marks the time Jesus has before he is to die. The disciples ask Jesus where he wants them to make preparations for the Passover meal. They have no home and it is the first day of the Feast of Unleavened Bread. The Feast of Unleavened Bread marks a time that Jesus at once shares and will reconfigure. He tells his disciples that they are to go into the city to a "certain man," again a man with no name, and tell him that "the Teacher says, My time is near; I will keep the Passover at your house with my disciples." Just as Jesus had sent the disciples into the village to bring the donkey and colt to him for his entry into Jerusalem, he now sends the disciples into the city to secure a room in which they can prepare the Passover meal.

Jesus tells the disciples that his time is near. Not yet is the time to which the disciples are being drawn, that is, the time of Jesus's death and resurrection. But he begins to draw them into his time through the meal he will share with them, a meal in which betrayal is ever present. As they are eating the meal in which they remember God's deliverance of Israel from the angel of death, Jesus tells the disciples that one of them will betray him. They have followed him this far. They share this meal with him. They cannot believe one of them will betray Jesus. They are distressed and say to one another, "Surely not I, Lord?" They will all betray him; sin is seldom recognized through self-reflection.

Jesus observes that the one who has dipped his hand into the bowl with him, who has washed his hands with Jesus, is the one who will betray him. The very gesture of cleanliness becomes the sign of betrayal. Jesus pronounces a woe on the one who betrays the Son of Man: it would have been better if his betrayer had not been born. What perfidy Judas enacts. He has been called to be a disciple of Jesus. He has been with Jesus, heard him teach, witnessed the healings of the blind, lame, deaf, mute, heard his disputations with the Pharisees, Sadducees, and elders, but still he will betray him. The devil, all that is evil, is parasitic on the good, but Judas, the devil's child, is parasitic on the *one* who is the good.

Judas responds with the other disciples: "Surely, not I, Rabbi?" The other disciples, however, had addressed their question to the "Lord," but Judas calls him "rabbi." Judas, of course, is not wrong to call him rabbi. Sending the disciples to the man with a house where they could celebrate Passover, Jesus had told them to say that the "teacher's" time had grown near. Judas rightly calls him rabbi, but Judas does not recognize that he is more than the teacher. Jesus's only response to Judas, as is his response to us, is to point out that Judas's own words incriminate him.

Judas's betrayal, however, cannot deter Jesus from his mission. While they were eating, Jesus took a loaf of bread, blessed it, broke it, and gave it to the disciples, commanding them to take it and eat it, for "this is my body." Jesus first gives thanks, making this a eucharist. He is not thanking his Father only for feeding us with bread, but he is thanking his Father for making him the bread that will give life. He breaks the bread, anticipating that his body will be broken on the cross, and gives it to his disciples. He tells the disciples to take and eat, for this is his body. The disciples begin to learn that they can take, they can act, because of what they are being given. Instead of the multiplication of the loaves that testified to God's abundance in the feeding of the five thousand and the four thousand, at this meal the disciples share directly in God's abundance.

Jesus then took a cup; again he gave thanks and shared the cup with them, commanding them to "drink from it, all of you; for this is my blood of the covenant, which is poured out for many for the forgiveness of sins." Moses, after he had received from the Lord all the ordinances to which the people agreed to obey, threw blood on the people, telling them, "See the blood of the covenant that the LORD has made with you in accordance with all these words" (Exod. 24:3–8). Jesus, God's covenant, now becomes for us the forgiveness that makes possible our participation in God's redemption of the world.

The forgiveness we become through baptism means that we are brought into the time created through Jesus's life, death, and resurrection. To be forgiven means that the disciples' betrayal, our betrayal, is subsumed by God's more determinative redemptive purpose for his creation. To be so redeemed makes possible the recognition of our betrayal, because sin is bounded by God's more determinative purposes. Forgiveness, therefore, is not a simple exchange between God and us, but rather the naming of a people who have become participants in a history that is an alternative to the history of the denial of God—a history of death that only leads to more death.

Jesus insists that "all of you" are to drink from the cup, making clear that Judas will also share the cup. Judas, however, drinks to his death, unable to join the kingdom of life. In his first letter to the Corinthians, Paul berates the Corinthians for abusing the Lord's Supper by ignoring those who hunger and by giving into self-indulgence, leading to drunkenness. Paul observes that when they abuse that which they have been given, they eat and drink judgment on themselves: "For this reason many of you are weak and ill, and some have died" (1 Cor. 11:30). Judas will commit suicide, unable to bear the sin of his betrayal.

The salvation wrought by Jesus is not ethereal. The salvation he has brought is as physical as the food we eat that is necessary to keep us alive. Jesus is our teacher, but what he has taught is inseparable from what he is and has done. The people of Israel are a people located on a land with a distinct history. Jesus is no less landed and provides no less a distinct history. The invitation to share his body and blood, his command that we eat his body and drink his blood, constitutes the creation of a people who are to be in the world as he was in the world.

Jesus's command that his disciples eat his body and drink his blood is a challenge to all accounts of Christianity that would separate the truth of the gospel from the flesh and blood of the Eucharist. The gospel is not a philosophical truth that can be known apart from its embodiment in a concrete body of people constituted by baptism and Eucharist. The Protestant emphasis on faith has too often had the unfortunate effect of making the gospel a provocative account of the human condition that can provide meaning for one's life. The gospel may provide meaning for many people, but it first offers a life and a people through which our bodies are inscribed into a world otherwise unavailable.

To let our attention be determined by questions of how or when this bread and wine becomes the body and blood of Jesus is an indication that the church has forgotten that more important than this issue is that the Eucharist is enacted. Too often accounts of how or when the elements became the body and blood are attempts to provide mechanistic explanations, assuming that God cannot get into his creation because creation is something "back there." But we must remember that "salvation is created in the midst of the earth!" (Pavel Tschcanikopf). The God who created us continues to create and redeem. The first sentence of Matthew's gospel made that clear. By being made sharers in Jesus's body and blood, we participate in the new creation.

The God who is in Christ, very God and very man, is also the God that has no difficulty in being found in the bread and wine made for us the body and blood of Christ. The church does not just remember Jesus when we do what he commanded we do, but in fact we become Jesus's memory for the world so that the world might be reconciled. We do not remind the world of Jesus as if he is dead and our memory keeps him alive. The exact opposite is true; because Jesus lives we can be made participants in his time. The Eucharist is the feast that makes Christ's time the time in which his people live. Thus we say: "Christ has died, Christ has risen, Christ will come again."

Therefore, Jesus tells his disciples that he will not again drink of the fruit of the vine until he drinks it anew with them in his Father's kingdom. The meal that he shares at Passover with his disciples becomes the meal he continues to share with the church through his resurrection and ascension and the sending of the Holy Spirit. This meal, therefore, becomes the meal of unity binding Christians through time and space to be one body, one Christ, for the world. That we have been made one makes it impossible, therefore, for Christians to contemplate killing other Christians with whom we share this meal. Such killing is not murder (although sometimes it may take that form), it is suicide.

Jesus had told his disciples that the Son of Man would give his life as a ransom for many (Matt. 20:28). Accordingly, the language of sacrifice often shapes Christian celebration of the Eucharist. Indeed, in the book of Hebrews we are told that by Jesus's death—a death in which we participate through the meal he has invited us to share—a "single offering" has been made, perfecting "for all time those who are sanctified" (Heb. 10:13–14). A sacrifice has been made, the sacrifice of Jesus's death, which has brought to an end all those sacrifices made in the hope that such sacrifices might remove our sins.

Sacrifice is the preeminent human action that embodies our desire to return all that is to God. God created us to be animals that sacrifice. God instructed Israel through the law to sacrifice to him, but Israel proved, as we all prove, capable of turning God's good gift of sacrifice into a device to serve the presumption that we are our own creator. In Jesus, God joined his life to our life, becoming one of us, to free us from the attempt to determine our relationship to him on our terms. The Father sent the Son, humbled in human form, obedient to the point of death, even the death on a cross, to end forever any sacrifice not determined by Jesus's cross. Our Father restrained Abraham, providing a ram in place of Isaac, but did not spare his only Son from becoming for us the sacrifice necessary to free us from our endless attempts to atone for our sins on our own terms. This is the forgiveness of sins we receive when we eat and drink with Jesus.

Matthew tells us that after the meal the disciples, like Moses, sang "the hymn" and went to the Mount of Olives. Matthew does not tell us what hymn the disciples sang, but it may well have been all or part of Ps. 114–18 because those psalms are often sung at the end of Passover to celebrate God's care of Israel and, in particular, the rescue from Egypt:

> When Israel went out from Egypt,
>   the house of Jacob from a people of strange language,
> Judah became God's sanctuary,
>   Israel his dominion.
> The sea looked and fled;
>   Jordan turned back.
> The mountains skipped like rams,
>   the hills like lambs.
> Why is it, O sea, that you flee?
>   O Jordan, that you turn back?
> O mountains, that you skip like rams?
>   O hills, like lambs?
> Tremble, O earth, at the presence of the LORD,
>   at the presence of the God of Jacob,
> who turns the rock into a pool of water,
>   the flint into a spring of water. (Ps. 114)

Much is made of this text by those who argue that Christians must be nonviolent as well as by those who argue that the sword has an appropriate place in God's care of the world. The latter argue that Jesus's command that the sword be put "back into its place" suggests, appealing to Rom. 13, that the sword has a proper role in government. Such a reading can be tested only by whether it does justice to the overall configuration of Jesus's teaching and ministry. At the very least it seems that such a reading bears the burden of proof. Jesus's general observation that those who use the sword will perish by the sword seems to apply equally to those who would use the sword on behalf of governmental authority. It is not irrelevant that in the book of Revelation we are told:

> Let anyone who has an ear listen:
> If you are to be taken captive,
>   into captivity you go;
> if you kill with the sword,
>   with the sword you must be killed. (Rev. 13:9–10)

However, Jesus's command that the sword be put away is not a conclusive text, committing his followers to some version of pacifism. Arguments for Christian nonviolence, just as arguments for the Christian justification of violence, depend on how the story is told and the kind of community that exists to tell the story. Jesus's command that the sword be put away is but one expression that testifies to his willingness to be given over to sinners and crucified so that we might be made part of the new age inaugurated by his birth, death, and resurrection. Therefore, Christian nonviolence cannot be a position separable from what it means to be a disciple. Rather, Christian nonviolence is, in the words of John Howard Yoder, the pacifism of the messianic community. Such pacifism would "lose its substance if Jesus were not Christ and would lose its foundation if Jesus Christ were not Lord" (1992, 134). Yoder observes:

Since Jesus is seen in his full humanity as responding to needs and temptations of a social character, the problems of our obedience to him are not problems in the interpretation of text. Nor is the question of our fidelity to him one of moralism, a stuffy preoccupation with never making a mistake. The question put to us as we follow Jesus is not whether we have successfully refrained from breaking any rules. Instead, we are asked whether we have been participants in that human experience, that peculiar way of living for God in the world and being used as instruments of the living of God in the world, which the Bible calls *agape* or cross.

When we speak of the pacifism of the messianic community, we move the focus of ethical concern from the individual to the human community experiencing in its shared life a foretaste of God's kingdom. Persons may severally and separately ask themselves about right and wrong in their concern for their own integrity. That is fine as far as it goes. The messianic community's experience, however, is different in that it is not a life alone for heroic personalities. Instead, it is a life

So sang the disciples celebrating God's care of Israel in a time in which Israel was anything but victorious. That they sang the hymn, or one like it, is a significant political act. Singing can be a form of resistance, because to sing not only witnesses to but creates community. Singing, next to eating, is the most physical and communal form of behavior. Our voice comes from our body. When we sing our bodies are joined, making possible a good in common that cannot be destroyed even when a people are under occupation or persecution or otherwise do not seem to be in control of their own destiny. The Psalms are testimony to Israel's understanding of how to survive as a people—the very form of survival is a song. It is, therefore, not surprising that a community bound in unity through the body and blood of Jesus is also a community that not only sings but must sing.

Jesus and the disciples return to the Mount of Olives. Jesus gives his disciples the unhappy news that all of them will desert him this very night. In Ezek. 34, God promises to seek out the scattered sheep of Israel, but Jesus quotes Zech. 13:7, where we are told that the shepherd will be struck down and the sheep of the flock scattered. Jesus will be left alone and he will die alone, but he tells his disciples that he will not desert them. Rather, he will go ahead of them to meet them in Galilee.

Peter again tries to distinguish himself from the rest of the disciples, denying that he would ever desert Jesus. Jesus knows better, telling Peter that before the cock crows Peter will deny him three times. Peter protests, claiming that he is even willing to die with him rather than to deny him. It seems that Peter, the same Peter who had rebuked Jesus for showing his disciples that he must go to Jerusalem to die, now understands that Jesus will be put to death. All the disciples in turn echo Peter's declaration of their willingness to die rather than to betray Jesus.

It is surely the case that most of us identify with Peter's and the other disciples' claims to be ready to follow Jesus to death, but we have no idea what we mean when we declare our willingness to die rather than desert Jesus. Christianity, at least in America, has made us safe, making it impossible for American Christians to know what it might mean to risk our lives because of our unwillingness to deny Jesus. It is not for us to try to create risk in Jesus's name in the hope that we may recover some sense of what it might be to be a disciple of Jesus. To do that would only further our temptation to "play" at being Christian. To try to create risk would be an attempt to be heroic rather than to be disciple. Not knowing what it would mean to follow Jesus to death, we can at least be a church that remembers that we are built on the blood of the martyrs. The blood of the martyrs is still the seed of the church, and we should thank God that even in our time we are given martyrs such as Oscar Romero.

It does not take long for the disciples, at least some of the disciples, to test their resolve not to desert Jesus. Jesus goes with the disciples to a place called Gethsemane. He told his disciples to sit while he went "over there" to pray. He takes with him Peter, James, and John, the disciples he had taken with him at the transfiguration. He began to be grieved and agitated, that is, he manifests the agony so often expressed in the Psalms:

> Why are you cast down, O my soul,
> and why are you disquieted within me?
> Hope in God; for I shall again praise him,
> my help and my God. (Ps. 42:11)

Jesus tells his disciples that he is deeply grieved, even to death, asking them to remain with him and to stay awake while he prays. He prays: "My Father, if it is possible, let this cup pass from me; yet not what I want but what you want." He has told the disciples many times that he must go to Jerusalem to be crucified. Jesus now faces not just death, but separation from his Father. On the cross he will cry, "My God, my God, why have you forsaken me?" Jesus, the Son of God, must undergo the terror of being alone, not just being abandoned by his disciples, but abandoned by his Father.

This is a terror that only Jesus can know, because only Jesus knows the intimacy of being the Son. Israel, God's beloved people, has intimated the agony that Jesus will undergo in its Psalms. Psalm 22, the psalm that begins with Jesus's cry from the cross, is a psalm that begs the Lord to "not be far away! / O my help, come quickly to my aid" (22:19). Such a plea draws from the depths of God's love of Israel. In Isaiah, we know that Israel's redeemer will be so marred that his appearance will be

> beyond human semblance,
> and his form beyond that of mortals—
> so he shall startle many nations. (Isa. 52:14–15)

This is the terror that Jesus encounters in Gethsemane. He is facing an aloneness no one has ever faced. He returns to his disciples and finds them sleeping. He says to Peter, "So, could you not stay awake with me one hour?" He tells Peter to stay awake and pray, as Peter was taught by Jesus in the Sermon on the Mount, to "not come into the time of trial." Jesus, who shares Peter's humanity, observes that Peter's spirit is willing but his flesh is weak. Peter's failure is not, however, that he cannot stay awake, but that he and the disciples with Jesus do not pray. Jesus again goes away to pray: "My Father, if this cannot pass unless I drink it, your will be done." He has shared the cup of his blood with his disciples, but now he asks as he taught us to ask, that the Father's will be done. He must, alone, undergo what only the Son of God can do.

Again he comes to the disciples and finds them sleeping. In the boat Jesus slept even though the boat was threatened by the chaos of a storm. The disciples, whose flesh is weak and faith little, asked Jesus to save them. In the garden, when

the chaos of the world threatens the kingdom, the disciples sleep, i[ndicating] that they have not yet learned what is the true danger. Like the maid[ens in the] parable of the ten bridesmaids, the disciples failed to understand the [importance] of being prepared. By sleeping they retreat into the dreams and fant[asies that] always tempt us as modes of escape from the reality of Jesus's agony.

This time Jesus does not try to awaken the disciples, but continue[s] his prayer of agony. Prayer, it seems, is the alternative to sleep, becaus[e to pray] is to make our lives vulnerable to God. Through his prayer, moreov[er, Jesus] knows that his hour has come. All that he has taught the disciples t[o expect] is now at hand. The Son of Man is betrayed into the hands of sinne[rs. Jesus] tells his disciples to get up, because his betrayer is at hand. Jesus says, [let us] be going." Remarkably he continues to address his disciples as "us"; [he has] promised not to abandon them or us even as we desert him.

But while Jesus was speaking, Judas arrives with a large crowd fr[om the] chief priests and elders to arrest him. The crowd comes with clu[bs and] swords. Jesus, who has preached against retaliation and commanded [us to] love our enemies (Matt. 5:38–48), is besieged by an armed crowd. W[e do] not know if any in this crowd were among those amazed and astonish[ed by] what Jesus taught or the cures he performed, or if these are among [those] who welcomed him to Jerusalem. Regardless, that a crowd has come [to ar]rest him suggests that it is never sufficient to admire Jesus. Admiratio[n too] easily turns to betrayal.

Judas, however, has been a disciple. Even being among those who [have] been privileged to be called by Jesus does not mean that we will be safe [from] betraying him. Indeed the betrayal is all the more poignant because of Ju[das's] closeness to Christ. Judas betrays Jesus with a kiss—a gesture of love use[d to] betray love. Just as he had at the Last Supper, Judas addresses Jesus as "rab[bi,"] identifying him so that the crowd will know on whom they are to lay their ha[nds.] Jesus addresses Judas as "friend," commanding him to do what he has c[ome] to do, that is, betray his master. In the parable of the vineyard, the landow[ner] had addressed those hired at the beginning of the day as "friend," indicat[ing] he had done them no wrong (Matt. 20:13). Jesus now uses the same addre[ss] making clear that he has done Judas no wrong, but Judas wills not to be p[art] of a kingdom of friendship.

Suddenly, one of those with Jesus puts his hand on his sword, draws it, a[nd] cuts off the ear of the slave of the high priest. Matthew does not tell us if th[is] was one of the disciples. That anyone with Jesus, anyone who has listened [to] Jesus's preaching, would carry as well as use a sword seems odd, but knowin[g] that his disciples will abandon him should alert us to the weakness of the flesh. Jesus commands that the sword be put "back into its place; for all who tak[e] the sword will perish by the sword." Jesus intimates that, if he asked, his Fathe[r] would send twelve legions of angels to protect him, but to do so would mea[n] that the scriptures would not be fulfilled.

for a society. It is communal in that it is lived by a covenanting group of men
and women who instruct one another, forgive one another, bear one another's
burdens, and reinforce one another's witness. (Yoder 1992, 134–35)

It is, therefore, the cross that is the crucial event that determines how we
are to understand Jesus's command to put away the sword. Jesus could ask the
Father to send legions of angels, but that would not fulfill the scripture. The
cross is the fulfillment of scripture. Jesus, as we know from Isa. 53:7–9, will be
the lamb that is to be led to slaughter, who will not open his mouth but remain
silent, who will be cut off from the land of the living by a perversion of justice,
stricken for the transgressions of his people. Such is the fate that awaits Jesus.

Accordingly, Jesus challenges the crowd, asking why they have come to
Gethsemane with swords and clubs to arrest him as if he were a bandit. Bandits do their work under the cover of night and hide during the day. Day after
day Jesus taught in the temple, but they did not try to arrest him there. Jesus
tells them they are part of a larger drama: "all this" has taken place so that the
scriptures and the prophets may be fulfilled. Matthew's whole gospel has been
an ongoing instruction that we might understand what Jesus says to the crowd
who has come to arrest him. Jesus's life and death fulfill the trajectory that has
been at the heart of Israel's life with God. Jesus is the work that God has always
desired for Israel through the law and the prophets.

His disciples desert Jesus and flee. We knew that this was to happen, but
that it happens now, in a moment, seems surprising yet quite revealing. That
Jesus is arrested, that Jesus is bound over to his enemies, that Jesus will be
tried, could well frighten the disciples. But Jesus has also just refused to fight
or to be defended in the way that the world understands fighting or resisting.
Jesus is a king but he will not triumph as kings triumph. Jesus has no army
other than an army of angels. He will face death unarmed. The disciples desert
him because they see no way to defend him. They have not yet understood
the radical character of the kingdom that would challenge the violence of the
world by refusing to respond on the world's terms.

Oddly enough, the crowd that came to arrest Jesus understood that he was a
political threat. He may well have looked like a bandit to them, particularly if
the bandit was one who was a political rebel. What they failed to understand was
that Jesus is more radical than those who rebel against Rome or other empires
using the force of arms. Rome knows how to deal with those who oppose it on
its own terms. What Rome and all empires fear are those who refuse its terms
of battle. Jesus has more time than Rome to engage in the work of calling into
existence a people who have learned to live trusting in the goodness of God.

Jesus, as he knew he would, now must face the world alone. The world takes
the form of Caiaphas, the high priest, who has gathered the scribes and elders
to his home so that evidence against Jesus might be fabricated. Matthew reports
that Peter followed at a distance, coming as close as the courtyard, sitting with

the guards "to see how this would end." "Following at a distance" is a wonderful description for the way most of us follow Jesus. We want, as Peter wanted, to see how all this will end before we commit ourselves. Unfortunately, that strategy means that we cannot help but end up sitting with the guardians of the established order.

The chief priests and the whole council were looking for those who would give false testimony against Jesus so that they might put him to death. However, in order to put someone to death at least two witnesses must agree in their testimony (Deut. 17:6). Many false witnesses came forward but their testimony could not be made to agree. At last, however, two came forward claiming that Jesus had said, "I am able to destroy the temple of God and to build it in three days." Jesus had certainly cleansed the temple (Matt. 21:12–17), he had predicted that the temple would be destroyed (24:1–2), but he had not said that he would destroy the temple of God and rebuild it in three days.[2]

Yet there is some truth in the accusation. Jesus has acted as the one who will be the temple in his person. His crucifixion is the "desolating sacrilege" spoken of by Daniel the prophet. He is the end of the sacrifices of the temple. He will be resurrected after three days, becoming the one alone worthy of worship. So from the lips of false witnesses comes truth, but it is a truth neither they nor their hearers can understand, for to understand this truth requires that they have learned to read their scriptures through the life of Jesus.

The high priest has finally heard what he has wanted to hear. The prophet Nathan told David that only one appointed by God could build the temple (2 Sam. 7:12–13). For anyone to claim the right to destroy the temple would be equivalent to the claim that they are God. Therefore, to claim that one can destroy the temple would be blasphemy. The high priest, therefore, challenges Jesus to respond to his accusers, but he remains, as we were told he would in Isa. 53:7, silent. Jesus will also remain silent before Pilate, but that silence is the silence necessary to challenge uncomprehending political power. Jesus refuses to speak in response to the high priest's challenge because his truthful response cannot be heard as true.

Yet the high priest says to him, "I put you under oath before the living God, tell us if you are the Messiah, the Son of God." The high priest puts under oath the one who has forbidden his followers to take oaths (Matt. 5:33–37). The high priest, just as the devil had when he tempted Jesus (4:3), challenges Jesus to say if he is the Messiah, the Son of God. Jesus responds, as he responded to Judas at the Last Supper: "You have said so." Jesus, however, has more to say: "But I tell you" that "from now you will see the Son of Man / seated at the right hand of Power / and coming on the clouds of heaven" (quoting Dan.

---

2. In John 2:19 Jesus does say he will rebuild the temple in three days, but he is speaking of his resurrection.

7:13). Jesus answers by making clear that the Son of God and the Son of Man are the same. The nearer Jesus comes to crucifixion the various titles used to identify him become one.

The high priest tears his garment, accusing Jesus of blasphemy. Jesus—the one who had said every sin but blasphemy can be forgiven (Matt. 12:31–32)—is now accused of blasphemy. Jesus, the one alone incapable of blasphemy, is identified by the high priest as being a blasphemer. The high priest declares that witnesses are no longer required because they are all witnesses to Jesus's acknowledgment that he is the Son of God. The chief priest asks for the council's verdict, knowing the answer will be, "He deserves death." Then they spit in his face (Isa. 50:6), strike him, slap him, and taunt him, saying, "Prophesy to us, you Messiah! Who is it that struck you?"

Soon the crowd will pronounce judgment on themselves when they say in response to Pilate's declaration of Jesus's innocence that Jesus's "blood be on us and on our children" (Matt. 27:25). In a terrible and terrifying ironic judgment, in similar fashion Jesus's tormentors who spit, strike, and slap him and ask him to prophesy become the fulfillment of prophecy. They confirm, just as the sham trial that Jesus has endured before the chief priest, scribes, and elders has confirmed, that he is indeed the Messiah, the Son of God.

We are tempted to think that if we had been there, we would have recognized Jesus for who he was and is, but Peter was there and failed to see that Jesus is the fulfillment of prophecy. Moreover, Peter saw "how this would end," but seeing Jesus mocked and tormented did not confirm for him his expectations of what the Messiah would be. Peter, who had identified Jesus as "the Messiah, the Son of the living God" (Matt. 16:16), in answer to a servant girl's question whether he was not one of those associated with Jesus the Galilean, denies that he even knows what the girl is talking about. There is truth to Peter's response. He does not know what the young servant asks, because he has failed to understand why Jesus must die.

Peter is identified by another servant girl to the bystanders as a man who had been with Jesus of Nazareth. Again he denies that he has been a follower of Jesus, even swearing an oath that he does "not know the man." Peter, who had heard Jesus command his followers not to swear oaths (Matt. 5:33–37), now swears an oath to deny that he has been associated with Jesus. Just as it has been clear that to follow Jesus requires a new way of life, it is equally true that to deny him means that we will find ourselves living a quite different life than Jesus described in the Sermon on the Mount.

Peter, however, is identified by the bystanders by his accent. He is, as the servant girls noted, a Galilean. His accent has betrayed him. This is the first suggestion we have that Jesus's and his disciples' Galilean roots might make them stick out in Jerusalem. But Peter is determined to dissociate himself from Jesus. He not only swears by an oath that he does not know Jesus, but he curses. Matthew does not tell us what kind of curse Peter uses, but cursing seems to have been his attempt to show that he is a very different person than those who have followed Jesus.

At that moment a cock crows and Peter remembered that Jesus had told him that before the cock crows he will deny Jesus three times. Peter is devastated by being forced to recognize, in spite of his declaration never to desert Jesus, that he has denied him three times. He leaves the vicinity of the courtyard of the high priest and weeps bitter tears. This is the last time we will hear of or from Peter in Matthew's gospel. Peter is left, as we are so often left, in tears, mourning our unfaithfulness to Jesus.

It is well that Jesus has named Peter to be the rock on which he will build his church. Peter's bitter tears must always be the tears of the church, for the church, like Peter, finds itself in the position of having denied that we know Jesus. Even worse, the Jesus we claim to know has little relation to this Jesus who has been handed over to the chief priest, scribes, and elders. Jesus has rightly directed us to Peter as the rock on whom the church will be built, because he is the first among sinners.

MATTHEW 27

Crucifixion

Jesus was tried and condemned by the chief priests, scribes, and elders under the cover of night. They now bring to light what was done in darkness in order to confirm their previous unjust judgment. They play an old and well-established game: Jesus must be guilty, because he is now under arrest. The very fact that he is to be handed over to Pilate confirms their judgments against him. Those in prison must deserve to be in prison because they are in prison.

The chief priests and elders, moreover, are unrelenting in their desire to bring about Jesus's death. It is not enough that he has been beaten and ridiculed. He must be killed. Yet the right to kill belongs to Rome. So the chief priests and elders hand him over to Pilate the governor. Jesus's fate will be determined by a Gentile, a minor official of Rome, who has the responsibility to keep order among what the Romans consider to be a troublesome people.

Pilate's name plays a crucial role in Christian theology. In the Apostles' Creed we affirm that Jesus "suffered under Pontius Pilate." Karl Barth observes that Pilate's name makes it unmistakably clear that

> this Passion of Jesus Christ, this unveiling of man's rebellion and of God's wrath, yet also His mercy, did not take place in heaven or in some remote planet or even in some world of ideas; it took place in our time, in the centre of the world-history in which our human life is played out. So we must not escape from this life. We must not take flight to a better land, or to some height or other unknown, nor to any spiritual Cloud-Cuckooland nor to a Christian fairyland. God has come into our life in its utter unloveliness and frightfulness. That the Word became flesh also means that it became temporal, historical. It assumed the form which belongs to the human creature, in which there are such folk as this very

Pontius Pilate—the people we belong to and who are also ourselves at any time on a slightly larger scale! It is not necessary to close our eyes to this, for God has not closed His either; He has entered into it all. The Incarnation of the Word is an extremely concrete event, in which a human name may play a part. God's Word has the character of the *hic et nunc*. There is nothing in the opinion of Lessing that God's Word is an "eternal truth of reason," and not an "accidental truth of history." God's history is indeed an accidental truth of history, like this petty commandant. God was not ashamed to exist in this accidental state. To the factors which determined our human time and human history belong, in virtue of the name of Pontius Pilate, the life and Passion of Jesus as well. We are not left alone in this frightful world. Into this alien land God has come to us. (Barth 1959, 109)

Israel's life was always intertwined with the lives of other people and nations. She could not escape from the world. After Babel, she was called, through Abraham, to be a people to dwell among the peoples of the world so that they might witness to the holiness of God. Israel was seldom in control of its fate, more often she was subject to the will of more powerful nations. Through it all she learned to survive, but survival sometimes was but a word for unfaithfulness. Jesus came to offer Israel more than survival. He came to offer her redemption, but instead he finds himself handed over by the chief priests and elders of the people to Pilate. Yet again, representatives of Israel try to use the powers of the world for their own ends but they cannot avoid being used in return.

Judas, like Peter, has witnessed Jesus's condemnation, and, for reasons that Matthew does not disclose, Judas changed his mind about what he had done. He brings back to the chief priests and elders the thirty pieces of silver, confessing, "I have sinned by betraying innocent blood." Judas tries to be faithful to the law, using the language of Deut. 27:25: "Cursed be anyone who takes a bribe to shed innocent blood." Judas attempts to undo what cannot be undone. What he has done cannot be undone because those with whom he is dealing do not understand the forgiveness that Jesus enacts.

"What is that to us? See to it yourself." Judas discovers that he is but a minor player in a larger game. Ironically, the very words that the chief priests and elders use in response to Judas will also be used by Pilate to place the responsibility of Jesus's death on the "whole people" (Matt. 27:24–25). Judas, however, is but one man caught in a decision that has consequences so dark that he cannot comprehend how his life can continue to be lived. He hangs himself.

Some in the Christian tradition have wondered if Judas's so-called repentance means that he has escaped damnation. Such speculation risks focusing on Judas rather than on the one whom Judas betrayed. What Judas did is not beyond the forgiveness enacted in Jesus's crucifixion. Indeed, Judas's betrayal can be remembered because it is not and cannot be the last word about Judas's life or our own. The last word about Judas or us is not ours to determine because the last word has been said in the crucifixion. The challenge is not whether Jesus's forgiveness is good, but whether any of us, Judas included, are capable of facing as well as acknowledging that, given the opportunity, we would be willing to betray Jesus for thirty pieces of silver.

Judas threw the thirty pieces of silver into the temple, but the chief priests observe that it is not lawful to put the money into the treasury because it is "blood money." The chief priests who have no difficulty conspiring to put an innocent man to death become quite concerned about what to do with the money they regard as tainted. Again, the law is used not to force the priests to change their lives, but to keep up appearances. Jesus's depiction of the "blind guides" whose primary concerns are with the externals of the law is confirmed by the way the chief priests and elders deal with the blood money (Matt. 23:16–22).

After conferring together, the chief priests and elders agree to use the money to buy the potter's field as a place to bury strangers and foreigners. Matthew observes that this was done so that the prophetic action of Jeremiah in buying a field during the siege of Jerusalem might be fulfilled (Jer. 32:6–15). However, Matthew uses the words of Zech. 11:13 concerning the shepherd's disposing of the thirty pieces of silver to indicate how the prophecy of Jeremiah has come to fruition.

After his resurrection, Jesus will send his disciples to the nations to baptize in the name of the Father, Son, and Holy Spirit, but without knowing that they do so those who have conspired against Jesus begin to enact his gathering of the nations into Israel by buying a field in which those foreign to Israel can be buried. Israel cannot avoid the reality of Jesus. Even the process of having him killed results in the fulfillment of what he has come to do. Just as there can be no church without the continuing presence of the people of Israel, so there can be no Israel without the church.

But Jesus is subject not only to the chief priests and elders, but also to Rome in the person of Pilate. Jesus now stands before Pilate the governor, who asks him, "Are you the King of the Jews?" Pilate is a state official. He asks the question that is the concern of a state official. Jesus has been called the son of David; he has even accepted that title after he has cleansed the temple and cured the blind and the lame in the temple (Matt. 21:14–17). Pilate's question, however, is a question of a Gentile. He does not ask if Jesus is the son of David, but rather if he is the king of the Jews. He wants to know if Jesus may be a rival to Herod. One suspects that it would never occur to Pilate that, in reality, Jesus is a rival to Caesar.

Jesus answers Pilate with, "You say so," the same answer he had given Judas in response to Judas's attempt to hide his betrayal with the rhetorical "surely not I?" Jesus had also given the same response when the high priest demanded that he say whether he is the Son of God. "You say so" is a response that confounds those, including the representative of Rome, who would have Jesus condemn himself. He is a king, but his kingship is not that which Pilate can recognize.

Pilate's inability to understand the politics of Jesus does not mean that Jesus is any less a threat to Rome. Rather, it means that the politics that Jesus represents is a more radical threat to Rome than Rome is capable of recognizing.

The chief priests and elders, however, come to Pilate's aid, making accusations against Jesus. Matthew does not tell us what accusations they make against Jesus. But they are clever men who recognize that a representative of Rome might care little that Jesus claimed to have a special relation to God the Father. Nor would Rome have any particular concern about Jesus's prophecy concerning the temple. Rome, as we shall see, wants order. Pilate is not disposed to try to settle arguments between the people of Israel. Indeed he seems to have no reason or interest to help the chief priests and elders kill Jesus.

Yet Jesus, as he had earlier, remained silent when accused by the chief priests and elders. Pilate is disposed to come to his aid. Pilate asks Jesus if he does not hear the many accusations they make against him. Yet just as Jesus had not responded to the chief priests and elders, he remains silent before Pilate, answering not one of the charges made against him. His silence remains the silence described by Isaiah:

> He was oppressed, and he was afflicted,
>   yet he did not open his mouth;
> like a lamb that is led to the slaughter,
>   and like a sheep that before its shearers is silent,
> so he did not open his mouth. (Isa. 53:7)

Not to answer the chief priests and elders is one thing. It is quite another thing to remain silent before Pilate. Jesus now confronts the power of Rome. That power has no capacity to acknowledge the truth that comes in the form of a suffering servant. That power, moreover, is the power of the old age exposed and rendered futile by the coming of the Son of God. Jesus's silence before Pilate, therefore, is the sign of the end of the power that the Pilates of the world represent. Pilate's power will crucify Jesus, but "when power crucifies truth, it signals to all the world that it has come to its effective end" (Lehmann 1975, 66).

Jesus is silent because he is the new order of truth on which a community of peace is possible. A community of peace is possible only when order does not rest on lies and injustice. Bonhoeffer observes that when a community of order built on lies and injustice is confronted by a community of peace a battle must ensue. What must be recognized is that the only tolerable ground for any community of peace is the forgiveness of sins. According to Bonhoeffer, there is a community of peace for Christians because one will forgive the other for their sins. The peace made possible by forgiveness is the peace of God, which cannot help but challenge all orders that claim to provide peace yet are based on the denial of God (1956, 168–69).

Jesus's silence before Pilate is, therefore, the silence of truth required when confronted by an order built on lies and injustice. Jesus's silence before Pilate is the silence of the church whenever it is faithful to the witness of Jesus before those who would tempt us to confuse order with peace. Jesus's silence before Pilate is the silence necessary to unmask the pretensions of those who would have us believe that the violence they call justice is the only alternative we have to chaos. Jesus submits to Pilate, but his submission cannot help but subvert Pilate's authority. Such is the power of truthful silence.[1]

The governor was "greatly amazed." Pilate, like the crowds who heard Jesus's teaching and witnessed his cures, is amazed. He has not encountered one such as this before. He is used to dealing with the chief priests and elders, who seek to accommodate him in the interest of sustaining their positions. Pilate, however, has nothing that Jesus wants. Jesus does not even ask Pilate for his life. Pilate stands helpless before the one to die, making apparent that he is the one in captivity.

But Pilate seems to be rescued from having to kill Jesus to please the chief priests and elders by the custom that during Passover the governor should release a prisoner for the crowd. Pilate, therefore, has Jesus Barabbas, a notorious prisoner, brought out to give the crowd the choice of releasing or crucifying Jesus or Barabbas. The crowd is gathered and Pilate asks whom they want released. Pilate pits Jesus against Barabbas, hoping to confound the chief priests and elders because Pilate knew that they had handed Jesus over out of jealousy. Pilate seems to have thought the crowd would ask him to release Jesus rather than Barabbas.

Pilate, moreover, has a further motivation to seek the release of Jesus. Pilate's wife has reported to him that she has suffered from a dream she has had about Jesus. Like Joseph's dream about Mary and the wise men's dream about Herod, Pilate's wife had a dream that told her that Jesus is an "innocent man." She sends word to Pilate that he is to have nothing to do with Jesus. Pilate's wife, unlike Herodias, does not desire Jesus's death. Yet the outcome is the same, caught as they are in a politics of death.

Pilate is unable to heed his wife's advice. The chief priests and elders have been at work among the crowd gathered before Pilate. They have persuaded the crowd to ask Pilate to release Barabbas and to crucify Jesus. So when Pilate asks the crowd who they would have him release, they ask for Barabbas.

---

1. Jesus's silence before Pilate does not mean that Christians will always assume a stance of opposition before the governing authorities. Christians are appropriately thankful for those in authority that make possible lives of godliness and honesty (1 Tim. 2:2). Rulers can rule modestly, securing the peace of the earthly city (Rom. 13). Yet we also know, given Jesus's crucifixion, that such rule is rare and fragile. Our task, as those who follow Jesus, is to be for those who rule the truth-determined silence that invites rulers to be no more than God intends them to be. It is, therefore, not unthinkable that those who rule could do so without returning evil for evil (Rom. 12:17). At the very least, however, we can ask them to be honest.

Pilate does not think that to be the end of the matter, so he asks them what he should do with "Jesus who is called the Messiah." This time Pilate does not identify Jesus as the king of the Jews, but identifies Jesus in a manner that the people of Israel would recognize, namely he calls Jesus the Messiah. He is careful, however, not to say he is the Messiah. Rather, Pilate says only that he is "called" the Messiah.

The crowd is unrelenting. They shout, "Let him be crucified!" Pilate is puzzled. He asks the crowd why they would have Jesus killed, because he does not appear to have done anything that is evil. But they shouted "all the more, 'Let him be crucified!'" We cannot help but wonder if any who called for Jesus's crucifixion were among those who heard him deliver the Sermon on the Mount, heal the lame, deaf, and blind, or dispute with the Pharisees, Sadducees, and scribes.

Crowds are fickle and untrustworthy because they depend on opinion. During his ministry, Jesus has had compassion on the crowd, but he has never shown trust in the crowd. Instead, he has taught that if anyone would follow him they must take up their cross and follow him (Matt. 10:37–39). The alternative to the crowd is not to know how to think for oneself, but rather to be a follower of Jesus. Indeed, there are few more conformist messages than the suggestion that we should escape from the crowd by learning to be autonomous. Jesus's call to discipleship is an alternative to the crowd and to our attempt to escape from the crowd on our own.

Pilate, the governor appointed by Rome, cannot escape the crowd. He sees that he can do nothing to avoid doing what the crowd desires, that is, to crucify Jesus. A riot is beginning. Pilate fears a riot worse than he fears the injustice of killing an innocent man. He has been in the middle of the process that condemned Jesus, but now he wishes to free himself of any responsibility. He asks for some water and before the crowd, following the procedures outlined in Deut. 21:1–9 for absolving guilt of one who finds a body outside of the city limits (either murdered or killed by beasts), Pilate washes his hands, saying, "I am innocent of this man's blood; see to it yourselves." Now the crowd, the chief priests, and the elders are in the same position as Judas was when he tried to undo what he had done to Jesus: "See to it yourself."

We know that Jesus will die. That has never been in doubt. But John Milbank rightly asks:

> Who then really killed Jesus and why? And why did Jesus submit to this? The only consistent thread in these narratives is that Christ was constantly handed over, or abandoned to another party. Judas betrayed his presence; the disciples deserted him; the Sanhedrin gave him up to Pilate; Pilate again to the mob who finally gave him over to a Roman execution, which somehow, improperly, they co-opted. Even in his death, Jesus was still being handed back and forth, as if no one actually killed him, but he died from neglect and lack of his own living space. (Milbank 2003, 82)

Milbank's question and observations take on peculiar urgency in the light of the response of the people to Pilate's gesture to free himself from responsibility for Jesus's death: "His blood be on us and on our children!" This declaration has been used by Christians through the centuries to blame Jews for Jesus's death. Many Christians named Jews "Christ killers" and treated them as murderers. Matthew's identification of "the people as a whole," moreover, has made it difficult to deny that it is not just the crowd or the elites that are guilty but all of Israel.

Who killed Jesus, however, cannot be determined by any one text. That it is unclear from the gospels and especially from Matthew who killed Jesus, is not accidental. Matthew, as we have seen from the beginning, has written his gospel in which we cannot avoid being a disciple of Jesus, one of the elites, or a member of the crowd. The answer to the question of who killed Jesus, therefore, is that we all killed Jesus. The disciples killed Jesus by deserting him. The crowd killed Jesus because they were a crowd. The elites of Israel killed Jesus because they feared his call to holiness. Pilate killed Jesus because he had the responsibility to maintain order. "The people as a whole" killed Jesus because they had nothing better to do. We all killed and continue to kill Jesus. So let us all say that "his blood be on us and on our children!"

Jesus must be killed because Jesus is the Son of God. Jesus must be killed because Jesus has called into existence a new people who constitute a challenge to the world order based on lies and deceit. Jesus must be killed because he is a threat to all who rule in the name of safety and comfort. Jesus must be killed because we do not desire to have our deepest desires exposed. Jesus must be killed because we do not want our loves governed by his love. Jesus must be killed because we refuse to forgive our enemies. Jesus must be killed because we do not believe in a God who creates us and who would come among us after our likeness. So we have learned from Matthew.

Pilate releases Barabbas and, after having Jesus flogged, hands Jesus over to be crucified. Why did Pilate have Jesus flogged? Why did Pilate hand Jesus over to his soldiers who would degrade him as Caiaphas and the scribes had done after they had supposedly tried him? Matthew does not tell us why Pilate had Jesus flogged or handed over to the soldiers, but surely one of the reasons is to preserve the humanity of those who will kill Jesus. They are going to kill an innocent man. It, therefore, becomes all the more important that he go to the cross degraded and unrecognizable as a human being. It is easier to kill those who have been literally stripped of all humanity before they are subjected to death. Those doing the killing, therefore, are able to comfort and delude themselves with the thought that they do only the inevitable.

Yet the soldiers of Pilate are more creative than the high priest and elders. They can be so because they are innocent of the traditions and hopes of Israel. They strip Jesus, cover him with a scarlet robe, crown him with a crown of thorns, put a reed in his right hand, and kneel before him, mocking him, "Hail,

King of the Jews!" They literally do not know what they do, but what they have done is acknowledge that this is a king who has come to serve rather than to be served. Their cruelty seems beyond belief. They were incapable of recognizing their cruelty even as they degraded the one who is the very embodiment of kindness. It is not at all clear that we, people who think we are civilized, would have done any better.

They mock Jesus, spitting on him and striking him on the head. But they tire of this game, so they strip him of the robe of scarlet, put his own clothes back on him, and lead him away to be crucified. Jesus is abandoned. Jesus is alone. Jesus says nothing. Jesus endures. This is not what he wants, but it is what the Father wills. The Son must suffer so that we might not only know, but be participants, in the life made possible by Jesus. This is what the Father has desired since Adam and Eve betrayed their creator.

The sadness that we must feel in the face of Jesus's suffering is wonderfully captured by Paul Gerhardt's great hymn:

> O sacred Head, now wounded,
> with grief and shame weighed down,
> now scornfully surrounded
> with thorns, thy only crown,
> how art thou pale with anguish,
> with sore abuse and scorn!
> How does that visage languish
> which once was bright as morn!
>
> What thou, my Lord, hast suffered
> was all for sinners' gain:
> mine, mine was the transgression,
> but thine the deadly pain.
> Lo, here I fall, my Savior!
> 'Tis I deserve thy place;
> look on me with thy favor,
> vouchsafe to me thy grace.
>
> What language shall I borrow
> to thank thee, dearest Friend,
> for this thy dying sorrow,
> thy pity without end?
> O make me thine forever!
> And should I fainting be,
> Lord, let me never, never
> outlive my love to thee!

On their way to crucify Jesus the soldiers come upon a man from Cyrene named Simon and compel him to carry Jesus's cross. Simon does not get to volunteer. He is compelled to carry the cross by the soldiers who will crucify Jesus. To be compelled to carry Jesus's cross is not a result that Jesus's cross is meant to achieve. Jesus has invited us to take up our cross, but he does not compel us to do so. Yet to be so compelled, to receive the gospel under coercive conditions, does not mean that the gospel has not been received. It is surely a judgment on the churches of mainstream Protestantism in America that the most nearly faithful form of Christianity among us came to those in slavery.

They came to a place called Golgotha, which Matthew tells us, means "Place of a Skull." We are given no reason why it was so named, but the name does justice to the evil work that will be done there. The soldiers offer Jesus wine, mixed with gall, to drink, but when he tastes it he will not drink it. His refusal to drink echoes Ps. 69:21, where we are told that the persecuted will be given vinegar to drink. Matthew's account of the crucifixion of Jesus is suffused with echoes of the Psalms and, in particular, Ps. 22. Some may wonder if Matthew is forcing the crucifixion to correspond to these psalms. That very suggestion, however, fails to recognize that Jesus is God's psalm for the world. It is not an accident that the Psalms became the hymnal of the church. When we pray them, we pray Jesus.

"And when they had crucified him"—what more can be said? Matthew does not elaborate. All we need to know is that Jesus is crucified. He is nailed to a cross. That cross, moreover, is the icon of God. No matter how hard Christians try to make our faith confirm our presumption that we can follow Jesus without suffering, we confront the stark fact of his crucifixion. We should like to think that his crucifixion was some terrible mistake, a failure in communication, but the reality is unavoidable. He was crucified.

Why did he have to die? Why did he have to die on a cross? The latter question seems easily answered. He had to die on a cross because that is the way Romans executed those they regarded as a threat to their interest. Hang them high so that all could see what happens when one challenges Rome. But that answer is not sufficient for us to understand why he had to die on a cross. He died on a cross to reveal the heart of God. The cross is where God's life crosses our life to create a life otherwise unimaginable. Timothy Radcliffe observes that the forgiveness of the cross is not God forgetting Good Friday, because

> if forgiveness were forgetting then God would have to suffer the most acute amnesia, but it is God's unimaginable creativity, which takes what we have done and makes it fruitful. The medieval image of God's forgiveness was the flowering of the cross. The cross is the ugly sign of torture. It is the sign of humanity's ability to reject love and to do what is utterly sterile. But the artists of the Middle Ages showed this cross flowering on Easter Sunday. The dead wood put out tendrils and flowers. Forgiveness makes the dead live and the ugly beautiful. (Radcliffe 2004, 11–12)

The cross, Jesus's cross, now determines the character of the universe. The cross is not a symbol to explain inexplicable suffering. One does not need Jesus to explain or to contain our rage when faced by the tragedies of the world. Rather, Jesus's cross is his alone, making possible a people who do not need an explanation for inexplicable suffering. Love, not explanation, is required when faced by the tragedies of life. Our task, a task made possible as well as demanded by the cross, is not to turn away but to be present to one another when there is quite literally nothing we can do to save ourselves.

Yet why did Jesus have to die? Christians have developed explanations for why Jesus had to die called atonement theories. For example, some suggest that Jesus had to die as a satisfaction for our sin, to serve as a moral exemplar for us, or to defeat the devil and the powers that have revolted against their creator. There is scriptural warrant for each of these accounts of Jesus's death, but these theories risk isolating Jesus's crucifixion from his life. Matthew's gospel, Matthew's story of Jesus's mission to Israel, Matthew's understanding of discipleship, Matthew's description of the beginnings of the church—all climax in the death of Jesus.

His death cannot be isolated from his life, because his death is the result of his life. He died because he had challenged the elites of Israel who used the law to protect themselves from the demands of God; he died because he challenged the pretentious power of Rome; and he died at the hands of the democratic will of the mob.[2] He died because he at once challenged and offered an alternative to all forms of human polity based on the violence made inevitable by the denial of God. Robert Jenson, therefore, rightly observes that the gospels

> tell a powerful and biblically integrated story of the Crucifixion; this story *is* just so the story of God's act to bring us back to himself at his own cost, and of our being brought back. There is no other story behind or beyond it that is the real story of what God does to reconcile us, no story of mythic battles or of a deal between God and his Son or of our being moved to live reconciled lives. The Gospel's passion narrative is the authentic and entire account of God's reconciling action and our reconciliation, as events in his life and ours. Therefore, what is first and principally required as the Crucifixion's right interpretation is for us to tell this story to one another and to God as a story about him and about ourselves. (Jenson 1997, 189)

In Hebrews we are told that Jesus was made a little lower than the angels and that all things would be subjected to him. Accordingly, he tasted death for everyone of us—the death richly deserved because of our sin (Heb. 2:7–18). This is the death of the Son of God, who has undergone for us what only he could do. Thus he is "the captain of [our] salvation" (2:10 King James Version), having died for us so that we might live.

2. I am indebted to Milbank 2003, 96 for some of this wording.

The soldiers keep watch over Jesus. While they wait, they divide up his clothes by casting lots, fulfilling what was said in Ps. 22:17–18:

> They stare and gloat over me;
> they divide my clothes among themselves,
> and for my clothing they cast lots.

They put over his head their understanding of why he is crucified: "This is Jesus, the King of the Jews." These are Pilate's men. Like Pilate they assume that Jesus is put to death because he claims to be a king. Like Pilate they are right to declare him a king, but like Pilate they fail to understand what kind of king he is. They fail, as we continue to fail, to understand how the one born to be king can die such a humiliating death.

It seems that all those who surround Jesus's cross fail to see Jesus for who he is. Those who pass by deride him, shaking their heads (Ps. 22:7), saying, "You who would destroy the temple and build it in three days, save yourself! If you are the Son of God, come down from the cross." Pilate's soldiers identify him as the king of the Jews. Now he is taunted in a manner that draws on the narrative of the people of Israel concerning the temple. He again is subject to the same temptations he faced in the desert when the devil placed him on the pinnacle of the temple and said to him: "If you are the Son of God, throw yourself down" (Matt. 4:6). This time, suffering even more than he did when he faced the devil, Jesus refuses to give the sign that would confirm his tormentors' presumptions of what the priest-king of Israel will be. His crucifixion is that sign for which they ask, but they cannot see what is before their eyes.

He is also mocked by the chief priests, scribes, and elders. They acknowledge that he has saved others. He has healed the blind, the deaf, the mute. He has brought deliverance to the poor and the hungry, but they point out that surely one so powerful can save himself. If he is the king of Israel, they say, let him come down from the cross so they will believe in him. Again they desire a sign that makes it reasonable within the world as they know it to believe in him. But Jesus remains on the cross.

The elites of Israel have one more taunt available to them, a taunt that goes to Jesus's heart: "He trusts in God; let God deliver him now, if he wants to; for he said, 'I am God's Son.'" This taunt is directed not only at Jesus, but to the Father. This is the agony that Jesus knew that he and his Father would endure. The Father has willed that his very Son be subject to our fears so that we might learn to trust as Jesus trusts the Father. The Father will deliver the Son, but not before he has undergone death itself. The temple will be restored, but the restoration will be in the form of a body, the body of Jesus.

James and John had asked to be on Jesus's right and left hand and we can now clearly see, as Jesus said, they knew not for what they asked. But now, like all the disciples, they have deserted him. Instead, on Jesus's right and left hand are two bandits who have been crucified with him. Even these bandits taunt Jesus in the same way the passersby and the elites have derided him. In this case, common suffering does not produce sympathy or commonality. Jesus, the only true human being, is devoid of all human connection. Even the women looked on him "from a distance" (Matt. 27:55). Those crucified with him, the passersby, the elites, the soldiers, are all witnesses; we too are witnesses to this "desolating sacrilege."

From noon until three in the afternoon darkness covers the whole land. From the very beginning of the gospel of Matthew we have known that cosmic forces are in play with the birth of Jesus (Matt. 2:2). We should, therefore, not be surprised that as his death grows near all of creation will respond. In the book of Amos the Lord promises that "on that day"

> I will make the sun go down at noon,
> and darken the earth in broad daylight. (Amos 8:9)

That day has arrived. A day of judgment. A day of redemption. At about three o'clock Jesus cried aloud, "My God, my God, why have you forsaken me?" We cannot suppress the thought: "If you are the Son of God, should you be saying this? If you are God, if you are the second person of the Trinity, how can you be abandoned?" Our temptation is to try to explain, to protect Jesus from this abject cry of abandonment. Yet Jesus's cry, a cry learned from Ps. 22, is the cry that only Israel's Messiah can say. His cry is not an indication that he is less that the second person of the Trinity, but rather the prismatic exemplification of the love that is the life of the Trinity. It is the love that is Jesus,

> who, though he was in the form of God,
>   did not regard equality with God
>   as something to be exploited,
> but emptied himself,
>   taking the form of a slave,
>   being born in human likeness.
> And being found in human form,
>   he humbled himself
>   and became obedient to the point of death—
>   even death on a cross. (Phil. 2:6–8)

In Jesus's cry from the cross we see, as Rowan Williams puts it, "the sheer, unimaginable *differentness*—of God" (2000, 37). Jesus's words from the cross, the cross itself, mean that the Father is to be found when all traces of power, at least as Pilate and the elites of Israel understand power, are absent; that the Spirit's authoritative witness is most clearly revealed when all forms of human authority are lost; and that God's power is to be found exemplified in this captive under the sentence of death.

In truth we stand with the Pilates of this world. We want God to be a king with armies. We do not want to give up our understanding of god as the one capable of putting everything right on our terms. We do not want Jesus to be abandoned because we do not want to acknowledge that the one who abandons and is abandoned is God. We seek to explain these words of dereliction, to save and protect God from making a fool out of being God, but our attempts to protect God reveal how frightening the God of Jesus Christ is. That God rightly frightens us. Yet God is most revealed when he seems to us the most hidden: "Christ's moment of most absolute particularity—the absolute dereliction of the cross—is the moment in which the glory of God, his power to be where and when he will be, is displayed before the eyes of the world" (Hart 2003, 327).

In the cross of Christ God refuses to let our sin, the sin of his tormentors, determine our relation to him. God's love for us means that he can only hate that which alienates his creatures from the love manifest in our creation. Cyril of Jerusalem observes that by calling on his Father as "my God," Christ does so on our behalf and in our place. Hear these words, "My God, my God, why have you forsaken me?" and know that the Son of God has taken our place, become for us the abandonment that our sin produces, so that we may live confident that the world has been redeemed by this cross.

So redeemed, any account of the cross that suggests that God must satisfy an abstract theory of justice by sacrificing the Son on our behalf is clearly wrong. Indeed, such accounts are dangerously wrong. The Father's sacrifice of the Son and the Son's willing sacrifice is God's justice. Just as there is no God who is not the Father, Son, and Holy Spirit, so there is no God who must be satisfied that we might be spared. We are spared because God refuses to have us lost.[3] Such is God's justice.

Some of the bystanders hear Jesus's cry and speculate that he must be calling for Elijah. They fill a sponge with sour wine to touch his lips in hope they can better understand him. Others protest their action, suggesting that they should wait to see if Elijah will come to save him. Cruelty knows no bounds. But Elijah will not come, because Elijah has already come (Matt. 11:14; 17:12–13). The one who was received into heaven without dying had already come to witness to the one who will defeat death itself.

"Then" Jesus cried out in a loud voice and died. The Son of Man has died. Jesus is really dead, because he is really fully human. The Father has not died, but rather the Son has done the will of the Father and entered death itself. God is the great enemy of death, but death can be overcome only by the Son's willingness to be subjected to death's darkness. The death that the Son becomes is not "not to be," but the more terrifying death of being separated from the Father. As Hans Urs von Balthasar puts it, "This day exists, when

---

3. Some of the reflections on Jesus's words from the cross are taken from Hauerwas 2004a, 59–70.

the Son is dead, and the Father, accordingly, [is] inaccessible. . . . At the end of the Passion, when the Word of God is dead, the Church has no words left to say" (1990, 49).

The curtain in the temple is torn from top to bottom, as it was in the earlier desecration of the temple. The earth shakes and rocks are split in two. The temple, Jesus's body, is broken. As prophesied in Dan. 12:2, graves are opened and the bodies of the saints who had fallen asleep are raised and, after his resurrection, enter the holy city. Jesus's descriptions of the apocalypse (Matt. 24:7), descriptions drawn from Israel's life (2 Sam. 22:8; Ps. 68:8; Joel 2), surround his crucifixion and death. God commanded Ezekiel to prophecy to the valley of bones so that they might live (Ezek. 37:1–14). Jesus's death now is the breath of God giving life to all. The dramatic events that accompany Jesus's death mark the end of the old age and the beginning of the new.

When the centurion, who had kept watch with the soldiers, saw the earthquake and all that took place at Jesus's death, he was terrified. He confesses that "truly this man was God's Son!"—a confession that he may well have learned from those who tormented Jesus. Yet his confession is in the past tense. He has still to learn that this crucified one, who is dead and will be buried, will be raised, offering hope to him and his comrades. He has witnessed the triumph of God over the power of death so that he and all soldiers might be free to never kill again.

Matthew tells us that many women also were there and witnessed Jesus's crucifixion and death. The disciples had deserted him, but these women followed Jesus from Galilee to provide for him. Matthew does not tell us what they provided, but it is good to know that people were present to Jesus other than the twelve. Moreover, Matthew gives us their names: Mary Magdalene, Mary the mother of James and Joseph, and Zebedee's wife—the mother of James and John. The mother of the sons of Zebedee now knows what she had asked for her sons, but she still remains present with Jesus.

Just as we discover after Jesus's death that women had followed him from Galilee, Matthew tells us about another follower of Jesus we had not earlier met. Joseph of Arimathea, who was a disciple of Jesus, went to Pilate to ask for Jesus's body. Matthew identifies Joseph as a rich man who owns a new tomb, but rather than using the tomb for himself, desires to bury Jesus in it. Given Jesus's strictures about wealth (Matt. 6:24; 19:23–26), some think it strange that Jesus could have a rich disciple. Yet we see that Joseph, who has not deserted Jesus, does not try to use his wealth as a form of protection. To ask Pilate for Jesus's body, to ask for the body of one killed by Rome, could get one in trouble. But Joseph does not hesitate to request from Pilate that Jesus's body be given to him. Pilate readily agrees.

Joseph took Jesus body and wrapped it in a clean linen cloth and laid it in the tomb hewn from a rock. Jesus is dead. His body is cared for as a dead body should be treated. Joseph rolls a large stone in front of the door of the tomb and went away. Like the Joseph who cared for the baby in Mary's womb, so this Joseph cares for the dead body of Jesus. He went away, however, but Mary Magdalene and the other Mary sat opposite the tomb. The women wait because they trust what Jesus has told them. He is to be resurrected. These women sit across from the tomb, expectant and faithful witnesses to that resurrection.

But they are not the only ones who remember that Jesus has said that after three days he will be raised (Matt. 16:21; 17:23; 20:19). The chief priests and Pharisees also remember that Jesus said he would rise after three days. The day after his crucifixion, therefore, the chief priests and Pharisees gather before Pilate to remind him that the "imposter" said "while he was still alive" that after three days he would rise again. The Pharisees suddenly reappear in league with the chief priests. They have not been among those who conspired to kill Jesus, but now they join with the chief priests to control any further news about Jesus that might go to the people.

The chief priests and Pharisees ask Pilate to command that the tomb be made secure until the third day. They suggest that the disciples may try to steal the body in order to tell the people he has been raised from the dead. The chief priests and Pharisees assume that the resurrection means no more than that Jesus's body is missing. They suggest to Pilate that if the people were to believe the disciples, that deception would be worse than their having stolen the body. The chief priests and Pharisees obviously do not trust the people, but ironically they are right to worry about the role of the disciples as witnesses to Jesus's life, death, and resurrection.

Accordingly, they ask Pilate to secure the tomb. Pilate agrees to do so and makes a guard of soldiers available so the tomb can be secured. The guard was not only stationed at the tomb, but the stone in front of the tomb was sealed in place. The chief priests, Pharisees, and Pilate assume that a stone can hold Jesus, the Son of God, in place. They have learned nothing from the earthquake and rocks that were split at Jesus's death. They are obtuse, but that they are so makes them unwitting witnesses to Jesus's resurrection.

MATTHEW 28

Resurrection

Mary Magdalene and the other Mary believe what Jesus has promised, that after three days he will be raised. After the Sabbath, on the first day of the week, Mary Magdalene and Mary go to the tomb. Matthew indicates the time, because time is now refigured. The two Marys will be the first to witness the one whose resurrection will reconfigure the time in which we live. Indeed, a new Sabbath will be created because he is the new creation. Matthew's gospel began "in the beginning," and we have now come to the end that which opens all to the new beginning.

"Suddenly" there is an earthquake, and an angel of the Lord descends from heaven and rolls back the stone in front of the tomb and sits on it. His appearance is like lightning, and his clothing is as white as snow. An angel of the Lord had appeared in a dream to Joseph to tell him that he should take Mary as his wife because the child she carried had been conceived by the Holy Spirit (Matt. 1:20). An angel had also appeared to Joseph in a dream to tell him to take his family to Egypt (2:13). Angels had waited on Jesus after his temptation in the desert (4:11). But this angel has come to announce that Jesus had been raised.

Confronted by the blinding light of this fiercesome angel, the guards who had been posted to insure that nothing would happen to Jesus's body were so gripped by fear that they shook and became like dead men. That they became like dead men indicates the transformation that Jesus's resurrection has effected. Those who had thought they were alive now discover that what they took for life is death. Jesus's resurrection creates a life freed from the death that grips our everyday lives. This is life reborn, revealing to us how death has determined our living. And yet it is possible to remain dead, to live as dead men, as the behavior of these guards will make clear.

The guards are frightened to death, but the angel tells Mary Magdalene and Mary that they do not need to be afraid: "I know that you are looking for Jesus who was crucified. He is not here; for he has been raised, as he said. Come, see the place where he lay. Then go quickly and tell his disciples, 'He has been raised from the dead, and indeed he is going ahead of you to Galilee; there you will see him.' This is my message to you." This extraordinary speech contains the whole gospel. "Do not be afraid." Jesus has made it possible to live unafraid. The disciples are often afraid of the elites and the crowds, but Jesus has given them all they need not to be afraid. He has done so by drawing them, and us, into a way of life so compellingly true that we have no time to be afraid.

Yet Matthew tells us that Mary Magdalene and Mary left the tomb quickly with "fear and great joy," but now their fear is that commensurate with joy. They leave the tomb in awe, knowing that they are now participants in the kingdom of God. The fear they have as they leave the tomb is the fear that protects them from the fears that would have us deny the resurrection. The fear and joy that possess their lives saves them from the fears derived from the attempt to create lives of security in the face of death.

The fear and joy they now experience is that made possible by the resurrection. But they have not seen the resurrection. The angel rolled back the stone before the tomb to allow them to see the empty tomb. They had come to see the tomb. Matthew has been training us to "see" from the beginning of his gospel. One does not come to see the tomb unless one has learned to follow Jesus to his crucifixion. Mary Magdalene and Mary have seen the crucifixion, they have seen the tomb. They are, therefore, our first witnesses to the good news that the one crucified has been, as the angel announces, raised.

The Father has raised the Son from the dead in honor of the Son's perfect obedience even to the cross. Jesus was handed over, made subject to sinners and death itself, but he has been made victorious. The Father has raised his Son, but the Son wills to be with the Father, having done the Father's will. We now see that the crucifixion cannot be separated from the resurrection. Robert Jenson puts it this way:

> The Crucifixion put it up to the Father: Would he stand to *this* alleged Son? To *this* candidate to be his own self-identifying Word? Would he be a God who, for example, hosts publicans and sinners, who justifies the ungodly? The Resurrection was the Father's Yes. We may say: the Resurrection settled that the Crucifixion's sort of God is indeed the one God; the Crucifixion settled what sort of God it is who establishes his deity by the Resurrection. Or: the Crucifixion settled *who and what* God is; the Resurrection settled *that* this God is. And just so the Crucifixion settled also who and what we are, if we are anything determinate. (Jenson 1997, 189)

The resurrection of Jesus, however, cannot be seen. We can no more see the resurrection than we can see creation. We can see only the empty tomb and the resurrected Jesus. The resurrection is not a resurrection of one who had lived, died, and then lived again. Jesus raised Lazarus from the dead, but Lazarus was still to die. Resurrection is not the resuscitation of a corpse. Jesus is raised from the dead to be freed from death itself. He will never die again. Jesus's resurrection cannot be seen by us, because God cannot be seen. Jesus has been raised from the dead, defeating death itself. The resurrection therefore is the climax of the history begun with Mary's conception by the Holy Spirit.

Mary Magdalene and Mary rush from the tomb to tell the disciples, but suddenly Jesus meets them. It is Jesus, resurrected. It is the crucified one who is the resurrected. Jesus greets them in a familiar way, and they come to him. They saw him and recognized him. They took hold of his feet and they worshiped him. The resurrected Jesus can be touched. The resurrection of Jesus is not an idea. His body has been raised. The one born of Mary, the one baptized by John, the one who called the disciples, the one who delivered the Sermon on the Mount, the one who cured the lame, the blind, the deaf and mute, the one who disputed with the Pharisees and Sadducees, the one who endured humiliation by trial and cross—he has been raised.

We know that Jesus was raised bodily because, as he promised at the Last Supper with his disciples, he continues to share his body with us (Matt. 26:26–29). His body, through the agency of the Holy Spirit, he shares with us. That sharing is made possible because he has been raised from the dead. Jesus has assumed his place at the right hand of the Father, making possible his bodily presence. We are fed with the spiritual food of his body and blood, but "spiritual food" does not mean that we are only pretending that this is Jesus's body and blood. Rather, it means that the resurrected Jesus is the crucified Jesus.

Jesus's bodily presence does not prevent Mary Magdalene and Mary from worshiping him. One worships only God. Yet they worship him. They had not worshiped the angel who had announced Jesus resurrection, but they now worship Jesus. These women of Israel, formed by Israel's commandment to worship God alone, worship Jesus. If this is not the Son of God then they are surely idolaters. But this is the crucified Jesus, the Son of God, who alone is worthy of worship.

That they worship Jesus marks the central activity of the new reality aborning, that is, the church. What makes the church the church is the worship of Jesus. The worship of Jesus will take many different forms across time and space. But where the word is preached and the sacraments are enacted, we know that Jesus is present among us. By baptism and eucharist we participate in Jesus's life, death, and resurrection, making us an alternative to the world. Being the alternative is not, however, an invitation for self-righteousness. Rather, it enables us to witness, as Mary Magdalene and Mary do, to our having been given the time in a world that thinks it has no time to worship Jesus.

Jesus tells them not to be afraid, but to go tell his brothers to go to Galilee where they will see him. Jesus, who has been abandoned by his disciples, tells Mary Magdalene and Mary to tell his disciples that they will be able to "see" him. They have deserted him, but that they have done so does not mean they will not be able to see him. Jesus, moreover, calls them his brothers. Jesus has come to call into the world a new people. He calls the disciples "his brothers," indicating that they are the seedbed of the new family made possible by his life, death, and resurrection. Jesus's brothers—humans—will bring forth life. Again we see the beginnings of the church.

Jesus began his ministry in Galilee (Matt. 4:12), and it is to Galilee that he will return. The disciples had been called in Galilee, they are now to be regathered in Galilee; later, it will be from Galilee that they are sent forth. Jesus unleashes the disciples to go into the world not from Jerusalem, the center of power, but from Galilee. Galilee becomes the staging area for the disciples to go to the nations to announce the new age begun in Jesus.

While Mary Magdalene and Mary were going to tell the disciples, some of the guards who had been present at the tomb went into the city and told the chief priests everything that had happened. Again the chief priests conspired with the elders, deciding that their best course of action is to bribe these soldiers with a large sum of money to say that while they were asleep his disciples had come by night and stole his body. They are clearly becoming desperate, because this is not a convincing cover story. If the guards were asleep, how would they know that the body was stolen or that the body had been stolen by his disciples? Some worry that belief in the resurrection requires us to suspend our normal understanding of how we know anything to be true. There is some truth to that, but it is not because the resurrection is irrational. Of course we cannot see the resurrection, because God cannot be seen. But we do see Jesus, who has been resurrected. Accordingly, the resurrection is the condition that now makes it possible for us to see truthfully all that is in God's good creation. That is why followers of Jesus must be relentless truth tellers and seekers.

The resurrection, of course, is not a "knockdown sign" that establishes that Jesus is the Son of God. The soldiers were scared to death by the angel, but that did not incline them to believe in Jesus or the resurrection. They remain under the power of the chief priests and elders and seem more than willing to do their bidding. The truth that is Jesus is a truth that requires discipleship, for it is only by being transformed by what he has taught and by what he has done that we can come to know the way the world is. The world is not what it appears to be, because sin has scarred the world's appearance. The world has been redeemed—but to see the world's redemption, to see Jesus, requires that we be caught up in the joy that comes from serving him. That is what it means to live apocalyptically.

The chief priests and elders seem to realize, however, that they have not developed a convincing story concerning the empty tomb. One lie leads to another lie, less believable than the original lie. So, they reassure the soldiers to whom they have offered the bribe that if the news of disappearance of Jesus's body comes to the ears of the governor, they will satisfy him and keep them out of trouble. The implication seems to be that they will also pay off the governor. So the guards took the money and did as they were directed.

Matthew reports that the guards tell the story created by the chief priests and elders, which explains why the story that the disciples stole the body of Jesus "is still told among the Jews to this day" (Matt. 28:15). That such a story was required testifies that the Jews had inherited the stories and practices that make Jesus's crucifixion and resurrection intelligible. A people who believe that God had raised Israel from Egypt might well believe that Jesus had been raised from the dead.[1] Indeed, as we have seen, Matthew's gospel is an ongoing commentary on God's care of Israel, which witnesses to Jesus as Israel's long-expected Messiah.

Unfortunately, no longer does anyone need to be bought off to deny the resurrection. For us, that is, for anyone schooled in modernity, the resurrection is quite simply unbelievable. The resurrection is the miracle of miracles, and miracles are unbelievable. Of course, the resurrection is the miracle of miracles, but not because it defies belief. The resurrection is the miracle of miracles because it is the resurrection of Jesus, the Messiah of Israel. But little will be gained in trying to convince anyone that the resurrection *might* have happened. To do so threatens to isolate the resurrection from the life and crucifixion of Jesus in a manner that distorts the witness that Matthew has trained us to be. The problem, after all, is not belief in the resurrection, but whether we live lives that would make no sense if in fact Jesus has not been raised from the dead.

The eleven disciples go to Galilee, to the mountain to which Jesus had directed them, and when they see Jesus they worship him. They had previously worshiped him after he had walked on water (Matt. 14:33), but now they worship him as the one who has returned to life. But some doubt. Again we see Matthew's absolute candor. There is nothing to hide. Even after the resurrection some of Jesus's disciples doubted. Matthew does not tell us what form their doubt took, but one doubts that they doubted that he had been raised. Rather, their doubt regarded their ability to obey and follow Jesus. They have not forgotten that they deserted him.

Jesus, however, reminds them who he is. He tells them that "all authority in heaven and on earth has been given to me." For the last time Jesus uses the language of the book of Daniel that we might identify him:

> I saw one like a human being
> coming with the clouds of heaven.

1. I have rephrased Jenson's contention that "God is whoever raised Jesus from the dead, having before raised Israel from Egypt" (1997, 63).

And he came to the Ancient One
    and was presented before him.
To him was given dominion
    and glory and kingship,
that all peoples, nations, and languages
    should serve him.
His dominion is an everlasting dominion
    that shall not pass away,
and his kingship is one
    that shall never be destroyed. (Dan. 7:13–14)

The devil has lost. The devil had offered Jesus authority over all the kingdoms of the world if only Jesus would worship him (Matt. 4:8–11), but Jesus's whole life was a refusal of that offer. It was a refusal that required Jesus to endure rejection and crucifixion, but through that endurance he has triumphed. He alone now has the authority to send the disciples to the world to make disciples of all the nations. He first sent the disciples only to Israel (10:5–6), but now he sends the disciples to all the world to baptize them in the name of the Father, Son, and Holy Spirit.

What has been hidden from the foundation of the world, what has been hidden from the wise, is now revealed by the Son. The God of Israel is the God of all nations. The disciples are now equipped to be sent to the nations, baptizing them into the death and resurrection of Jesus to make them citizens of his death-defying kingdom. Israel is not to be left behind, but rather its mission is now continued in a new reality called church. Through the church all nations will learn to call Israel blessed.

The church, moreover, is but the name of a people who have been formed to worship the Father, the Son, and the Holy Spirit. To worship that God is to live a life described by Jesus in the Sermon on the Mount. Therefore, Jesus commands his disciples to teach those whom they baptize to obey all that he has commanded. Jesus's death and resurrection cannot be separated from the way he has taught us to live. The Sermon on the Mount, how we are to serve one another as brothers and sisters, the forgiveness required by our willingness to expose the sin of the church, is salvation. The teaching and the teacher are one. The salvation that Jesus entrusts to his disciples is the gospel of Matthew.

The disciples are to remember that the mission on which Jesus sends them is not one on which they must go alone. He is the resurrected Lord who will always be with those entrusted to witness to him and his work. He was in the beginning, which means that he can promise to be at the end of the age. But the age that he will be present at the end of is the age inaugurated by his birth, ministry, death, and resurrection. On that basis and that basis alone Christians are sent to the world with the message: "Repent, for the kingdom of heaven is present."

BIBLIOGRAPHY

Allison, Dale. 2005. *Studies in Matthew: Interpretations Past and Present*. Grand Rapids: Baker.

Aristotle. 1999. *Nicomachean Ethics*. Translated by Terence Irwin. Indianapolis: Hackett.

Augustine. 1955a. *Confessions and Enchiridion*. Translated and edited by Albert Outler. Philadelphia: Westminster.

————. 1955b. "On the Morals of the Catholic Church." In *Christian Ethics: Sources of the Living Tradition*. Edited by Waldo Beach and H. Richard Niebuhr. New York: Ronald.

————. 1961. *Confessions*. Translated by R. S. Pine-Coffin. Baltimore: Penguin.

————. 1977. *Concerning the City of God against the Pagans*. Translated by Henry Bettenson. Harmondsworth: Penguin.

Ayres, Lewis. 2004. *Nicaea and Its Legacy: An Approach to Fourth-Century Trinitarian Theology*. Oxford: Oxford University Press.

Bader-Saye, Scott. 1999. *Church and Israel after Christendom: The Politics of Election*. Boulder, CO: Westview.

Balthasar, Hans Urs von. 1990. *Mysterium Paschale*. Translated by Aidan Nichols. Grand Rapids: Eerdmans.

Barth, Karl. 1936–77. *Church Dogmatics*. Translated by G. W. Bromiley. Edinburgh: Clark.

————. 1959. *Dogmatics in Outline*. Translated by G. T. Thompson. New York: Harper.

————. 1960. *The Humanity of God*. Translated by John Newton Thomas and Thomas Wieser. Richmond: John Knox.

————. 1990. *The Göttingen Dogmatics: Instructions in the Christian Religion*. Translated by Geoffrey Bromiley. Grand Rapids: Eerdmans.

Bauckham, Richard. 2005. *The Theology of the Book of Revelation*. Cambridge: Cambridge University Press.

Berry, Wendell. 2000. *Life Is a Miracle: An Essay against Modern Superstition*. Washington, DC: Counterpoint.

Bonhoeffer, Dietrich. 1956. *No Rusty Swords*. Translated by John Bowden. New York: Harper & Row.

————. 1962. *Creation and Fall: A Theological Interpretation of Genesis 1–3*. Translated by John Fletcher. London: SCM.

————. 2001. *Discipleship*. Translated by Barbara Green and Reinhard Krauss. Minneapolis: Fortress.

————. 2005. *Ethics*. Translated by Reinhard Krauss, Charles C. West, and Douglas W. Stott. Minneapolis: Fortress.

Book of Common Prayer. 1979. New York: Church Publishing.

Bruner, Frederick Dale. 2004. *The Christbook: Matthew 1–12.* Revised edition. Grand Rapids: Eerdmans.

Burrell, David. 2000. *Friendship and Ways to Truth.* Notre Dame: University of Notre Dame Press.

Cantalamessa, Raniero. 1992. *Mary: Mirror of the Church.* Collegeville, MN: Liturgical Press.

Carter, Warren. 2003. *Matthew and the Margins: A Sociopolitical and Religious Reading.* Maryknoll, NY: Orbis.

Cartwright, Michael. 1988. "Practices, Politics, and Performance: Toward a Communal Hermeneutic for Christian Ethics." PhD diss., Duke University.

Cochrane, Arthur C. 1962. *The Church's Confession under Hitler.* Philadelphia: Westminster.

Davenport, Gene. 1988. *Into the Darkness: Discipleship in the Sermon on the Mount.* Nashville: Abingdon.

Davies, W. D. 1969. *The Sermon on the Mount.* Cambridge: Cambridge University Press.

Davis, Ellen. 2003. *Who Are You My Daughter? Reading Ruth through Image and Text.* Louisville: Westminster John Knox.

Day, Dorothy. 2002. *Writings from Commonweal.* Edited by Patrick Jordan. Collegeville, MN: Liturgical Press.

Dostoevsky, Fyodor. 2001. "The Grand Inquisitor." In *Remembering the End: Dostoevsky as Prophet to Modernity* by P. Travis Kroeken and Bruce K Ward. Boulder, CO: Westview.

Greer, Rowan. 1997. *Broken Lights and Mended Lives: Theology and Common Life in the Early Church.* University Park: Pennsylvania State University Press.

Griffiths, Paul. 2004. *Lying: An Augustinian Theology of Duplicity.* Grand Rapids: Brazos.

Hart, David Bentley. 2003. *The Beauty of the Infinite: The Aesthetics of Christian Truth.* Grand Rapids: Eerdmans.

———. 2005. *The Doors of the Sea: Where Was God in the Tsunami?* Grand Rapids: Eerdmans.

Hauerwas, Stanley. 1993. *Unleashing the Scripture: Freeing the Bible from Captivity to America.* Nashville: Abingdon.

———. 2000. *A Better Hope: Resources for a Church Confronting Capitalism, Democracy, and Postmodernity.* Grand Rapids: Brazos.

———. 2001. *Christian Existence Today: Essays on Church, World, and Living in Between.* Grand Rapids: Brazos.

———. 2004a. *Cross-Shattered Christ: Meditations on the Seven Last Words.* Grand Rapids: Brazos.

———. 2004b. *Performing the Faith: Bonhoeffer and the Practice of Nonviolence.* Grand Rapids: Brazos.

———. 2006. "Seeing Darkness, Hearing Silence: Augustine's Account of Evil." In *Speak No Evil: Moral Judgment in the Modern Age.* Edited by Ruth Grant. Chicago: University of Chicago Press.

Hays, Richard. 2005. "The Gospel of Matthew: Reconfigured Torah." *Harvard Theological Studies* 1.2.

Heschel, Abraham Joshua. 1951. *The Sabbath.* New York: Farrar, Straus & Giroux.

Huebner, Chris. 2002. "Unhandling History: Anti-Theory, Ethics, and the Practice of Witness." PhD diss., Duke University.

Jenson, Robert. 1997. *Systematic Theology: The Triune God.* New York: Oxford University Press.

John Paul II. 1994. "Veritatis splendor." In *Considering Veritatis splendor.* Edited by John Wilkins. Cleveland: Pilgrim.

Jones, L. Gregory. 1995. *Embodying Forgiveness: A Theological Analysis.* Grand Rapids: Eerdmans.

Kant, Immanuel. 1959. *Foundations of the Metaphysics of Morals.* Translated by Lewis White Beck. New York: Liberal Arts Press.

———. 1960. *Religion within the Limits of Reason Alone.* Translated by Theodore Greene and Hoyt Hudson. New York: Harper.

Lash, Nicholas. 1993. *Believing Three Ways in One God: A Reading of the Apostles' Creed.* Notre Dame: University of Notre Dame Press.

Lehmann, Paul. 1975. *The Transfiguration of Politics: The Presence and Power of Jesus of Nazareth in and over Human Affairs*. New York: Harper & Row.

Levering, Matthew. 2002. *Christ's Fulfillment of Torah and Temple: Salvation according to Thomas Aquinas*. Notre Dame: University of Notre Dame Press.

Lischer, Richard. 1987. "The Sermon on the Mount as Radical Pastoral Care." *Interpretation* 41.

Luz, Ulrich. 1993. *The Theology of the Gospel of Matthew*. Translated by J. Bradford Robinson. Cambridge: Cambridge University Press.

MacIntyre, Alasdair. 1995. *Marxism and Christianity*. 2nd edition. London: Duckworth.

MacKinnon, Donald. 1979. "Ethics and Tragedy." Pp. 182–95 in *Explorations in Theology*, vol. 5. London: SCM.

Manlio, Simonetti. 2001. *Matthew 1–13*. Ancient Christian Commentary on Scripture. Downers Grove, IL: InterVarsity.

———. 2002. *Matthew 14–28*. Ancient Christian Commentary on Scripture. Downers Grove, IL: InterVarsity.

Marvin, Carolyn, and David Ingle. 1999. *Blood Sacrifice and the Nation: Totem Rituals and the American Flag*. Cambridge: Cambridge University Press.

McCabe, Herbert. 1987. *God Matters*. London: Chapman.

McClendon, James. 1990. *Biography as Theology: How Life Stories Can Remake Today's Theology*. Philadelphia: Trinity.

Milbank, John. 2003. *Being Reconciled: Ontology and Pardon*. London: Routledge.

Minear, Paul. 2000. *The Good News according to Matthew: A Training Manual for Prophets*. St. Louis: Chalice.

Niebuhr, Reinhold. 1953. *Christian Realism and Political Problems*. New York: Scribner.

———. 1986. "The Wheat and the Tares." In *The Essential Reinhold Niebuhr*. Edited by Robert McAfee Brown. New Haven: Yale University Press.

O'Donovan, Oliver. 2004. "The Political Thought of *City of God* 19." In *Bonds of Imperfection: Christian Politics, Past and Present* by Oliver O'Donovan and Joan Lockwood O'Donovan. Grand Rapids: Eerdmans.

Origen. 1926. *Commentary on Matthew*. Ante-Nicene Fathers. New York: Scribner.

Pinches, Charles. 2002. *Theology and Action: After Theory in Christian Ethics*. Grand Rapids: Eerdmans.

Radcliffe, Timothy. 2004. *Seven Last Words*. London: Burns & Oates.

Radner, Ephraim. 2004. *Hope among the Fragments: The Broken Church and Its Engagement of Scripture*. Grand Rapids: Brazos.

Rogers, Eugene. 2005. *After the Spirit: A Constructive Pneumatology from Resources outside the Modern West*. Grand Rapids: Eerdmans.

Rosenzweig, Franz. 1999. *Understanding the Sick and the Healthy: A View of World, Man, and God*. Translated by Nahum Glatzer. Cambridge: Harvard University Press.

Senior, Donald. 1998. *Matthew*. Nashville: Abingdon.

Thomas Aquinas. 1981. *Summa theologica*. Translated by Fathers of the English Dominican Province. Westminster, MD: Christian Classics.

Turner, Denys. 2004. *Faith, Reason, and the Existence of God*. Cambridge: Cambridge University Press.

Vanier, Jean. 1979. *Community and Growth*. Translated by Ann Shearer. London: Darton, Longman & Todd.

Wells, Samuel. 2004. *Improvisation: The Drama of Christian Ethics*. Grand Rapids: Brazos.

———. 2006. *God's Companions: Christian Ethics and the Abundance of God*. Oxford: Blackwell.

Wilken, Robert. 2003. *The Spirit of Early Christian Thought: Seeing the Face of God*. New Haven: Yale University Press.

Williams, Rowan. 1994. *Open to Judgment: Sermons and Addresses*. London: Darton, Longman & Todd.

———. 2000. *Christ on Trial: How the Gospel Unsettles Our Judgement*. London: Fount.

———. 2002. *Ponder These Things: Praying with Icons of the Virgin.* Norwich: Canterbury.

Yoder, John Howard. 1964. *The Christian Witness to the State.* Newton, KS: Faith & Life.

———. 1971. *The Original Revolution: Essays on Christian Pacifism.* Scottdale, PA: Herald.

———. 1984. *The Priestly Kingdom: Social Ethics as Gospel.* Notre Dame: University of Notre Dame Press.

———. 1992. *Nevertheless: Varieties of Religious Pacifism.* Scottsdale, PA: Herald.

———. 1994a. "The Disavowal of Constantine: An Alternative Perspective on Interfaith Dialogue." In *The Royal Priesthood: Essays Ecclesiological and Ecumenical.* Edited by Michael Cartwright. Grand Rapids: Eerdmans.

———. 1994b. *The Politics of Jesus: Vicit Agnus Noster.* Grand Rapids: Eerdmans.

———. 2003. *The Jewish-Christian Schism Revisited.* Edited by Michael Cartwright and Peter Ochs. Grand Rapids: Eerdmans.

SUBJECT INDEX

abortion, 41
Abraham, 26–27, 28, 36, 220, 230
abundance, 82
Adam, 100
adultery, 69–70, 143, 148, 170
afterlife, 191
allegories, 18
Allison, Dale, 68n8
alms, 76, 81
altruism, 193
American Christians, 110, 130, 147, 221
Ananias and Sapphira, 174–75
Andrew, 56
angels, 244
anger, 68, 69, 184
anointing, 214
Antiochus IV Epiphanes, 205
antithesis, 67–68, 72
apocalyptic, 24, 110, 127, 172, 201, 204–5
    in parables, 133, 134
    and waiting, 207
apostles, 105–6
Apostles' Creed, 229
apostolicity, of church, 107–8
Archelaus, 42, 56
Aristotle, 75, 193
atonement, 60, 238
Auden, W. H., 98
Augustine, 29, 30n5, 51, 65n5, 70n10, 75,
    85–86, 131–33, 169–70, 203
autonomy, 88–89
Ayres, Lewis, 25, 30n5

Babel, 27, 230
Babylonian captivity, 31
Bader-Saye, Scott, 177n2
Balthasar, Hans Urs von, 241
banquet, 188–89
baptism, 70n9, 218, 219, 246, 249
    of John the Baptist, 47–49, 185
Barabbas, 233
Barmen Declaration, 178–79
Barth, Karl, 34–35, 100, 173–74, 175, 178,
    229
Bathsheba, 31
Beatitudes, 61, 63, 115, 118
Beelzebul, 121, 123
beginning, 23
Berry, Wendell, 140, 148
Bethlehem, 39–40, 41
Bethsaida, 115
Bible, as weapon of truth, 109
blasphemy, 99, 122, 227
blessedness, 63, 115, 118, 149
blind, 103, 183–84, 185
blindness, 129
    of scribes and Pharisees, 199
blood money, 231
blood of the covenant, 218
blood of the martyrs, 221
boat, 97
body, 70n9, 80, 221
body and blood, 218–19
Bonaventure, 124n4

Bonhoeffer, Dietrich, 52, 58, 60–61, 63,
        69–70, 71, 73, 74, 75, 84–85, 86, 90,
        92n5, 108–9, 232
Book of Common Prayer, 33, 189
Bruner, Frederick Dale, 41, 73
burdens, 196
Burrell, David, 34n7

Caesar, 190
Caesarea Philippi, 149–53
Caiaphas, 214, 225
Cain and Abel, 68
Canaanite woman, 32, 144, 180
Cantalamessa, Raniero, 36
Capernaum, 94, 115
capitalism, 81, 212
Carter, Warren, 38
categorical imperative, 88
Catholicism, 60
celibacy, 69, 171
centurion
        confession of, 242
        faith of, 94–95, 144
ceremonial law, 65–66
Chalcedon, 35, 124
character, 75
charity, 111, 145
"cheap grace", 60
chief priests, 184–87, 214, 216, 226, 232, 233,
        239, 243, 247–48
children, 41, 191
        humility of, 116
        and kingdom, 160–61, 172
        in temple, 184
Chorazin, 115
Christian humanism, 99
Christians, and Jews, 187, 197
Christology, 20, 60, 117
        and discipleship, 91, 128–29
Chrysostom, 35, 128
church, 87, 129, 165–67
        apostolicity, 107–8
        as ark, 97, 141, 206
        beginning of, 238, 246–47
        faithfulness, 107
        and Israel, 231, 249
        and kingdom, 150–51
        mission of, 104
        mixed character of, 131–33
        in northern and southern hemispheres, 131
        visibility of, 61–63

as way of life, 30
wealth of, 215–16
and world, 87
cleanliness, 217
coercion, 108, 178
communion, with God, 88
community
        ethics of, 61–63
        and parables, 126
        of peace, 232
        and truth, 91
compassion, 63
compromise, 131
Constantinianism, 62, 91, 133n3, 177, 203, 204
conversion, 125
cornerstone, 186
covenant, 177n2
creation, 23–24, 26, 84, 85, 169, 219
cross, 237–41
crowd, 234, 235
crucifixion, 28, 245
cynicism, 121
Cyril of Jerusalem, 241

daily bread, 78, 82, 144–45
dance, 117–18
Daniel, 204, 205, 206
darkness, 95, 209, 229
Davenport, Gene, 68n7
David, 26, 27, 31, 33, 120, 181, 194
Davies, W. D., 59n1, 61
Davis, Ellen, 32n6
Day, Dorothy, 211–12
death, 55, 151, 198, 233
debts, 78–79
defiling, 142–43
demons, 95, 97–98, 104, 121–22, 124
desolating sacrilege, 205, 226, 240
despair, 121
devil, 51–53, 152, 217, 249
disabled, 116
discernment, 90–91, 206
disciples, 25–26, 63, 75, 148–49
        calling of, 56
        and crowd, 58, 85
        deserted Jesus, 225, 239
        faith, 185
        killed Jesus, 235
        public responsibilities, 73
        sleeping, 222–23
        undistinguished character, 105–6

discipleship, 19, 56, 179, 238, 247
  as alternative to crowd, 234
  and Christology, 91, 128–29
  and freedom, 130
  as journey, 90
  radical demands, 82
  as status, 161
  visibility of, 74
divorce, 69–70, 148, 168–70
Dodd, C. H., 127
donkey, 181–82
Dostoevsky, Fyodor, 52–53, 55
doubt, 141
downcast, 189

earthly city, 233n1
earthquake, 242, 243, 244
Eastern Christianity, 30
ecclesiology, 177n2
egoism, 193
Egypt, 40, 42
elders, 185–86, 214, 232, 233, 239, 247–48
Elijah, 44–45, 50–51, 96, 115, 156, 157, 241
Elisha, 96
Elizabeth, 44
Emancipation Proclamation, 119
emperor, 80, 189–91
end of the age, 201, 207, 210, 211
endurance, 111, 202
Enlightenment, 88n3
envy, 210
eschatology, 23
ethics, 89
Eucharist, 52, 69, 218–20, 246
eunuchs, 170–71
evangelicalism, 46
evangelism, 103, 107
Eve, 52
evil, 51, 85–86, 98, 125, 131, 216–17
excommunication, 165
exile, 31
exorcisms, 121–22, 124
Ezekiel, 242

faith, 102, 145, 185
faithfulness, 107, 112, 134, 143, 172, 202
false gods, 54
false messiahs, 206
false prophets, 90, 91, 205
family, 108–9, 125
fasting, 80, 102, 114

Father, 77, 196, 239
fear, 39, 41, 55–56, 82, 87, 141
  of God, 108, 155
Feast of Unleavened Bread, 217
feeding
  of five thousand, 139–40, 149, 188
  of four thousand, 144–45, 149, 188
fig tree, 184–85, 187, 206
food, 139, 144–45
forgetfulness, 74–75, 79
forgiveness, 59–60, 67, 78–79, 87–88, 165–67,
  218, 220, 230–31, 237
fornication, 143
freedom, 130
friendship, 70, 172, 193, 223
fruits, 134

Galilee, 42, 56, 247
genealogy, of Jesus, 23, 26, 31–33
Gennesaret, 142
Gentiles, 31, 32, 33, 76, 121, 187
gentleness, 63, 118
Gerhardt, Paul, 236
Gethsemane, 138, 178, 221–25
gifts, 210
goats, 210
God
  abundance, 55, 188, 218
  faithfulness, 169, 208
  hospitality, 189
  justice, 176
  as love, 193
  mercy, 82
  patience, 37, 55, 207
  promise to Israel, 187
  time, 74
godliness, 233n1
Golden Rule, 88–89
Golgotha, 237
good soil, 129
gospel, 46
  as dangerous, 129
  embodiment of, 106, 219
  proclaimed in parables, 127
greed, 198
Greek and Roman philosophers, 75
Greer, Rowan, 202–3
Griffiths, Paul, 70n10
guards, 247–48

Hart, David Bentley, 24n1, 29n3, 99n1
hatred, 202

Hauerwas, Stanley, 61, 51n1, 63n3, 111n1
Hays, Richard, 27
healing, 94, 99–104, 123, 142
Herod, 18, 37–42, 137–38, 214, 231
Herodians, 190, 192
Herodias, 137–38, 233
Heschel, Abraham, 119
Hilary, Adolf, 51
history, 204–5
Hitler, 147
Hobbes, Thomas, 202
holiness, 45, 77, 101–2, 151, 183, 195, 235
Holy Spirit, 33–34, 48, 219
    blaspheming against, 122
    and body of Christ, 246
homosexuality, 143, 169
honesty, 233n1
hope, 145, 192, 207
Hopkins, Gerard Manley, 155
hospitality, 107, 211
humanism, 99
humiliation, 162
humility, 63, 86, 116, 118, 132, 161–62, 197
hypocrisy, 66, 195–200

idolatry, 185, 190
imagination, 43, 191
impatience, 55, 128
incarnation, 20
infants, 116
injustice, 82, 212, 232–33
innocence, 107
integrity, 200
irony, 97
Isaac, 220
Isaiah, 56
Israel
    and the church, 231, 249
    judgments against, 197
    mission to, 106, 112
    raised from Egypt, 248
    recapitulated in life of Jesus, 27
    restoration of, 31
    unfaithfulness, 169, 208, 230
    as vineyard, 175–76
    in wilderness, 139

James, 56, 177–78
jealousy, 210
Jenson, Robert, 238, 245, 248n1
Jerusalem, 39, 180, 181–82, 200, 247

Jesus
    as apocalyptic, 172
    authority, 92, 99
    baptism, 33, 48–49, 149, 156
    betrayal of, 216–18, 223
    birth, 33–34, 38
    as bread of life, 118
    compassion, 139, 144, 234
    as cornerstone, 186
    crucifixion, 70, 148, 160, 205, 236–42
    death, 30, 200, 238, 241
    descent, 93
    exorcisms, 121–22, 124
    extravagance, 216
    flogging of, 235
    fruits of ministry, 114
    as fulfillment of law and prophets, 102,
        192
    glorification, 154
    greater than Moses, 113
    as great high priest, 205
    healing ministry, 94–104, 123
    humanity, 3, 34, 100
    as image of invisible God, 124
    as the law, 93
    lordship, 94
    as new Moses, 40, 58
    obedience, 50, 245
    and Paul, 59n1
    person and work, 30
    politics of, 179–80, 183, 232
    prayer of, 138, 221–23
    pronounces judgment, 115–16
    as prophet, priest, and king, 54, 182
    recapitulates Israel's life, 27
    rejection of, 115, 135–36
    resurrection, 30, 124, 148, 200, 243,
        244–49
    as revelation of God, 150
    sacrifice, 28–29
    as second Adam, 100
    silence, 232–33
    suffering, 96
    taken to Egypt, 40
    teaching in temple, 214
    as temple, 205
    temptation in wilderness, 50–56, 122
    touch, 155
Jews, as "Christ killers", 235
John, 56, 177–78
John Paul II, Pope, 173, 174

John the Baptist, 43–49, 157, 185, 187, 199
   arrest, 56
   death of, 137–38
   more than a prophet, 115
   imprisonment, 113–14
Jonah, 124, 147–48
Jones, L. Gregory, 79n5, 165n2
Jordan, Clarence, 57
Joseph, 35–36, 42
Joseph of Arimathea, 242–43
Joshua, 36
journey
   discipleship as, 90
   kingdom as, 40
jubilee year, 45, 78, 114, 166, 183
Judaism, 44
   as religion of law, 60, 194
Judas Iscariot, 105, 216–18, 223, 230
Judges, 214
judgment, 84–85, 86, 106, 115–16, 167, 195
justice, 45, 63, 75, 176, 198, 212

Kant, Immanuel, 88–89
keys, of the kingdom, 150
kingdom of death, 108
kingdom of God, 21
   as alternative, 38, 67, 108
   and church, 150–51
   coming of, 78
   and exorcisms, 122
   and Gentiles, 56
   gentleness of, 118
   as journey, 40
   as mixed in composition, 67
   as movement, 103
   rejection of, 107
   time and space of, 135
   visibility of, 68
knowledge, and virtue, 147

lame, 183–84, 185
language, 123
l'Arche movement, 162
Lash, Nicholas, 24
Laura Hodgkinson Sunshine Home (Sydney,
   Australia), 117–18
law, 65–66, 113, 198
   and love, 89, 194
law and gospel, 47, 59–60, 145
law and the prophets, 89, 102, 156, 192
lawlessness, 202

Lawrence (Saint), 215–16
legalism, 120
lepers, 93–94
Levering, Matthew, 66n6
lies, 70–71n10, 232–33
Lischer, Richard, 61
little faith, 117, 124, 141, 149, 158
loneliness, 70
losing ones life, 153
lost sheep, parable of, 163–65
love, 34, 192–94, 238
   for enemies, 72, 79
   as fulfillment of law, 89
   for God, 89, 173, 192–93
   as judgment, 195
   for neighbor, 89, 165, 173, 192–93
   overcoming violence, 115
lust, 69, 169–70
Luz, Ulrich, 128

MacIntyre, Alasdair, 81
MacKinnon, Donald, 41
male and female, 168–71
manna, 52
marriage, 69–70, 168–71, 191
Martyrdom of Jerome, 24
martyrs, 221
Mary Magdalene, 242–43, 244–47
Mary (mother of Jesus), 35–36, 161, 246
Mary (mother of James and Joseph), 242–43,
   244–47
Matthew, 100–101
Maurin, Peter, 211–12
McCabe, Herbert, 32–33
McClendon, James, 57
meal, 219
memory, 79
mentally handicapped, 162
mercy, 101, 103, 120, 211–12
Messiah, 27, 149–53, 184, 194, 196–97, 201,
   226–27, 234, 240
messianic consciousness, 43
Milbank, John, 75–76n2, 88, 234–35
Minear, Paul, 25–26
miracles, 140, 248
mission to the nations, 187
modernity, 38, 43, 140, 189, 248
monasticism, 107, 202–3
moral exemplar theory of atonement, 238
morality, 193
moral law, 65

Moses, 31, 40, 58, 93, 113, 139, 140, 156, 213
mountain, 93
Mount of Olives, 181, 201, 220–21
Mount Sinai, 58, 93
mourning, 64
mustard seed, 133, 158–59
mutuality, 88

national renewal, 114
natural law, 65n5
Nazarenes, 44
Nazareth, 42, 135
net, of the kingdom, 134
new age, 115, 172
new beginning, 31
new community, 125
new creation, 24, 25, 36, 82–83, 120, 155, 244
Nicea, 35
Niebuhr, Reinhold, 131–33
Noah, 206
nonviolence, 20, 21, 72, 110, 224

oaths, 70, 73, 143
O'Donovan, Oliver, 133n3
Origen, 38, 64n4, 171

pacifism, 72, 73n11, 130, 224
parables, 126–35, 185–87, 188–89
    and waiting, 207–10
paralyzed man, 98–99
Passover, 214, 217
patience, 72, 86, 110, 128, 133, 134, 207
Paul, 163
    and Jesus, 59n1
    on marriage, 171–72
    on poverty, 64
    on resurrection, 191
    on wisdom, 116
Paulinus of Pella, 203
peace, 95, 151, 165–66, 183, 204, 232–33
peacemaking, 64–65
penance, 165
perfection, 72
persecution, 64–65, 107, 129, 202
Peter, 105, 140–41, 175
    confession of Jesus as Messiah, 28, 149–51
    denial of Jesus, 221, 227–28
    on Jesus as cornerstone, 186
    rebukes Jesus, 151–52
    as rock, 150–51

as stumbling block, 166
at transfiguration, 156–57
Pharisees, 18, 46–47, 52, 65–67, 101–2, 119–22, 123, 152, 243
    ask for sign, 146–48
    blindness of, 199
    on divorce, 170
    hypocrisy of, 66, 195–200
    on Jesus's healing, 104, 142–43
    plot to trap Jesus, 189–90, 192, 194
    as the rejected, 187
piety, 74, 196
Pilate, 226, 227, 229–35, 239, 241, 243
Pinches, Charles, 194n2
politics
    of Jesus's birth, 38
    of kingdom, 30
    of Matthew, 20
    in modernity, 183
    of murder, 41
    and sacrifice, 28–29
    and worship, 54
poor, 64, 184, 185, 189, 211–12, 215–16
poor in spirit, 63–64
possessions, 81
power, 94, 138, 158, 183, 189, 197
prayer, 76–81
preaching, 246
precious pearl, parable of, 134
prediction, 206
prestige, 196, 197
pretense, 162
pride, 86, 88, 97
problem of evil, 85–86
progress, 134
prophets, 25, 65, 149, 198
prostitutes, 186
Protestantism, 219
Protestant Reformation, 47, 59–60
Protestant scholasticism, 100
providence, 136
Prudentius, 215
Psalms, 71, 123, 128, 220–21, 222, 237
punishment, 111–12

rabbi, 196, 217–18, 223
Rachel, 41
Radcliffe, Timothy, 237
Radner, Ephraim, 18, 130n1
Rahab, 31
reason, 89

reconciliation, 68–69, 79, 151, 166
rejection, 107
religion, 52
    as private, 38
renewal, 114
repentance, 45–47, 56, 63, 114
rest, 118–19
resurrection, 191–92, 248
reward, 111–12
rich young man, 173–75
righteousness, 64, 198
Rilke, Rainer Maria, 24
rock, 150–52
Rogers, Eugene, 33
Rome, 37, 133, 189–90, 225
    fall of, 203
    violence, 67
Romero, Oscar, 221
Rosenzweig, Franz, 77n4
rulers of this world, 178
Ruth, 31, 32

Sabbath, 119–21, 154, 183
sacraments, 246
sacrifice, 28–29, 88, 101, 220
Sadduccees, 46–47, 52, 146–48, 152, 191–92, 234
salvation, 27, 218–19
Satan, 151
satisfaction theories of atonement, 60, 238
scarcity, 55, 82
scribes, 18, 52, 65–67, 92, 96, 123, 184, 234, 239
    blindness of, 199
    challenge Jesus's work, 142–43
    hypocrisy of, 195–200
self-deception, 196
self-indulgence, 198
self-sacrifice, 109
Senior, Donald, 127
sentimentality, 35, 89, 129
Sermon on the Mount, 30, 58–73, 81, 84, 92, 126–27, 144, 249
servants, 178–79
sex, 169
    as public, 143
sharing, 67
sheep, 163–64, 210
shepherd, 163–64
sign, 123–24, 146–48, 201–2, 204, 210
Simon, 56. See also Peter

Simon of Cyrene, 236
simplicity of life, 81
singing, 220–21
slavery, 79, 119–20, 237
socialism, 212
Sodom, 115
Solomon, 124
Son, reveals Father, 117–18
son of David, 103, 184, 194, 231
Son of God, 61, 63, 226–27, 231, 238
Son of Man, 96, 99, 149, 178, 206, 226–27, 241
sower, parable of, 128, 129–31, 210
speech, 70–71, 143
Stalin, Josef, 108
status, 161, 196, 197
St. Elizabeth's Church (Norwich), 163–64
stewards, 81
striving, 135
stumbling block, 152, 161–63, 164–66
success, 107
suffering, 67, 95, 116, 188, 205, 238
suicide, 219
swine, 98
sword, 223–25

talents, parable of, 207, 209–10
Tamar, 31
tax collector, 100–101, 186
taxes, 189–90
temple
    cleansing of, 182–84, 187
    destruction of, 44, 200, 226
    Jesus's teaching in, 191, 214
temple tax, 158–59
temptation, 200
ten bridesmaids, parable of, 207–9, 210
Ten Commandments, 173
Thomas Aquinas, 65–66, 75, 111, 211
thrones of judgment, 175–77
time, 37
    recreation of, 120, 153
tomb, 243, 244
Torah, 68n7
transfiguration, 154–57
treasure in field, parable of, 134
Trinity, 116–17, 192, 240
triumphal entry, 181–82
trust, 83, 143
truth, 70–71, 90–91, 147, 166, 185, 188
Turner, Denys, 124

two ages, 87
two cities, 131–33
two slaves, parable of, 207
tyranny, 178–79, 189

unchastity, 170
utilitarianism, 193

Vanier, Jean, 162
Vatican I, 39
vineyard, 175–77, 186
    parable of, 176–77
violence, 37, 67, 73, 82, 108, 130, 183–84,
    224
virgin birth, 34–36
virtues, 65, 74–75, 81, 145, 147
visibility
    of discipleship, 74
    of kingdom, 68
voluntary society, 67

waiting, 207–10
war, 30, 204
watchfulness, 208
weakness, 197
wealth, 80–81, 128, 129, 130, 174–75, 215
wedding banquet, 208, 210

Wells, Samuel, 82, 161, 163–64
Western church, 30
wheat and tares, parable of, 128, 131–33
wilderness wanderings, 45
Williams, Rowan, 90, 117–18, 240
wind, 97
wisdom, 107
wise men, 40–41
witness, 105–7, 110, 125, 150
woes, 196–200
women, in genealogies of Israel, 31–32
words, 122–23
work, and watchfulness, 208–10
worrying, 82
worship, 184
    of Jesus, 141–42, 246
    and justice, 198
    and politics, 54

yeast, of Pharisees and Sadduccees, 148–49
Yoder, John Howard, 27, 29n4, 45–46, 62,
    63n3, 67, 87, 155, 157, 179, 204, 224
yoke, 118, 196

Zebedee's wife, 160, 177, 242
Zechariah, 44, 201

SCRIPTURE INDEX

Acts
2:10–11 45
3:1 187
4:11 186
5 174
12:2 178
17:32 92

Amos
5:18–24 197
8:9 240

Colossians
2:11–12 66n6

1 Corinthians
1:18–31 116
6:1–8 68
6:13–15 70
11:30 218
12:5–11 130–31
12:12–20 163
14:22 39
15 87
15:20–22 192

2 Corinthians
3:6 65n5
3:7 156
11:2 208

Daniel
7:13 96, 227
7:13–14 206, 210, 248–49
9:27 205
11:31 205
12:2 242
12:11 205

Deuteronomy
5:15 119
6:5 192
6:16 53
8:3 52
17:6 226
17:19 54
21:1–9 234
23:1 170
24 170
24:1–4 168
25:5–10 191
27:25 230
31:24 213
32:44–47 213

Ephesians
5:21–23 208
5:21–33 171
5:31–32 172

Exodus
3:6 78, 191
3:13–15 77n4
12 214
13:21 174
16 139
19:16–25 58
20:3–5 54
20:4–5 190
24:1–2 156
24:3–8 218
24:15–18 156
32:19 93
32:30–34 140
34:29 93
34:29–35 156

Ezekiel
2:1 96
2:3 96
2:6 96
11:19 47
20:21 119
32:7 206
34 221
34:11–19 163
37:1–14 242

Galatians
4:6 77
5:24 70

Genesis
1:1 23
1:26–27 168
1:28 169
2:4 23
2:18–24 168
3:1 52
4:1–16 68
5 32
10 32
11 32
38 31
45:7–8 136

Hebrews
2:7–18 238
2:8–9 155
4:12–13 109
4:14–16 77
7:19 66n6
8–9 205
10:5–7 101
10:10 28
10:12 101
10:13–14 220
10:14 101

Hosea
2:1–20 208
6:6 28, 101, 120
11:1 27
11:1–2 40

Isaiah
2:3–4 95
5:1–2 175
5:7 175
7:14 36
9:1 56
9:6–7 56
10 197
13:10 206
29:13 142
40:3 45

42:1–4 121
49:24–25 122
50:6 227
52:14–15 222
53:4 95
53:7 226, 232
53:7–9 225
53:12 96
54:1–8 208
56:6–8 183
61 45

Jeremiah
7:1–15 198
7:11 183
8:13 184
13:27 197
31:15 41
31:32 208
31:33 12
32:6–15 231

Joel
2 242

John
1:18 117
2:19 226n2
4:44 135
6:35 148
6:44 174
10 164
11:25 148
11:45–46 147
12:6 216
20:30–31 43

1 John
4:11 193

Jonah
1:4–6 97

Joshua
2 31

Judges
2:11–15 214
16:17 44

1 Kings
1 31
1:39 214
19:4–9 50
19:19–21 96

2 Kings
1:8 44

Leviticus

5:7 184
13:46 93
14 94
15:11 142
18:6 137
19:17 192
19:17–18 165
19:18 173, 192
20:21 137
21:17 183
21:20 170
25 45, 78
25:8 166
27:30–33 198

Luke

1:5–25 44
1:44 44
1:68–69 44
15 164
24:26 96

1 Maccabees

4:54 205

Malachi

2:14–16 169
3:1 115
4:4–6 44
4:5 115

Matthew

1:18–25 38
1:20 244
1:23 38
2:2 240
2:13 244
2:15 27
2:23 42
3:2 38
3:7 199
3:16 33
3:17 141, 149
4:3 52, 141, 152, 226
4:6 141, 152, 239
4:8–11 249
4:10 54
4:11 244
4:12 138, 247
4:13 158
4:17 38, 45
4:18–22 125
4:23 94
5 84
5–7 59
5:7 102
5:14 63
5:16 65, 74

5:17 102
5:21–26 151
5:22–26 122
5:31–32 170
5:32 70
5:33 143
5:33–37 122, 198, 226, 227
5:38–48 195, 223
5:39 59n1
5:43–48 165
5:44 59n1
6:1 74, 196
6:7 122
6:8–13 127
6:19–21 78
6:24 174, 190, 242
7:1 59n1
7:4–5 122
7:12 165
7:21–22 122
7:24–27 127
7:28 113
8–9 113
8:5–13 143, 211
8:14 158
8:18–22 125
8:21–27 39
8:22 96
8:23–27 185
8:29 141
9:5 99
9:10–13 35
9:14–17 114, 127
9:27 194
10 113
10:5–6 249
10:16–23 125
10:22 111
10:34–35 102
10:34–39 125
10:37 109
10:37–39 234
10:38 151
11 149
11:1 112
11:4 78
11:4–6 45
11:6 115
11:14 44, 157, 241
11:19 114
11:20–24 114
11:27 34, 76, 141
11:28–30 196
12:1–8 142
12:2 122
12:5–6 183
12:7 28
12:19–21 121
12:22–32 104
12:23 194
12:31–32 227

12:38–42 148
12:43–45 127
13 207
13:1–9 210
13:8 130
13:13 127
13:22 128
13:31 158
13:40 131
13:42 127
13:49–50 127
13:51 129
13:52 128
13:53 113
13:57–58 182, 198
14:1–11 114
14:13–21 211
14:31 97
14:33 248
15:1–9 66
15:21–28 32, 180, 211
15:32–39 211
16 113
16:1 123
16:1–4 201
16:13–23 28
16:16 227
16:18 151
16:21 160, 243
16:23 161
16:25 92
17:12 96
17:12–13 241
17:22 160
17:23 243
18:1–5 116, 172
18:15 150
18:15–20 68, 192
18:20 38
19:1 113
19:23–26 242
20:13 223
20:18 96
20:19 160, 243
20:25–26 178
20:28 96, 102, 214, 220
21:1–2 39
21:4–5 54
21:12–17 226
21:14–17 231
21:42 187
21:43 189
22:11–14 208
22:13 95
22:15–22 80
22:37–40 89
22:39 165
23:2 84
23:2–3 147
23:23 66
23:16–22 231

23:25–26 66
23:37 182
24 48
24:1–2 159, 226
24:13 202
24:36 204
24:51 95, 201–12
25 72
25:31–46 111
25:35–36 208
26:1 113
26:2 96
26:24 96
26:26–29 139, 178, 246
26:36–46 28, 156, 178
26:60–62 159
26:61 200
27:22–23 57
27:24–25 230
27:25 227
27:46 50, 117
27:55 240
28:4 56
28:15 248
28:19 106, 187
28:19–20 33
28:20 38

Micah
4:1–8 95
5:2 39
6:8 198
7:6–7 108

Numbers
28:9–10 120

1 Peter
2:1–8 186

2 Peter
1:5–7 157
1:16–18 157

Philippians
2:5–8 64
2:6–8 240

Psalms
2:7–9 48–49
8:1–2 184
22 237, 240
22:7 239
22:17–18 239
22:19 222
23 164
42:11 222
68:8 242
69:21 237

72:12–14 103
77:19 140
78 128
78:1–3 127
91:11–12 53
99 31
110:1 194
114–18 220
118 182
118:22–23 186
118:26 200

Revelation
3:5 155
5:11–12 77
19:7 208
21:1–4 155

Romans
1:24–25 214
5:12–21 100
6 70n9
9–11 47, 136, 176
9:15 86
9:30–33 47
11:11–12 176
11:24 177
12:14 59n1
12:14–21 179
12:17 59n1, 233n1
13 179, 233n1

13:9–10 224
14:10 59n1

Ruth
3:9–10 32n6

1 Samuel
16:12–13 214
21:1–7 120

2 Samuel
5:8 183
7:12–13 226
11–12 31
15:30–31 181
22:8 242

2 Thessalonians
3 81

1 Timothy
2:2 233n1
2:5 86

Zechariah
9:9 181
11:7–17 217
11:13 231
13:7 221
14:1–5 181, 201

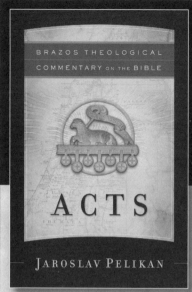